THE ART OF PRECOLUMBIAN GOLD

The Jan Mitchell Collection

THE ART OF PRECOLUMBIAN GOLD

The Jan Mitchell Collection

EDITED BY

Julie Jones

COLOUR PHOTOGRAPHY

Justin Kerr

A NEW YORK GRAPHIC SOCIETY BOOK

LITTLE, BROWN AND COMPANY   BOSTON

First published in England by
George Weidenfeld and Nicolson Limited
First United States edition

Library of Congress Cataloging in Publication Data

Mitchell, Jan.
The art of precolumbian gold.

Exhibition shown at the Metropolitan Museum of Art,
New York, May 9 to August 11, 1985.
Bibliography: p.
1. Indians of Central America—Goldwork—Exhibitions.
2. Indians of South America—Colombia—Goldwork—
Exhibitions. I. Jones, Julie. II. Metropolitan Museum of Art
(New York, N.Y.) III. Title.
F1434.2.G6M57   1985   739.2′278′07401471   84-22035

International Standard Book Number: 0-8212-1594-9

New York Graphic Society books are published by
Little, Brown and Company
Published simultaneously in Canada by
Little, Brown and Company (Canada) Limited

This book is published
in conjunction with the exhibition
The Art of Precolumbian Gold, the Jan Mitchell Collection
shown at The Metropolitan Museum of Art, New York,
May 9 to August 11, 1985.

Editor: Elizabeth P. Benson
Designer: Trevor Vincent
Set in Monophoto Palatino by
BAS Printers Limited, Over Wallop, Hampshire
Colour separations by Newsele Litho Limited, Italy
Printed and bound in Italy by Printers Srl
for L.E.G.O., Vincenza

Contents

List of contributors

WARWICK BRAY
Institute of Achaeology, University of London

PALOMA CARCEDO MURO
Universidad de Madrid

RICHARD G. COOKE
Smithsonian Tropical Research Institute, Panama

ANA MARÍA FALCHETTI
Museo del Oro, Bogotá

JULIE JONES
The Metropolitan Museum of Art, New York

HEIDI KING
The Metropolitan Museum of Art, New York

PRISCILLA E. MULLER
The Hispanic Society of America, New York

CLEMENCIA PLAZAS
Museo del Oro, Bogotá

IZUMI SHIMADA
Harvard University, Cambridge

MICHAEL J. SNARSKIS
Universidad de Costa Rica, San José

Acknowledgements

It is axiomatic that no exhibition can be drawn from a collection without the aid and encouragement of its collector, yet special note must be made of Jan Mitchell for his ever-gracious involvement with *The Art of Precolumbian Gold*. Mr Mitchell was always available when needed, and his good will never failed when he was dealing with the countless details encountered in preparing both exhibition and publication. I am most grateful to him for his help.

To the staff of the Metropolitan Museum of Art I am also grateful, for without recourse to its many specialized skills the work would not have been accomplished. The Department of Primitive Art and the Department of Objects Conservation are chiefly to be thanked, but there are many other departments and persons whose assistance was indispensable. Among them are the members of the staff of the Registrar's Office, the resourceful watchdogs over the objects for which the Museum is responsible, and without whom no loan exhibition ever takes place, and the Design Department, for it plans and manages the final, and very visible, installation of the exhibition itself.

During the course of working on this book, I have had the pleasure of working with photographers Barbara and Justin Kerr and experiencing at first hand their deep respect for Precolumbian art, a respect that is, I believe, apparent in the photographs of the Mitchell collection that appear in this Catalogue. Elizabeth P. Benson, who served as editor, was as always quick and efficient and, equally important, a comfort and support as well, because of her long experience in the Precolumbian field. The authors of the accompanying texts were most appreciated, for they managed to answer my request for contributions, and found time, midst already overburdened schedules, to accede to the requests for enlightenment on their various topics.

Individual mention must be made of Heidi King, who, with the greatest of enthusiasm, took on the painstaking task of describing the objects, in the small amount of allotted time; of James H. Frantz, Richard E. Stone, and Ellen Howe of Objects Conservation, who answered the hundreds of technical questions that Precolumbian gold objects elicit; of Wendy Schonfeld, who willingly cooperated on the most tedious of tasks; and of Susan Ebersole, who not only typed the many drafts of the Catalogue but also helped in pulling together the many parts of *The Art of Precolumbian Gold*, making its achievement infinitely less difficult. I thank them all.

JULIE JONES

Foreword

Precolumbian art—the art of the Americas made before the sixteenth century—has long had a place in The Metropolitan Museum of Art. The Museum first acquired a Precolumbian gold object in 1886, and, with the inauguration of the Michael C. Rockefeller Wing in 1982, the Metropolitan's commitment to ancient American art was made permanently visible. The new galleries show, in a wide variety of form and material, the astounding skill and inventive genius of the indigenous peoples of our hemisphere. Those people, and their art, are becoming better known as we enlarge our understanding of what comprises our 'American' heritage. As the ancient horizon is broadened through the advances in modern archaeology, we see that part of our heritage reaches back to the dawn of civilization in the Western Hemisphere.

It is therefore with great pleasure that I introduce the special exhibition *The Art of Precolumbian Gold, The Jan Mitchell Collection.* Jan Mitchell, initially an enthusiast and collector of objects made of gold, could not help but be drawn to the Precolumbian pieces that were brought to his attention. A pendant in the form of an engaging small musician with flute and rattle, acquired in the early 1950s, was his first Precolumbian purchase. Thus, Jan Mitchell became intrigued by Precolumbian gold when few collectors paid serious attention to these exotic objects. He succeeded, in time, in forming a most important collection. Indeed, objects from it were made available to the Metropolitan to accompany its own holdings in an exhibition sent to the Soviet Union in 1976, *Gold of Precolumbian America.* The exhibition opened at the Hermitage in Leningrad and subsequently travelled to Moscow and to Kiev. It was very well received by a public totally unfamiliar with its contents, and it thus increased the audience for the as yet little-known art of the ancient New World.

We were most grateful to Jan Mitchell for his participation in the Metropolitan's exchange show of 1976, as we are grateful now for the opportunity to show, in New York, such a substantial portion of his collection. It is not the first time that the New York public has had such an opportunity. Jan Mitchell has been generous in lending objects to museum exhibitions, but it is the Metropolitan's special privilege to present a sizable and representative part of the collection itself.

PHILIPPE DE MONTEBELLO
DIRECTOR, THE METROPOLITAN MUSEUM OF ART

Introduction

JULIE JONES

Countless American treasures from a great number of American lands fall into the category labelled Precolumbian gold. It is a category that shares in the universal attraction of gold. Gold, both wonderful to look at and very valuable, was as much a status symbol in the ancient New World as it is anywhere today. Malleable and, furthermore, almost indestructible, gold can be made into a thousand shapes, and, then, when new purposes demand, it can be made into yet another thousand. And so it has been used in the New World, as in the Old, except on those occasions when an antiquarian interest was strong enough to stall the needs of finance and the dictates of fashion. Some quantity of objects, produced in other times by other peoples, remains. It is, however, only a small percentage of the total number of gold works fabricated in the Precolumbian world.

The story of American gold is known, in part, by all. In the 16th century, the quantity of gold discovered by the Spanish conquerors among the peoples of the Americas was so great that it quickly led to the devastation and subjugation of the native American kingdoms. Their gold was just as quickly gathered, weighed, and exported. Such was the amount of gold crossing the Atlantic that it unsettled the economic and political structure of Europe and underwrote the first global empire in the history of the world, that of the Holy Roman emperor, Charles V, King of Spain and Emperor of the Indies. In the 16th century, America gained its reputation as a golden land; it was then, for example, that the legend of El Dorado, the Gilded One, was born. The legend, which had its origins in a ceremony performed in the highlands of central Colombia, was a compelling one—evoking the original American dream—in the minds of treasure-seeking Europeans. Even today, Webster's Dictionary defines El Dorado as 'a place of fabulous wealth, abundance or opportunity.'

Other chapters in the story of America's ancient gold are less well known than that told by the extraordinary events of the 16th century. Its remote beginnings, for instance, and its long and complex history in those regions of wealth and power where gold and its technology were employed are not well understood today. In recent decades, though, archaeological excavation has created a framework of enough breadth and sufficient time-depth to advance the study of Precolumbian gold substantially. As yet, the earliest evidence for the working of gold in the New World comes from Peru, in South America. This evidence is in the form of tiny bits of gold foil, obviously worked by man, that date to the middle of the second millennium BC. The small pieces of gold were excavated, together with lapis lazuli beads, in the burial of a young man and in an adjacent refuse deposit. A metalworker's tool kit, with an anvil and three small hammers, was also found in the earliest occupation level of the same site, Waywaka,

located on a hill above the modern city of Andahuaylas in Peru's southern Andes (Grossman 1972).

This modest beginning—no bit of foil was more than a quarter of an inch wide and the largest was just over an inch and a half long—not only illustrates an early step in the working of the precious metal, but it shows that symbolic and/or religious value had already accrued to it. It was already proper for gold, without having been given either representational or ornamental shape, to be used as a mortuary offering, and the use of gold for mortuary purposes would remain proper in the New World throughout its Precolumbian history.

From the Andahuaylas gold foil of 1500 BC until the production of works of art in gold, there is a paucity of information. A gap of about a thousand years' duration exists in the known history of New World gold, but works of art were being produced in Peru by the middle centuries of the first millennium BC. The first salient works of art come from burials in northern Peru, where they were discovered by chance in the late 1920s near Chongoyape, in the Lambayeque Valley (Lothrop 1941). These works, of Chavín style, are important indicators of the primary use to which gold would be put in ancient America. They are personal ornaments—headdresses, pectorals, plaques, ear and nose ornaments, necklaces, pins, and the like—all the types of wearable jewelry for which gold would be principally reserved until very late preconquest times, when big, authoritarian kingdoms controlled resources sufficiently to put gold to even more flamboyant purposes, when it could be written of the Inca capital, Cuzco, that there was 'a garden, the clods of which were made of pieces of fine gold; and it was artificially sown with golden maize, the stalks, as well as the leaves and cobs, being of that metal' (Cieza de León 1883: 85).

Sufficient numbers of works are known, dated—by stylistic associations—to the last centuries of the pre-Christian era, to suggest a growing awareness of the artistic possibilities presented by precious metals and a developing technological sophistication in working them. It was perhaps during this time that goldworking technology diffused northward along the Andes. The earliest documented evidence for the working of gold in Colombia, on the northern tip of South America, is dated to the late 4th century BC. Three small gold threads, or wires, were found with many fragmentary ceramics in a deposit in the municipality of Tumaco on Colombia's coast near Ecuador (Bouchard 1979). The threads are almost as modest as the pieces of early Peruvian gold foil, but they are not as isolated in time. Extant Colombian works of art may be of approximately the same date, but proof is lacking. The subsequent history of gold in Colombia, as befits the land of El Dorado, is complex, as is well illustrated by its enormous stylistic diversity.

It is from Colombia that goldwork and its technology moved northward onto the Isthmus of Central America. Journeying, apparently by sea, from Caribbean Colombia to Caribbean Panama and Costa Rica, goldworking arrived in both places at about the same time, perhaps in the 5th or 6th century AD. That the Isthmian societies quickly adopted a sophisticated goldworking technology is attested by the objects excavated at Sitio Conte, in Panama (Lothrop 1937). Situated on the banks of the Río Grande in Coclé province, the cemetery at Sitio Conte was initially used in the mid-5th century, and many important gold objects were placed in its burials during the following centuries. Sitio Conte is believed to have been occupied by a relatively gold-rich people for some four hundred years.

While gold was being placed with the honored dead at Sitio Conte, other gold objects were being traded north to Mesoamerica. Most of the trade pieces were from Central America, but others came from Colombia, farther to the south. By the end of the first millennium AD, Mexico was making its own gold objects—again, with all the advantages of developed techniques. The technology was imported into Mexico—perhaps even the goldsmiths were—but the artistic character of the region marked the objects clearly for its own. A latecomer to the use of gold in Precolumbian America, Mexico nonetheless made works of highly individual style. It is a style best illustrated by the Mixtec tomb objects excavated at Monte Albán in the 1930s (Caso 1969). The tomb of a Mixtec ruler who died in Oaxaca sometime in the 15th or early 16th century held many gold pieces that were similar in both type and style to those in use in Mexico when the Spaniards arrived in 1519. Thus, they are good evidence of the kinds of gold objects that were seen—and eagerly amassed—by the Spanish conquerors. This gold was much commented upon, in the Old World as well as in the New, for the fineness of execution, the richness of materials, and the unexpected 'naturalness' of its imagery. It was an amazement to the perceptive and the learned who willingly came to see it when opportunity allowed, as in the case of the Mexican gold seen in the hoard of treasure that was sent to Charles V in 1519, that so impressed Albrecht Dürer with the artfulness of its makers in foreign lands.

An account of the excited 16th-century response to the gold of the New World is given in the pages that follow. 'The Old World and the Gold of the New' by Priscilla E. Muller, is the first essay to appear in *The Art of Precolumbian Gold*. Its subject is an unfamiliar one to those who follow the Precolumbian field, for its perspective is European, and it assesses the effect that the fabulous American gold had on Renaissance Europe. 'Ancient American Metallurgy: Five Hundred Years of Study,' on the other hand, looks at an interest that is as old as the Spanish conquest itself. How American man worked his gold is seen as an endlessly fascinating subject. This interest is often occasioned by vastly different concerns, and yet, in spite of this long and substantial involvement, the technology of Precolumbian gold is still far from being well understood.

The other papers here have a more topical focus. 'The Symbolism of Gold in Costa Rica and its Archaeological Perspective,' by Michael J. Snarskis, and 'The Goldwork of Panama: An Iconographic and Chronological Perspective,' by Richard G. Cooke and Warwick Bray, cover those respective regions of the Isthmus of Central America, outlining available archaeological information and reviewing ethnographic sources and natural phenomena in an effort to get at the meaning of some of the gold images. The 'Cultural Patterns in the Prehispanic Goldwork of Colombia' are discussed by Clemencia Plazas and Ana María Falchetti in a paper that gives an overview of that large, diverse country and tries to integrate its disparate gold styles into a more unified cultural whole.

'Behind the Golden Mask: The Sicán Gold Artifacts from Batán Grande, Peru' by Paloma Carcedo Muro and Izumi Shimada, tells quite another kind of tale. It is a specific one, of a unique time and place, and of an extraordinary use of gold. The Sicán Lords, of whose wealth the authors write, must surely have been among the most extravagant and ostentatious of ancient American rulers. In ambition they seem second to none, and it is a welcome addition to have their exploits—in life and in death—begin to take shape out of the dark past to which they had been consigned by the cataclysmic events of the conquest of America.

Fig. 1
Pendant, enamelled gold with emeralds and pearls,
16th century. Western European.
L. 3⅜ in. (8·6 cm.)
British Museum, London.
Photo: British Museum.

The Old World
and Gold from the New

PRISCILLA E. MULLER

The wondrously wrought Precolumbian gold ornaments now in public and private collections are familiar through exhibitions and reproductions; they may awe, but rarely surprise, the viewer. When first seen by Europeans almost five centuries ago, however, these—and other handcrafted treasures from distant, unknown places—were far more astonishing than the moonrocks, brought through space by 20th-century explorers, are to modern viewers. Ironically, the 'sweat of the sun and tears of the moon,' as New World natives called gold and silver, were marvelously worked by peoples who valued raw gold no more than a lump of clay, whereas the long-awaited, but unworked, moonrocks are hardly more than a lump of clay. Unfortunately, gold itself was, for Europeans, as it is today, vital to the sustaining of governments, economies, and wars. Initially found praiseworthy, the handsomely worked gold introduced from the New World was soon of little importance to Europeans; its pagan forms and images mattered only negatively, if at all. The pagan gold was most often tossed quickly into the smelting pots; in fact, as the Spanish conquerors pushed forward into Mexico, they rushed to smelt almost all the gold ornaments they encountered, hardly heeding the cries of uncomprehending astonishment that came from the natives, who valued craftsmanship above all else. Thus, while there survive outstanding Precolumbian objects of lesser intrinsic worth, though equally remarkable craftsmanship (for example, Moctezuma's cape of feathers in the Museum für Völkerkunde, Vienna), by the conclusion of the century in which they were carried to the Old World, only a few Precolumbian gold objects had endured to be recorded in European collections.[1]

Yet the worked gold and silver first gathered, and preserved, by the conquistadors in Mexico (and soon after in Central and South America) was of considerable interest for Europeans, many of whom avidly sought novel and exotic objects and materials that might enrich personal *Kunstkammern*, or curio cabinets, the predecessors of museums. Those who could not see the new imports as they arrived from the West eagerly looked forward to descriptive reports. From contemporary accounts, designed in large part to satisfy the inquisitive, and the acquisitive, much can be learned of the nature of the material that so greatly impressed Renaissance sophisticates; and more recently uncovered Precolumbian gold can visually enhance our knowledge of the precious ornaments and jewels once so heralded in Europe. If we are aware of European preferences in jewel forms and decorative motifs at the time of the Conquest, we can examine the extent to which the till-then entirely unknown Precolumbian gold objects may have given impetus to European craftsmen and their patrons.

The Old World, which welcomed the products of the New with unrestrained amazement, had only shortly before begun to witness a replacement of Gothic art forms and thought by new ideas and interests expressive of a renascence founded on known antiquity. As subjects and shapes reflecting study of the ancients came to supplant mediaeval preferences, Renaissance humanists indulged in antiquarian delights, developing, for example, emblemata, dependent in part even upon Egyptian hieroglyphs. Presenting the fruits of their studies in printed emblem books with brief explanatory texts that incorporated moralizations and, frequently, symbolic illustrations employing familiar animal and human figures as well as more enigmatic motifs, emblematists provided the informed few with less-than-obvious subject matter—indeed, it was often purposefully obscured. In the 16th century, devices found in these volumes became a mainstay in artists' and craftsmen's repertoires, superceding such earlier Gothic themes as could recall innocent troubadorish pleasures in picturing a knight, a lady, a garden, or horticultural motifs, and tame—if, at times, imaginary—animals.

In Spain, relative socio-economic unity and stability were recent as well, having been attained only in Columbus's time, when Ferdinand and Isabella at last succeeded in uniting under the banner of Catholicism what had been a factional, segmented Iberian Peninsula. Although Isabella contributed to the building in Rome of a Renaissance monument *par excellence*, Bramante's Tempietto, these Catholic monarchs observed and supported a continuation of Gothic construction in the areas of Spain that they had finally wrested from centuries-long Moorish rule. Jewel designs of this time in Spain also illustrate a continuing accommodation to Gothic motifs, with Renaissance influence all but imperceptible before *c.* 1520. Isabella's own jewels were largely of a late Gothic character, though they also exhibited (as did jewels elsewhere in Europe) Moorish elements, notwithstanding Isabella's expulsion of the Moors (and Jews) from Spain in 1492, as Columbus sailed west from Palos. Like Precolumbian objects brought from the New World, however, Isabella's jewels long ago ceased to exist; even while she lived, many were consigned to goldsmiths for remodelling or other purposes. In fact, her jewels were usually in pawn to obtain funds to support armies engaged in military campaigns. They were not at hand to guarantee the moneys Columbus begged for the sea voyage that would at best, it was hoped, discover a more direct route than was then known between Europe and the much-desired spices of the Far East.

Instead of spices, there came, from an unanticipated continent, items so rare that Dürer, a goldsmith's son as well as an artist, wrote on viewing them in Brussels, late in August 1520, that he never before had seen such wonderful, heart-warming, artistic things, all the more astonishing for having been created with subtle *jngenia* (cleverness) by natives of till-then unknown foreign lands.

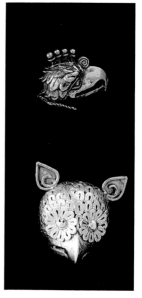

Fig. 2
Above
Eagle ornament of cast gold, 14th to early 16th century. Mexico.
H. ½ in. (1·3 cm.)
Below
Owl ornament of cast gold, 14th to early 16th century.
Reportedly from Achuitla, Oaxaca, Mexico.
H. 1 in. (2·5 cm.)
American Museum of Natural History, New York.
Photo: courtesy Library Services Department, American Museum of Natural History.

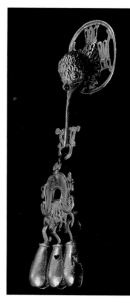

Fig. 3
One of a pair of gold ear ornaments with hummingbirds,
14th to early 16th century. Mexico.
H. 2⅜ in. (6 cm.)
Dumbarton Oaks, Washington (B-101 MIG).
Photo: Dumbarton Oaks.

The *Decades of the New World*, first published in 1516 and thereafter through 1526 by Isabella's Italian chaplain, Peter Martyr d'Anghiera, who was present in Barcelona when the Catholic monarchs received Columbus on his return from the New World, had been informing some Europeans of the veritable treasures of New World peoples: weighty gold discs, worn by them; an ingeniously wrought gold (or gilt-wood) mask, which was eventually brought to the Pope in Rome; beautifully worked buckles and delicately wrought gold collars, or necklaces, with pendants shaped like eagles, 'lions,' and other animals; and small gold birds, as well as other creatures. Anghiera planned to discuss such gold and gold-embellished ornaments—as marvelous in craftsmanship as in intrinsic value—with the Pope (Leo X: Giovanni de' Medici), with whom he had examined in Valladolid the first shipments that reached Spain from the New World.

Gifts presented to the Spanish conqueror, Cortés, by the Aztec ruler, Moctezuma, were made known and described in the conqueror's own letters to the Emperor. So beautifully crafted in gold, silver, and precious stones were these royal gifts that they were forwarded to the Emperor for his consideration, rather than being smelted at once. Thus, like Dürer, many Europeans could view and appreciate such New World wealth as we know solely from the contemporary reports: the massive gold and silver discs, the gold collars with beads shaped as shells (cf. fig. 4) and crabs with pendant bells, and gold ducks and other aquatic and land creatures, including a lizard (or crocodile) wound around with many gold wires.

In the share of another conquistador, Juan Ribera, were curious gold necklaces and rings, of which it was said that quadrupeds, birds (cf. figs. 2, 3), and fish were so precisely and faithfully reproduced in accordance with nature that they demanded great attention. Also displaying workmanship considered to exceed by far the value of the metal itself were small gold vases, as well as earrings, neck chains, and bracelets.

Anghiera reported that the worked gold gathered by Cortés and other conquerors was seen by everyone in Toledo, then the capital of Spain's central province of Madrid. In the spring of 1520, the New World treasures were displayed in Valladolid, which, at that time, boasted more goldsmiths and silversmiths than any two other cities in Spain. Soon after travelling north for his coronation as Emperor Charles V of Europe, Spain's King Charles I took the Cortés treasures to Flanders, where Dürer and others viewed them in late summer. The proud Charles should have been thankful that his order of the preceding year, requiring all worked gold obtained from the New World natives to be smelted for the Royal Fifth, as the King's share was known, had not been fully obeyed. As Bernal Díaz del Castillo noted subsequently in his *Discovery and Conquest of Mexico*, the royal arms, which were applied to designate the Royal Fifth, were not stamped on jewels judged so rich as to merit at least temporary preservation. Some— gold butterflies, a snail's head, an eagle with pendants, and a 'monster'— thus survived to be inventoried at the century's end among the belongings of Charles's son, King Philip II of Spain. Also listed then were similar objects of fairly low-quality gold: a butterfly, an eagle, a crayfish, and a 'lion.'

While hoards accumulated by other conquerors continued to arrive in Spain, Cortés, in Tenochtitlan in September 1526, registered for shipment gold collars with beads shaped as turtles with pendants (cf. fig. 5), and others

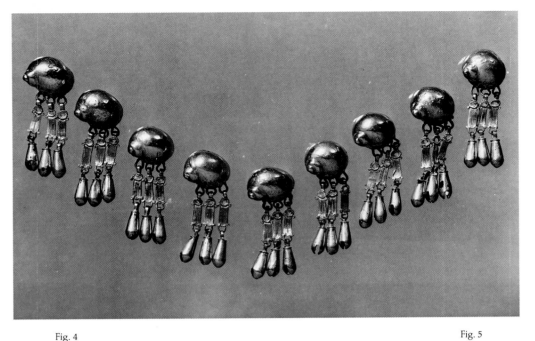

Fig. 4

Above
Shell-shaped gold necklace links with pendant bells,
14th to early 16th century.
Reportedly from the Soconusco region, Chiapas, Mexico.
L. of each element, 3⅛ in. (7·9 cm.)
Dumbarton Oaks, Washington (B-104 MIG).
Photo: Dumbarton Oaks.

Fig. 5

Below
Turtle-shaped gold necklace links with pendant bells,
14th to early 16th century. Mexico.
Total L. 20 in. (50·8 cm.)
Museum of the American Indian, Heye Foundation, New York (16/3451).
Photo: Museum of the American Indian, Heye Foundation.

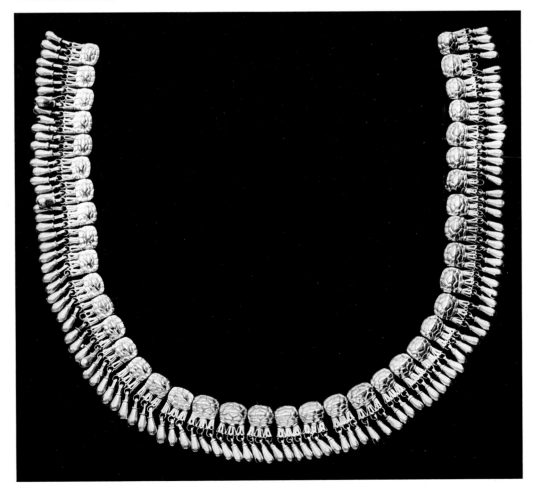

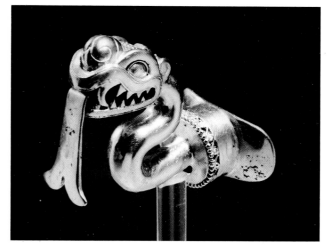

Fig. 6
Labret of cast gold in the shape of a serpent head
with a movable tongue, 14th to early 16th century.
Reportedly from Tlacolula, Oaxaca, Mexico.
H. 2¾ in. (7 cm.)
Collection Mr and Mrs Peter G. Wray, Scottsdale, Arizona.
Photo: courtesy Library Services Department, American Museum of Natural History.

Fig. 7
Jaguar pendant of cast gold with emerald inlay,
8th to 10th century.
Excavated at Sitio Conte, Panama.
L. 4⅜ in. (11·1 cm.)
University Museum, Philadelphia (40-13-27).
Photo: University Museum.

with firefly heads; an owl with pendants; a turtle with a firefly within; a snail and a small 'lion'; a winged lizard; butterflies; a tadpole; a bird; a 'tiger'; a cicada; an eagle and a 'tiger,' one within the other; and a coiled snake with pendants and a movable tail (cf. fig. 6). Cortés included Christian pieces in the shipment as well: crucifixes and Catholic images and medallions, quite possibly examples of the objects he had persuaded Moctezuma to have his goldsmiths copy. Very rich gold jewels, however, comparable to those that Moctezuma had initially presented to him—the collars of turtles and turtle-shells and those having snail- or cicada-shaped links, or such individual items as a gold skull, an eagle with bells in its tail, flowers with movable petals, and superb gold butterflies, snails, ducks, tigers, crayfish, and lizards—were, Cortés reported, no longer plentiful by 1524.

Many of the marvelous gold pieces that the Spaniards had gathered were lost during the frantic disorder of the *noche triste*, the 'sad night,' when, as July began in 1520, the Aztecs for once routed the conquerors, forcing them to flee the Mexican capital in panic. Thus, there disappeared into the swamps surrounding the city untold numbers of the tiny gold birds, animals, fish, serpents, and botanical creations so ingeniously crafted with unequaled facility by New World artisans that they were considered to have counterfeited nature's own creations.

Still, in 1532, Indians in Mexico gave to Cortés, who was by then the Marquis del Valle, striking and reportedly exceedingly well-made gold felines and other ornaments, together with a gold-handled fly swatter; he promptly ordered a trunkful of the precious gifts to be carried off to ships bound for Castile.

Of the worked gold objects assembled before the Spaniards in the Aztec capital for separation of the Royal Fifth, many were hollow-cast, and many, it is said, were technically beyond the abilities of Spanish goldsmiths. Such small masterpieces as a fish with scales of gold and silver, the two metals joined, not by soldering, but in the casting, amazed the Spaniards, as did miniature gold parrots having movable tongues, heads, and wings, and a fruit-eating gold monkey, whose head and feet could move. For these, as for their other artistic efforts, Indian goldsmiths could draw upon books they kept at hand, not, as we learn from Ribera, to be read, but as a source for pictorial designs. Color was often achieved in their handsomely wrought jewels by the incorporation of red and green stones (cf. fig. 7); and, according to López de Gómara's 1553 *Historia General de las Indias*, native goldsmiths could also enamel. Use of this technique is not verified, however, by surviving Precolumbian gold. López de Gómara may have had in mind other methods of coloring metals, or the adept native goldsmiths may, by 1553, have acquired the technique from the Europeans. We should also consider López's references to jewels lost in the rout of the conquerors, for he described these as including 'very natural' fish, birds, and snakes made of gold, silver, or stone with featherwork (*pluma*). As may be seen in some jewels (fig. 8) and other small metalwork objects of 16th-century design and character, areas of iridescent blue feathers, which serve as a background for diminutive metal or carved-wood figures, can ape enamel so convincingly that the technique passed unrecognized until fairly recently. Discovery of featherwork backgrounds in goldsmiths' work, encountered in several museum collections, has led some scholars to propose that such

Fig. 8
Cross pendant, gold with enamel, wood carving, featherwork, and pendant pearls,
late 16th to early 17th century. Western European style.
H. 3¾ in. (9.5 cm.)
*National Museum of American Art, Smithsonian Institution, Washington,
Gift of John Gellatly (1929.8.196).
Photo: Smithsonian Institution.*

Fig. 9
The so-called Ex-Voto of Cortés, brown ink and watercolor, *c.* 1777.
*Inventario del joyel de Nuestra Señora del monasterio, fol. 27.
Guadelupe, Archivo del Real Monasterio.
Photo: Priscilla Muller*

Fig. 10
'Winged lizard' pendant,
enamelled gold with emeralds, 16th century. Spanish.
H. 4⅜ in. (11.1 cm.)
The Wernher Collection, Luton Hoo, England. Photo: Wernher Collection.

Fig. 11
Frog pendant, cast gold with shell inlay, 8th to 12th century.
Reportedly from the Azuero Peninsula, Panama.
H. 2⅝ in. (6·6 cm.)
*The Metropolitan Museum of Art, New York, The Michael C. Rockefeller Memorial Collection,
Bequest of Nelson A. Rockefeller (1979.206.1072).
Photo: John T. Hill.*

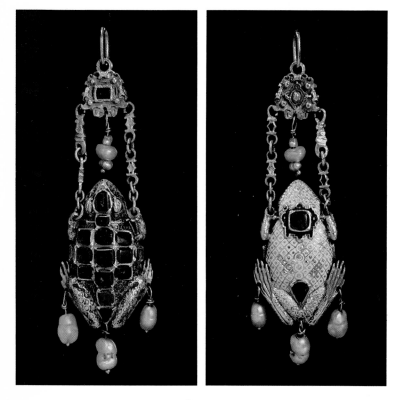

Fig. 12
Frog pendant, enamelled and jewelled gold with pendant pearls, 16th century. Spanish.
H. 3¼ in. (8·2 cm.)
*Formerly the Melvin Gutman Collection, New York.
Photo: The Baltimore Museum of Art.*

objects are Mexican rather than European in craftsmanship. The impact or influence in this adoption of a material, however, is limited to technique and ingredient; it does not involve style or design. In all other aspects, these objects are completely within the European tradition. Mexican featherwork did continue, however; mid-16th-century Mexican feather mosaic can resemble European embroidery, until closely examined. For this work, native artisans worked under the direction of Spanish Catholics, who provided religious books and prints as patterns.

During the early 16th century, workmanship as well as faithfulness to nature were the accomplishments of the New World artisans that aroused the greatest admiration among Renaissance Europeans. It may now be difficult to evaluate fully the character of this faithfulness on the basis of surviving Precolumbian art or to distinguish its role in the Renaissance Europeans' own awakening to naturalism, yet the focus on the lifelikeness of natural forms, cunningly replicated in gold and other precious materials, surely had an impact on Old World craftsmen and tastes (Muller 1972). It was in Spain, which enjoyed the closest contact with the newly introduced material, that natural animal forms were most used by jewellers in pendants created for their clients. Rarely seen in period portraits, these pendants on occasion served as ex-votos, as did one presented by Cortés to Spain's Guadalupe monastery in 1538. Described as a hollow, gold scorpion containing the carcass of the very insect that had nipped the conquerer, it would seem to have brought New World subject, form, and workmanship into a traditional Old World application. It is not possible to determine the true appearance of the piece, however, for, unfortunately, it was later confounded with an enamelled, winged-lizard pendant, whose thoroughly European appearance was pictorially recorded in a late-18th-century inventory of the monastery's jewels scheduled for smelting to acquire funds for new church doors (figs. 9, 10).

Turtle and frog pendants introduced in the work of 16th-century Spanish goldsmiths appear to exemplify an awareness of the validity of subjects that were found admirable in the highly respected work of New World craftsmen (fig. 11). Nonetheless, in many European examples, the praiseworthy fidelity to nature is compromised by superimposed patterns derived from European artistic traditions, as well as by a superabundance of pearls and gems, provided by the rich and ever-growing Indies trade (fig. 12). European pendants in the shapes of animals and sea creatures might represent also an adaptation to Renaissance interests; the pendants could act allusively and metaphorically for Europeans then preoccupied with emblematic references distinct from—if occasionally similar to—those of the inspiring New World peoples. Thus, if in alien cultures a golden frog pendant might call to mind or signify a rain god, and if the actual creature could be regarded as a source of poison by pagan as well as more civilized peoples, for Europeans it could also invoke, and had since pre-Christian times, the resurrection of the flesh; even the more sophisticated Europeans could regard the elaborate frog pendants as acceptable substitutes for the frogs, alive or dead, that were worn as amulets and prophylactics.

The highly colorful parrots of the New World, which came to be prized in the Old, together with knowledge of the tiny gold examples with movable tongues that were so admired in the work of New World artisans, stimulated European goldsmiths to create jewelled, brightly enamelled parrot pendants. When belonging to a Spanish poet, as one did, such a jewel quite possibly commemorated his powers of eloquence.

Northern European Mannerist gold- and silversmiths of the 16th century (whose designs, known in prints, were sometimes copied in Spain) were clearly inspired to integrate into their elaborate, complex creations not only the newly plentiful pearls and gems brought by the Indies trade, but such a figure as the feather-headdressed Indian, who became a widely recognized symbol of the New World. Combined with marine creatures who doubtless

signified the sea, which must be crossed to encounter the original, the New World Indian could even appear to be a substitute for, or confounded with, the Neptune of antiquity (fig. 1).

Thus did the Old World herald, esteem, and respond to the glistening discoveries from the New. Perhaps, as Precolumbian gold comparable in quality to that first brought for the Spanish conquerors—and so soon thereafter destroyed—is uncovered, we may appreciate even more its superb richness and craftsmanship, which so astonished the first European viewers.

[1] Complete bibliographical references, as well as specific citations for the sources here mentioned, appear in: Priscilla E. Muller, *Jewels in Spain, 1500–1800*, New York, 1972, especially Chapter II. In addition, re: jewels presented to the Marquis del Valle in 1532, see 'Información hecha en México sobre averiguar si los indios . . . regalaron al Marqués del Valle joyas y otras alhajas. . .,' in [Luis Torres de Mendoza], *Colección de documentos inéditos relativos al descubrimiento, conquista, y organización de . . . América y Oceania . . .*, XII, Madrid, 1869, pp. 531–

540; and re: the proposal that 16th-century European-style metalwork incorporating featherwork may have been created in the New World, see Charles Oman, *The Golden Age of Hispanic Silver, 1400–1665*, London, 1968, p. 57 ('Addendum'), and Theodor Müller, 'Das Altärchen der Herzogin Christine von Lothringen in der Schatzkammer der Münchner Residenz und verwandte Kleinkunstwerke,' in *Zeitschrift für bayerisches Landesgeschichte*, XXXV-1 (1972), pp. 69–77.

LAKE NICARAGUA

N I C A R A G U A

SANTA
ELENA
BAY

CULEBRA
BAY

Nacascolo

• Liberia

**Central Highlands-
Atlantic Watershed**

CARIBBEAN
SEA

• Filadelphia

La Ceiba ▲

**Guanacaste-
Nicoya**

*ARENAL
VOLCANO*

▲*Chaparrón*

Claudio Salazar

El Tres
▲

Guácimo •

*Ráventazón
River*

*Línea
Vieja*

• Nicoya

Tempisque River

GULF OF
NICOYA

SAN
LUCAS
ISLAND

NICOYA
PENINSULA

▲*La Fabrica*

San José •

Guayabo ▲

Turrialba •

Limon •

Cartago •

C O S T A   R I C A

▲*Hakiuv*

▲*Huaca de
la Reina*

Diquís

PANAMA

PACIFIC
OCEAN

Terraba •

*Río Grande de
Terraba or Diquís*

Palmar
Sur •

DIQUÍS
DELTA

▲*Coquito*

*Chánguina
River*

Jalaca

▲*Barriles*

Golfito •

OSA
PENINSULA

GULF OF DULCE

*La
Vaca* ▲

Carbonera
▲

• Puerto Gónzalez
Viquez

0   50   100km

▲ Sites
• Cities

BURICA POINT

Symbolism of Gold in Costa Rica and its Archaeological Perspective

MICHAEL J. SNARSKIS

The name Costa Rica, 'Rich Coast,' derives from the enthusiastic accounts of European conquistadors who had seen local chiefs arrayed in gold. The meeting place of two climatic realms, Costa Rica is also rich in biological diversity, a cornucopia of flora and fauna without equal elsewhere in the Americas. Strikingly different cultural traditions have long been associated with the two primary environmental zones. The generally more arid north-western quarter of the country, Guanacaste–Nicoya, had ties with Mesoamerica through much of prehistory. The eastern, central, and southern regions (usually combined into two archaeological zones, the Central Highlands–Atlantic Watershed and Diquís), all originally tropical rain forests, are closer culturally to Panama and northern South America. This frontier between two major cultural areas produced a rich and varied archaeological corpus.

THE RISE OF CHIEFDOMS, 300 BC TO AD 500

While chipped stone spear-points indicate man's presence c. 10,000 years ago (Snarskis 1979), and settled villages with well-made pottery date from 1000–500 BC (Snarskis 1984), the several centuries around the time of Christ represent a significant threshold in Costa Rican prehistory, with a dramatic increase in the number and size of sites, hence, of population, and the appearance of new elite artifacts: elaborate metates (grinding stones) of porous volcanic rock, ceremonial stone mace heads, figurines, ocarinas or flutes, rattles, and carved pendants of jade or similar hard green stones. Their quantity and placement in some burials, but not others, seem to indicate what anthropologists call chiefdoms, socio-political groupings between simple egalitarian bands and highly structured political states. Chiefdoms, ranging from hundreds to several thousand people, are usually organized around a partially hereditary hierarchy with a theocratic orientation, yet they lack rigid social stratification (Service 1975: 14–16). Craft traditions and mythico-religious symbolism are almost always highly developed to reinforce the status needs of a 'warrior-priest-chief.' In Costa Rica, two important kinds of symbolic artifacts possessed by elite individuals were of jade and of gold. Gold is almost never found in sites yielding jade artifacts, and vice versa. This complementary distribution has been revealed only recently through scientifically controlled excavations.

A hypothetical model suggests that the population expansion in Costa Rica around this time resulted from a dynamic feedback relationship between improved maize agriculture, new communities, and increasing competition for arable land, creating an increasing need to obtain land and insure its tenure, to ritualize cyclical agricultural procedures, and to administer the redistribution of food and other articles (Snarskis 1981, 1984). Warrior, priestly, and administrative classes formed a strongly ranked society

Fig. 1
Avian pendant of gold reportedly from Sierpe vicinity,
Diquís zone, after AD 500.
H. 4¼ in. (10·9 cm.)
Banco Central de Costa Rica, San José (760).
Photo: Dirk Bakker.

Fig. 2
Rectangular house foundations excavated at the site of
Severo Ledesma near Guácimo in the Atlantic Watershed, AD 1 – 500.
Photo: Michael J. Snarskis.

Fig. 3
Foundation of a circular house with entrance ramp
at the site of La Fábrica near Grecia
in the Central Highlands, after AD 500.
Photo: Juan Vincente Guerrero.

and a market for luxury items that were also badges of office, with agricultural symbolism. I believe that these 'badges' included ritual metates (a major sculptural vehicle for religious symbolism, associated with grain-processing), mace heads (possibly ritual digging-stick weights, associated with planting), and carved jade pendants (fig. 4), many of which incorporate the form of a celt, or polished axe (real celts were forest-clearing tools).

More intensive maize agriculture and/or better varieties, along with a reverence for carved jade amulets, must have been integral components in a mythical complex or politico-religious world view propagated in the northern half of Costa Rica through an elite-oriented trade or transfer network that included the heirs of the Mexican Gulf Coast Olmec cultural tradition. (Jade carving first appeared in the Americas in the Olmec culture, *c.* 1000 BC.) The Olmec symbolism of jade celts and avian effigies (the elements combined in the majority of Costa Rican 'axe-god' pendants) was linked to maize and water (Drucker 1952: 164; Joralemon 1976: 47–58). Other echoes of Mesoamerican Preclassic traditions are seen in the recently excavated rectangular houses in the Atlantic lowlands of Costa Rica (fig. 2), dating AD 1–400, and coeval bell-shaped storage pits, containing carbonized maize, found in the Central Highlands (Snarskis 1983).

CHANGE AND SOUTHERN INFLUENCE AFTER AD 500

Around AD 500, striking changes took place in most of Costa Rica. Gold-casting replaced lapidary jade as a source of ritually significant elite symbols (fig. 1); resist-painted ceramics became more numerous; and, probably in response to a shift in cosmogony, stone-cist tombs replaced rectangular tombs, without floor or lid, and circular houses replaced rectangular ones (fig. 3).

These traits existed earlier in South America, in the San Agustín region of Colombia, for example. We cannot be certain yet of the cultural dynamics that caused them to appear in Costa Rica. The archaeological data, however, admit the inference that the exchange network of chiefdom societies in eastern and central Costa Rica had expanded to the south. (Lines of communication between Tropical Forest peoples had probably been established much earlier.) A series of volcanic eruptions (Sheets 1984) and the fall of Teotihuacán, in central Mexico, in the 6th century AD—with consequent disruption in central lowland Maya centers and trade routes (Sharer 1984)— coincided approximately with the introduction to Costa Rica of cast-gold objects and then metallurgical techniques from Colombia and Panama. Elite-oriented gold objects and their associated mythology filled the vacuum produced by the sundering of Mesoamerican ties. The southern influence was eventually felt in all of Costa Rica, although Guanacaste–Nicoya apparently kept fingers on the faint Mesoamerican cultural pulse. The Central and Atlantic Watershed regions witnessed greater cultural flux through time. The 'edge effect' of shifting culture-area frontiers probably produced the incredible diversity of Precolumbian artifacts in Costa Rica. Their interpretation will constitute a puzzle for generations of archaeologists, anthropologists, and art historians.

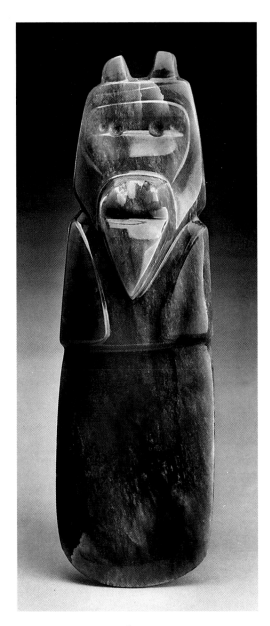

Fig. 4
Avian 'axe-god' pendant of jade from Tibás,
a site near the capital of San José, AD 1 – 500.
H. 8 in. (20·3 cm.)
Museo Nacional de Costa Rica, San José (1.5 [34]).
Photo: Dirk Bakker.

THE SYMBOLISM OF GOLD

Most of the first Spaniards to arrive were little interested in 16th-century Costa Rican images and tended to lump them as non-Christian 'devils.' The first ethnographic studies were made well into the 20th century, when most indigenous peoples were greatly acculturated. We can never be certain that beliefs recorded then are even derived from those of 500 or 1000 years ago. Helms (1977, 1979) suggests interpretive analysis of myths of surviving peoples, such as the Kuna, as a step toward understanding prehistoric beliefs in Panama (Cooke and Bray, this volume), but, given the absence of Precolumbian texts, there is no facile solution to this problem.

It seems safe to say that Costa Rican symbolism that is related to jade or jadelike stones had a Mesoamerican origin, while that of gold, and metallurgy in general, arose first to the south. Without consideration of the motifs it depicted, greenish-hued jade symbolized for Mesoamerican people (among other things) water and fertility (Thompson 1962: 110–111, 205–206, 260–261). Gold probably also had inherent meaning. The son of the Panamanian *cacique*, or chief, Comogre, disconcertedly watching the Spaniards melting artifacts into ingots, observed that unworked gold was the equivalent of an ordinary lump of clay until the goldsmith transformed it (Anghiera 1912: 221). In Diquís, one source of the considerable prestige of the cacique of Couto was that he was a talented goldsmith (Fernández 1886: 231). Helms (1979: 87) notes that, in historic times, the mythic culture hero of the Kuna was described as wearing 'golden clothing' as he confronted chiefly figures, who were in like array. Spanish chroniclers describe chiefs and warriors in Diquís similarly, and elite personages found in some tombs were literally covered in gold ornaments (Lothrop 1937: 46).

After analyzing Kuna myths, Helms suggests that 'golden clothing' symbolizes the celestial realms, particularly the Sun, a life-giving energy source for the world.

'. . . just as we may interpret the wearing of [gold ornaments] as indicative of the relative social status of an individual and as symbolically expressive of his membership in 'ordered' human society, so we can consider the more elaborate gold pieces worn by the elite both as signifiers of political power and as symbols of the supernatural realms from which this power was thought to derive. Conceivably, this was the thought expressed by the [cacique] of Darién [Panama] when he insisted to the Spaniards that his golden ornaments came from the sky . . . until the conquistadors forced him to identify a more earthly source.'
(Helms 1979: 87)

Bozzoli (1975), writing on the historic Bribri and Cabecar of southern Costa Rica, comments on the nature-culture dichotomy inherent in their myths. Certain clothing, adornment, artifacts, and behavior were considered necessary to designate 'men' or 'real people.' However, despite the comments of Helms (1977: 117, note 30) and other authors on the ubiquity of gold jewelry among all members of Central American cultures at Conquest time, the archaeological evidence of certain cemeteries indicates a lower per capita use of metals.

The human figure is shown in too many styles of Costa Rican Precolumbian gold for complete listing here. Both Panamanian and Costa Rican male figurines generally derive from the earlier Quimbaya style, of Colombia

(Bray 1981a), although without its technical sophistication. Casting techniques and gold/copper content help to distinguish some figures with recurved (feathered?) headdresses (Lothrop 1952: fig. 89d, h, i, fig. 97; Aguilar 1972a: fig. 29c; Bray 1978: nos. 227–229) as from Sinú (Colombia), Coclé, Veraguas (both Panama), or Costa Rica, but there was much hybridization of this style throughout the Isthmus (Bray 1984: 327). Human figures from Diquís or Central/Atlantic Costa Rica have disproportionately large, spatulate feet, with or without stylized toes; the downward-pointing feet look almost like swimming fins.

Some figures are called *maraqueros*, 'rattle-players,' for they hold round-headed objects in both hands, extended forward. Another style shows a drum in one hand and a ropelike object from the mouth to the other hand (fig. 5); Aguilar (1972a: 57–58, fig. 30) and others call them 'musicians,' identifying the ropelike element as a flute. Other figures hold in their hands a similar element that passes behind the legs. I believe that all these elements represent snakes (some have snake heads), held by ritual dancers or shamans. For the historic Bribri people of southern Costa Rica, snakes represent danger and incest; viewed as the bows and arrows of evil spirits, their bite is seen as demonic (Bozzoli 1975 :. 187). The handling of snakes with impunity may have enhanced spiritual or social power. Snakes are also phallic symbols for the Bribri; a snake head replaces the penis on many prehistoric gold figurines. Human figurines bearing snakelike elements are often double or bicephalic. Among the Bribri, twins portend approaching death, a general threat to the lives of all. Since warriors wore gold articles into battle, double-figure pendants may have been meant to inspire awe or fear. Some birds of prey (viewed by the Bribri as warriors or kinsmen) were renowned as snake-hunters; snakes held in their beaks may have inspired the poses of some gold figurines.

A frontal bird with spread wings and flared tail is seen on a large percentage of Costa Rican goldwork (see fig. 1). The motif may copy the posture of large birds in trees, drying damp feathers. Cooke (1984b) notes that the King Vulture (*Sarcorhamphus papa*), '. . . upon its arrival at a carcass, terrifies the other carrion-feeding species with a foreboding expansion of its bicolored wings.' The cere seen on many avian pendants connotes 'vulture,' not the 'eagle' described by the 16th-century Spaniards.

Analogues (probably earlier) of Costa Rican avian pendants are known from the Quimbaya, Sinú, and Tairona regions of Colombia, and the Coclé and Veraguas regions of central Panama. The early varieties were often elegant, smooth-lined, double-bird pendants, which, Bray (1984: 326) says, 'display none of the complex iconography of the later Isthmian styles . . . they are pure Colombian in spirit. . . .' This style (Stone and Balser 1967: pl. IId, e; Aguilar 1972a: fig. 16; Bray 1978: no. 406), found in Costa Rica with jadelike stone pendants, must date to *c.* AD 500. Annular ceramic pot stands of the earlier (AD 1–500) El Bosque phase (Detroit 1981: pls. 25, 26), in eastern Costa Rica, show at the top a row of modeled bird heads similar in form to the gold birds.

Later avian pendants from Diquís (which formed a cultural area with Chiriquí, Panama) frequently display a baroque abundance of ornament: false-filigree scrolls, alligator and serpent motifs, prey held in the beak, and dangling plaques. Often, anthropomorphic or other non-avian features are

Fig. 5
Human figure pendant of gold
from the vicinity of Palmar Sur, Diquís zone, after AD 500.
H. 4¼ in. (10·8 cm.)
Banco Central de Costa Rica, San José (963).
Photo: Dirk Bakker.

Fig. 6
Gold pendant in the form of two figures with danglers,
reportedly from United Fruit Company Farm 4,
Diquís zone, after AD 500.
H. 3⅛ in. (8·1 cm.)
Dumbarton Oaks, Washington (B-299 CRG).
Photo: Dumbarton Oaks.

added to make up fantastic creatures or to emphasize the symbolic or mythic union of traits of two or more animals.

A group of pendants from Diquís/Chiriquí features composite figures (men costumed as animals or believed to possess animal attributes) between two long, narrow, sheet-gold plaques, usually curved. The plaques anchor the elements between them, but the Bribri belief system suggests a further meaning. The Bribri conceive of an 'above-below' dichotomy in their world view, mediated toward a synthesis represented by their life on earth. Good and bad things may occur either above or below; they are mediated through other things. Large birds, jaguars, bats, the principal deity, and things male in general, for example, are *above*; things female, snakes, crocodilians, and water are *below* (Bozzoli 1975: 199–206). Could the man-animal figures between plaques symbolize powerful, multifaceted personages cognizant of the complex dualities inherent in worlds above and below? Some pendants have a curtain of square gold plaques hung from hooks in front of the main figures (fig. 6). The occluding plaques, apart from making the pendants showier, perhaps symbolized the protean aspect of a shaman-warrior-cacique who could assume animal shapes and attributes at will.

The jaguar (here designating the five or six wild cats of Central America) apparently gained in symbolic importance after AD 500 in Costa Rica, appearing frequently in all media. For the historic Bribri, the jaguar was 'hunter, killer, warrior, clansman, uncle, brother-in-law; symbol of power; equivalent to eagles [the Bribri word for 'vulture' is identical] above, crocodiles in the water, and to the *Xanthosoma* edible roots (*ñame*) in the vegetable world' (Bozzoli 1975: 180). Heavy, gold, Precolumbian jaguars convey a similar impression of power.

Monkeys appear in gold, often with tails circling over their bodies; the earlier, simpler prototype is perhaps recognizable in Veraguas. For the Bribri, monkeys are former men, and the spider monkey is a warrior. In historic (and probably late prehistoric) times, only jaguar and monkey clans could produce Bribri chiefs (Bozzoli 1975).

Linares (1977) notes that prehistoric Panamanian artifacts depict most often animals that bite, pinch, sting, are poisonous or somehow dangerous to man; dangerous animals were worthy adversaries, incorporating qualities that warriors should possess. The numbers of sharks, felines, snakes, spiders, scorpions, and crustaceans in Costa Rican gold tends to support this interpretation, but there are also innocuous creatures (for the Bribri, butterflies, dragonflies, and waterbirds are intermediaries between above and below, as are conch shells, symbols of sound and communication) and good protein sources (deer, peccary, tapir).

In the Bribri creation story, a giant tree was felled, later to become the ocean. The deer created a clearing around the tree to give it room to fall in the dense tropical forest.

'The deer makes a circular trail because God is creating the sea and leaving land in the middle. The Bribri conceive of the shape of the earth as a circle surrounded by water, which is what it looks like from the highest peaks. Why should the deer be the one to delineate the circular edges, the margins of earth and sea? The deer is associated with [the principal deity], with the above, as are usually all fast runners, whose mode of locomotion appears to be equated with flight.

There is an idea that deer, like [the deity], can look backwards without turning their head around . . . so there is also an association of this animal with good sight or perspective.' (Bozzoli 1975: 220)

Gold frogs have been found all over Costa Rica; the larger, more elaborate examples come from Diquís. Before AD 500, toads were more frequent symbolic effigies, primarily on pottery. Poison glands behind the neck of some toad species were emphasized; a hallucinogen was probably extracted from those glands. The gold pendants usually show the frog naturalistically, sitting with hind legs flexed; the rear feet are often oversized rectangular or trapezoidal plaques. The Bribri view the frog as a burial helper, who sits on a burial to prevent the deceased from arising to trouble the living; seats and sitting order are stressed in Bribri burial rituals (Bozzoli 1975: 210–216). Thus, the frog's ability to sit is critical. Emmerich (1965: 104) observes that the 'stylized spirals in the mouths of many [gold] frogs' must have special meaning. I view these spirals as water symbols; the Bribri believe that the frog played a role in the creation of the ocean and is 'a symbol of sterility on dry land, because it reproduces in water' (Bozzoli 1975: 216). Other frequent iconographic elements on frog pendants are snakes and crocodilians, who also have water associations.

METALLURGY: THE ARCHAEOLOGICAL EVIDENCE
As an archaeologist, I have a bias: inferences about prehistoric cultural processes should be based on evidence recovered in scientifically controlled excavations or collections. Priority is given, in this section, to evidence directly obtained by archaeologists, so that techniques like ceramic cross-dating and comparative dating of tomb structures are applicable. I am also a realist, however, aware that important data may come from nonscientific contexts, and that not a single Precolumbian metal artifact from Costa Rica has been radiocarbon-dated with charcoal directly associated.

Natural gold occurs in Costa Rica—as dust, flecks, and nuggets—primarily as a secondary deposit in watercourses, especially in the central and southern Pacific watersheds. Several Spanish chronicles note that indigenous peoples obtained gold from riverbeds, and panning goes on today in the Osa Peninsula. Bray (1981a) has observed that lower Central America and the donor cultures of Colombia made up a single metalworking province, characterized by a technology that emphasized lost-wax casting, gold-copper alloys (often called tumbaga), false-filigree decoration, and *mise en couleur*, or depletion gilding. The time around AD 500 must have been especially dynamic, with the introduction of metal objects, many local styles, and much copying and mixing of motifs.

Central Highlands—Atlantic Watershed
To date, the most important find from this period is a cemetery, in El Tres de Guácimo, Línea Vieja, of some 125 tombs, three of which were excavated by Stone and Balser (1965: 317–321). This cemetery yielded several slate-backed pyrite mirrors, typical of those manufactured in southern Mesoamerica c. AD 420–520, some of which were inscribed with Maya glyphs. In two tombs (not excavated by Stone and Balser), this kind of mirror was supposedly associated with jadelike pendants, ceremonial mace heads, metates, and gold or tumbaga artifacts. From one tomb came a gold frog, a 'curly-tailed-animal' pendant (probably a bird) from Coclé, Panama, and a double-spiral pendant, typically found in the Tairona and Sinú zones of Colombia (Bray 1984: 326). Another tomb contained two gold frogs, a double-headed, simply styled bird pendant like those of Coclé, two fragments of 'curly-tailed-animal' pendants, and a human-figure pendant of, or close to, the Quimbaya style of Colombia. The three pottery vessels illustrated from this site (Stone and Balser 1965: figs. 24, 25) can be reliably placed in the late El Bosque–early La Selva complexes, *c.* AD 400–600.

Stone (1977: 168–169) reports a superb Quimbaya-style head found at Hakiuv, Talamanca, and potsherds, supposedly found with it (ibid.: fig. 230), modally similar to some from the early La Selva–Curridabat phases (it is not clear who excavated these). From the La Fortuna site in the San Carlos region, Stone (ibid.: figs. 216, 217) illustrates a Coclé-style copper figurine and a Galo Polychrome vessel, *c.* AD 500.

These critically important associations combine elements of the Mesoamerican-affiliated symbolic complex with what must be considered the earliest southern metallurgy to appear in Costa Rica. The earliest gold objects seem to have been largely trade pieces; the sophisticated metallurgical technology would follow. Unfortunately, these valuable associations seem to rest solely on the word of a tomb-looter.

More recently, Aguilar (1980), during stratigraphic testing at the multi-component Tatiscú site, near Cartago, encountered a cache or tomb of river cobbles placed in a rough square. Within it was a group of broken ceramic *floreros* (small cups with very long, hollow, tripod supports), apparently broken there intentionally; their style was typical of the early Curridabat phase (AD 400–550) in the Central Highlands. With them was a fragmentary Coclé-style anthropomorphic pendant, of what Aguilar called solid copper. It might also be highly oxidized tumbaga, for Lothrop (1952: 94–105) has shown that similar Coclé figurines commonly contain from 20 to over 70 per cent copper; the Tatiscú piece has not undergone sophisticated metallurgical analysis. The slightly flexed legs and arm held forward (head and one arm are missing) indicate that the figurine belongs to the Coclé and Veraguas class of men holding rattlelike objects. The high copper content suggests a Coclé affiliation (Lothrop 1937: table IX). Aguilar (1980) illustrates a similar complete specimen, and, noting that both pieces are high in (he says pure) copper and are solid, not hollow-cast, he suggests the possibility of a different, although Coclé-influenced, manufacturing site.

The pottery associated with the metal figurine has its counterpart in the La Selva phase of the Central Atlantic Watershed. At the La Montaña site, near Turrialba, virtually identical floreros were found (occasionally smashed) by the Museo Nacional de Costa Rica in long, rectangular cobblestone tombs, some of which also contained greenstone pendants and necklaces (Snarskis 1978: 181–188).

La Fábrica (10–LF–A)   During the construction (1978–80) of the National Liquor Factory near Grecia, in the Central Highlands, a large prehistoric village, with circular house foundations and cobble-paved causeways, came to light. Juan Vicente Guerrero, an archaeologist at the Museo Nacional de Costa Rica, in charge of salvage excavations, mapped thirteen structures, along with other domestic and funerary features. La Fábrica showed evidence of several different occupations, although the house forms are typical of the AD 800–1500 period in central, eastern, and southern Costa Rica. Oddly, the vast majority of the more than 700 vessels recovered are mid- to late Curridabat phase, *c.* AD 500–700, and a metate–jade–mace-head burial suggests that part of an associated cemetery is even earlier. Several radiocarbon assays give a chaotic picture, so the enigma remains.

Near the principal circular structure (15 m. diameter, with two opposing rectangular east-west entryways), two copper bells were found, both like Lothrop's Style D bells (1952: fig. 80). One was just outside the stone foundation to the north. These did not appear to be associated with a burial or mortuary offering, although there were at least five burials beneath the principal house (all without associated grave goods).

Barrial de Heredia (26–CN–H)   In 1978–79, less than 10 km. west of San José, construction of a produce market revealed archaeological remains, and Aida Blanco, of the Museo Nacional de Costa Rica, was placed in charge. Eight structures were excavated; at least as many more remain untouched in an adjacent coffee field. As work progressed, it seemed that square or rectangular foundations were those of domiciles (many had prestige tombs beneath the floor and lacked cooking or food-processing areas), while ovate foundations contained no prestige burials, but had larger quantities of domestic rubbish, hearths, and ovens (Snarskis 1983). The largest quadrangular structure (*c.* 15 × 10 m.) was directly adjacent to the largest ovate one, indicating that the occupants of the latter had to do with the domestic maintenance of the former, a pattern since noted at many Costa Rican sites. Of the eight structures excavated, this quadrangular one yielded the most evidence for elite occupation. One of several tombs beneath its floor contained five types of polychrome ceramic vessels, all imported from several manufacturing sites in Guanacaste–Nicoya, and a tiny cast-gold 'eagle' (fig. 11) which rested virtually alone at less than 1 cm. beneath the house floor, with no skeletal remains apparent. Some 60 m. away was a Tayutic brown incised serving dish, a type made in the Central Highlands-Atlantic Watershed. The gold pendant falls into Aguilar's (1972a: 37–39) Línea Vieja Type 1 class, characterized by stylized avian figures with a vertical suspension ring. Although simple, these little figurines are usually cast from high-carat gold and are heavy for their size. Aguilar considers them to be local (i.e., confined to the Línea Vieja in the Central Atlantic lowlands), yet, like similar little frog pendants, they have been found by archaeologists in several parts of the country. Three good radiocarbon dates for the structure at Barrial all cluster *c.* AD 900.

Guayabo de Turrialba   This national park, the only archaeological site in Costa Rica that is even partially restored and maintained, has been extensively described (Aguilar 1972b; Fonseca 1979, 1983). It was undoubtedly an important socio-political and ceremonial regional center, probably *c.* AD 800–1200. (The single radiocarbon date, from mixed mound fill, is AD 712 ± 240.) Although Guayabo is impressively large and complex, including 20-ton stone-slab bridges and functioning underground aqueducts, there are probably hundreds of similar sites throughout the southern half of Costa Rica.

During initial excavations in the 1960s (Guayabo had already been

heavily looted), Aguilar found two cast-gold frog pendants (only the lower half of one remained) in earth fill covering a cobble-paved street near the two major mounds. There was no evidence of a funerary context; they may have been redeposited. The pendants are of a style Aguilar (1972a: 77–78, fig. 50a) calls 'Frogs with spiral mouth ornaments.' Modelling is rather crude; suspension rings form the front feet.

El Cristo (39–EC–C)   In 1981, Aida Blanco directed the excavation of 164 stone-cist tombs placed along a hillside on the Continental Divide, between San José and Cartago. The site has since been destroyed by the building of a highway. El Cristo apparently contained about 200 stone-cist tombs, including those excavated fifteen years ago by Carlos Aguilar and those lost to looting. The tombs were constructed of natural flagstones, almost all volcanic (in one tomb they were calcareous), and some river cobbles. The tombs are typically coffin-sized, with floor, walls, and lid of stone. A tomb sometimes contained more than one skeleton, and there is evidence for sequential interment, with the bones of the initial burial pushed or bundled to one side. The cemetery was probably used by a single lineage or residential group over at least a hundred years. The tombs may have been marked above the ground, so that the group could identify and reutilize them. In the Central Highlands–Atlantic Watershed, stone-cist tombs are seldom more than 1 m. deep.

In one tomb, Blanco found a simple copper bell like Lothrop's Style D (1952: fig. 80) with an appliqué like band added near the suspension ring and a tiny quartz crystal as a clapper. There were dental remains from two individuals, one 14–18 years and the other 20–30. The copper bell must have been in the mouth of the latter, for many teeth were stained a bright green on all surfaces. Other grave goods included an elaborate ceramic rattle, a brown incised dish (both local), and an imported polychrome vessel from Guanacaste–Nicoya.

At the large site of Aguacaliente, Cartago (less than 5 km. from El Cristo), in early 1984, Ricardo Vázquez excavated an almost-identical bell in a stone-cist tomb containing skeletal remains of three individuals; associated with the bell was an unusual ceramic vessel with an annular base incorporating appliqué monkeys (fig. 7).

Hacienda Molino (27–HM–C)   In this salvage excavation of a housing project just south of Cartago, Vázquez (1982, n.d.) dug and analyzed 34 stone-cist tombs of the type described for El Cristo. At Hacienda Molino, the tombs uncovered (some had been disturbed by looters) seemed to be organized in an unusual concentric-circle pattern, with the more elaborate edifices near the center. This deviation from the usual east-west orientation may derive from the symbolism of coeval circular houses.

Vázquez found an anthropomorphic copper figurine at one side of an undisturbed tomb. He thinks that it probably belonged to a group of offerings, mostly ceramic, that rested upon the unopened tomb lid; this pattern was common at the site. Since the tomb contained remains of five individuals, the piece might have been thrown out when later burials were put in. Although fragmented and corroded, I believe that it can be grouped with the simple cacique type with vertical topknot (Emmerich 1965:

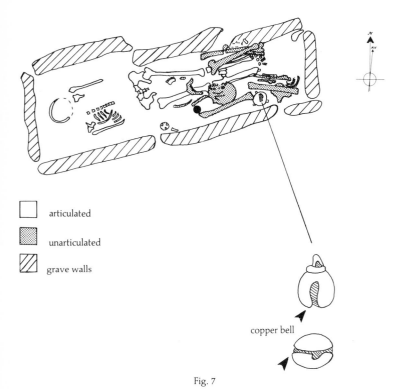

copper bell

Fig. 7

Stone cist tomb excavated at Aguacaliente site near Cartago.
The tomb contained at least two burials, the earlier one (shaded)
was perhaps pushed aside to make room for the later, AD 800–1200.
Drawing: Eugene Fleury, after Ricardo Vázquez.

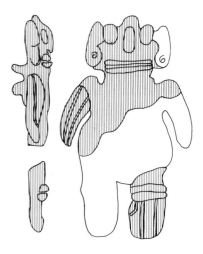

Fig. 8

Fragmented copper or tumbaga pendant excavated at Hacienda Molino site
in the Reventazón Valley-Línea Vieja region, AD 700–1000.
The pendant appears to be of the cacique type.
H. *c.* 1¼ in. (3·2 cm.)
Museo Nacional de Costa Rica, San José.
Drawing: Eugene Fleury, after Ricardo Vázquez.

fig. 148; see Aguilar 1972a: fig. 28 for a related style). This type is supposedly indigenous to the Reventazón Valley–Línea Vieja region; Hacienda Molino (AD 700–1000) lies near the Reventazón headwaters. Vázquez sees an avian aspect in the arms/wings; the figure may be human, with bird costume or mask (fig. 8).

Orosi Almost a century ago, at Orosi, near Cartago, in one of the more than 60 stone-cist tombs emplaced in a large circular mound (18 m. diameter, 3 m. high), Hartman (1901: pl. 63) found some ragged pieces of metal ('gilded copper-foil'), probably part of a headband or disc; its greenish oxide had discolored the nearby skull. Hartman noted the presence of tombs in many, but not all, of the circular foundations, which, he realized, were those of domiciles.

Claudio Salazar (36–CS–A) In this small cemetery near Chaparrón, San Carlos region, the stone-cist tombs were constructed of carefully chosen, rounded river cobbles. Several tombs had vertical basalt columns or elongated cobbles at their heads, like a tombstone, a trait of many Guanacaste–Nicoya sites after AD 800, but existing several hundred years earlier at the La Fortuna, San Carlos site (Stone and Balser 1965).
   During Museo Nacional de Costa Rica excavations in 1977, two metal artifacts were found along the inner wall of tombs, as if they had been placed in the spaces between the cobbles. One is a tiny copper (?)—oxidized light green—object less than 1 cm. in length. Two tiny projections at one end suggest that it may be complete, but I believe it to be the corroded head of a cacique figurine, similar to that from Hacienda Molino. The other artifact, a frog (fig. 9), apparently gilded by the *mise en couleur* process, is identical to a frog said to come from the Diquís zone (Stone and Balser 1967: pl. IVa).

Guanacaste–Nicoya

Culebra Bay, Guanacaste Northwestern Costa Rica has yielded few Precolumbian metal artifacts, a puzzling paucity, for the region has gold-bearing rivers, and early Spanish chroniclers describe the collection of quantities of gold from Gulf of Nicoya peoples.
   During test excavations at the Nacascolo site in 1978, Accola (1980) found an elite burial incorporating the primary remains of an adult male, several male and female skulls, bone bundles, a stone celt, and eleven complete ceramic vessels, including many local polychromes with Feathered Serpent and other Mexicanoid motifs. Incorporated in a shell-bead bracelet was a copper bell, with its suspension ring missing (Lange and Accola 1979: 26). Its pear shape, with teardroplike ornamental loops, place it in Lothrop's Style D5 (1952: fig. 84b). Citing the Papagayo/Pataky-type polychrome ceramics associated with the bell, Accola dates it *c.* AD 1000–1200. Although some native copper is present in Costa Rica, Precolumbian copper bells are usually taken as evidence of northern trade. Bell-making centers are postulated for Honduras, Oaxaca–Central Mexico, and West Mexico, but it is not clear which of these (or other) centers produced the bells found in Costa Rica. Lothrop noted that, on the basis of metallurgical analysis, the Style D5 bells appear not to have been made in the Valley of Mexico.

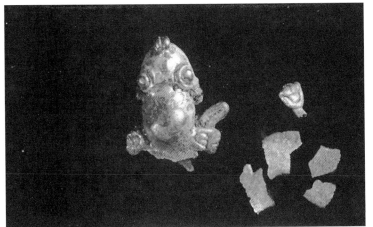

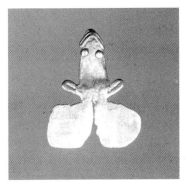

Fig. 10
Gold frog pendant discovered at Guacamaya near Culebra Bay,
Guanacaste, AD 800–1200.
H. ⅞ in. (2·1 cm.)
Museo Nacional de Costa Rica, San José.
Photo: Frederick W. Lange.

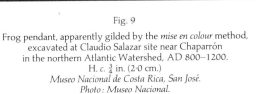

Fig. 9
Frog pendant, apparently gilded by the *mise en colour* method,
excavated at Claudio Salazar site near Chaparrón
in the northern Atlantic Watershed, AD 800–1200.
H. *c.* ¾ in. (2·0 cm.)
Museo Nacional de Costa Rica, San José.
Photo: Museo Nacional.

Lange and Accola (1979) see this bell as indicating the shift in Costa Rican trade routes, hence, in cultural influence, from lowland Maya to Mexican contacts.

Teams directed by Lange found, in 1976, a clay mold for a metal frog pendant (Bray, this volume, fig. 3). Two years later, at another site near Culebra Bay, they picked up a similar gold frog from a refuse midden (fig. 10). These finds suggest that metallurgical techniques were known in Guanacaste–Nicoya and that casting was done locally (Lange and Accola 1979). Both frog figures show tiny bent legs and large splayed feet (the mold shows that these were cast, not hammered). The mold also has four spiral false-filigree elements around the mouth, placing it in Aguilar's (1972a: 78, fig. 50b) class of 'Frogs with mouth decoration of spirals B.'

Arenal Volcano In the spring of 1984, a team directed by Payson Sheets found another small, gold, avian pendant (fig. 12), like those from Barrial and the Gulf of Nicoya, outside a tomb in a Middle Polychrome (AD 800–1200) cemetery on the Continental Divide between Guanacaste and San Carlos. The cemetery contained a modified variety of stone-cist tombs (mostly flagstones) placed at much greater depth (*c.* 3 m.) than those of the Central Highlands–Atlantic Watershed; it represents the first recorded instance of stone-cist tombs—*c.* AD 1000—in Guanacaste.

Gulf of Nicoya Winifred Creamer (1983) excavated a child's burial on San Lucas, one of the two largest islands in the Gulf of Nicoya. Grave goods included three simple monochrome pots, the annular base of a polychrome vessel, bone earspools, and a necklace composed of shell beads, drilled human teeth, and a tumbaga, bird pendant (fig. 13) like that described for Barrial de Heredia. Creamer's ceramic analysis suggests that her example dates 300–500 years later than the Barrial occupation. Her excavations,

the first controlled recovery of Precolumbian metals in Nicoya, show that the late prehistoric inhabitants of the Gulf were in touch with eastern or southern Costa Rica, and probably with places much farther away.

La Ceiba (Tempisque River) During 1982 and 1983, Juan Vicente Guerrero and Aida Blanco excavated an elite burial ground (AD 800–1200) near the town of Filadelfia. The tombs contained primary extended skeletons and secondary bone bundles, as well as quantities of ceramics of many styles. While only sometimes could the sex of the skeletal remains be designated (preservation was relatively poor), polished and chipped axes or projectile points were thought to indicate men, whereas spindle whorls and larger amounts of plain culinary ceramics pointed to women. Carved tripod metates were found with both sexes.

Associated with the cemetery was a culinary zone with large numbers of cigar-shaped or long (over 4 m.) rectangular, fired adobe hearths. Since no houses or domestic debris were noted, the tightly packed parallel hearths are thought to represent funerary-rite feasts. The identification of a carbonized chocolate pod (*Theobroma cacao*) among quantities of maize, and other foods reinforces this interpretation (C. Earle Smith, Jr., personal communication).

In one of two adjacent burials with many ceramic goods, three tiny copper bells appeared as part of a bracelet on the wrist area (fig. 14); they can be classed as Lothrop's Style D (1952: fig. 80), with an added circumferential molding near the suspension ring. These bells, now broken, were 1–2 cm. long when complete. In the adjacent burial (a male), an anthropomorphic pendant was found in the chest area, probably originally hung around the neck (fig. 15). It is a large (over 6 cm.) cacique pendant of Aguilar's 'feathered headdress' type (1972a: 53, fig. 28). Two diagonal projections (feathers) frame a vertical cylindrical element on the head. Aguilar

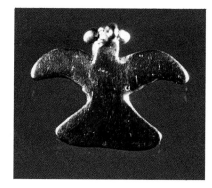

Fig. 11
Avian pendant of cast gold excavated at Barrial de Heredia
near San José, AD 900–1100.
H. ¾ in. (2 cm.)
Museo Nacional de Costa Rica, San José.
Photo: Museo Nacional.

Fig. 12
Avian pendant of cast gold excavated at a site
at Arenal volcano, Guanacaste, AD 800–1200.
H. 1 in. (2·5 cm.)
Museo Nacional de Costa Rica, San José.
Photo: Francine Mandel-Sheets.

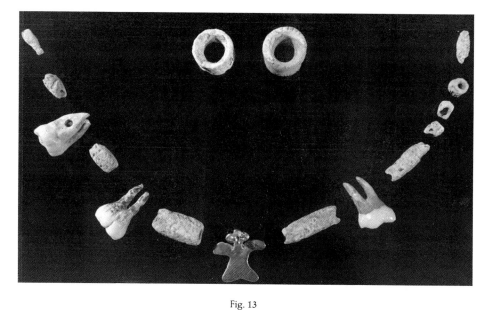

Fig. 13
Gold avian pendant and beads, apparently from a necklace,
and a pair of bone ear ornaments.
Excavated at San Lucas Island, Gulf of Nicoya, AD 1200–1500.
Museo Nacional de Costa Rica, San José.
Photo: Winifred Creamer.

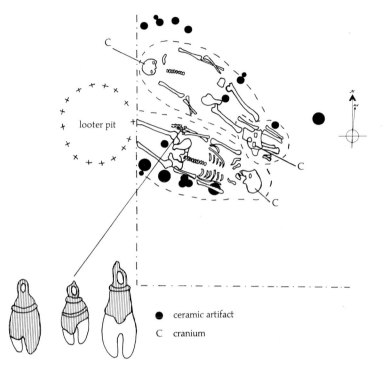

Fig. 14

Two adjoining burials excavated at La Ceiba site, Guanacaste, AD 800–1200, were accompanied by numerous ceramic vessels. The lower individual also had three copper bells at his wrist.
Drawing: Eugene Fleury, after Ricardo Vásquez.

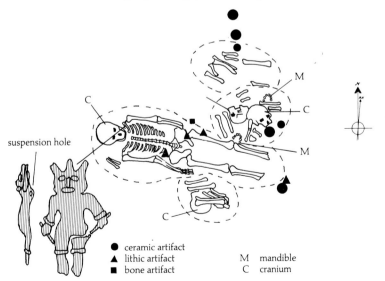

Fig. 15

A primary and three secondary burials excavated at La Ceiba site, Guanacaste, AD 800–1200.
In the primary burial, a copper or tumbaga cacique-type figure was found at the neck area suggesting that it was worn on interment. In the hands of the tumbaga figure is a ropelike element that may be a double-headed snake.
Drawing: Eugene Fleury, after Ricardo Vázquez.

sees a relationship with some Darién-style figurines from Colombia; the open-back casting recalls Veraguas. However, the numbers of similar pendants found in Costa Rica, as well as the flat, splayed, paddlelike feet, indicate that it is not an import. There is an avian look to the face/mask, and the cord held in both hands must represent a snake. The surface is eroded light-green copper oxide, but the weight of the piece suggests that it is of tumbaga with a high copper content.

Diquís

This region, with the greatest quantity and diversity of Precolumbian gold, has the fewest controlled archaeological data on tomb associations; hence, chronology is insecure. In early publications, it is often not clear if the authors carried out the excavations or if they relied on information from *huaqueros*.

MacCurdy (1911: 214–215) commented on the large quantities of gold ornaments taken from a cemetery called Huacal de los Reyes near Térraba. During the last 60 years, sites that have become famous for the quantities of gold artifacts brought out by looters include Coquito, Huaca de la Reina, La Vaca, Puerto González Víquez, and United Fruit Farms 4, 5, and 7, in the delta near Palmar Sur. One of three rich tombs opened in 1956 on Farm 4 contained 88 artifacts of metal, including 34 cast pendants of different styles in gold and tumbaga, 30 plain discs, ten headbands, five discs with geometric embossed decoration, five bells, two gold crescents (probably worn on the chest), and two gold cuffs (Lothrop 1963: 93–94). Many pieces were apparently made specifically for burial; flaws or casting errors were not repaired, and suspension hooks show no wear.

At Jalaca (Stone 1963), burials 1–5 m. deep were not individually marked or formed by slabs (there were occasional lids), and were covered by gravel and earth brought from elsewhere. Children were present; skulls were missing from some graves. The gold and tumbaga objects were placed in the neck and chest areas, probably worn by the deceased. Large avian figures with ornate head decoration fall into Aguilar's (1972a: 21–26) Veraguas and Jalaca types. Also present were bells, a rattle, a turtle with a twisted 'rope' in its mouth and front feet, and a cacique-type figurine (Aguilar's [1972a: fig. 28] 'Humans with feathered headdresses'). Most pieces discussed here were probably made AD 600–1550. Stone (1954) tells of finding, near the Chánguina River, beads made from rolled strips of gold alloy, along with iron tools and millefiori glass beads, signs of the Spanish presence.

ACKNOWLEDGEMENTS

The author was helped by conversations with colleagues Maria Eugenia Bozzoli, Carlos Aguilar, Oscar Fonseca, and Ana Cecilia Arias of the Universidad de Costa Rica, as well as Ricardo Vazquez, Aida Blanco, Juan Vicento Guerrero, and Maritza Gutierrez of the Museo Nacional de Costa Rica, some of whom generously gave permission to use unpublished data and photos from their excavations. Thanks also go to Frederick Lange, Francine Sheets, Winifred Creamer, and The Detroit Institute of Arts, the Museo Nacional de Costa Rica, and the Banco Central de Costa Rica for allowing photographs to be reproduced.

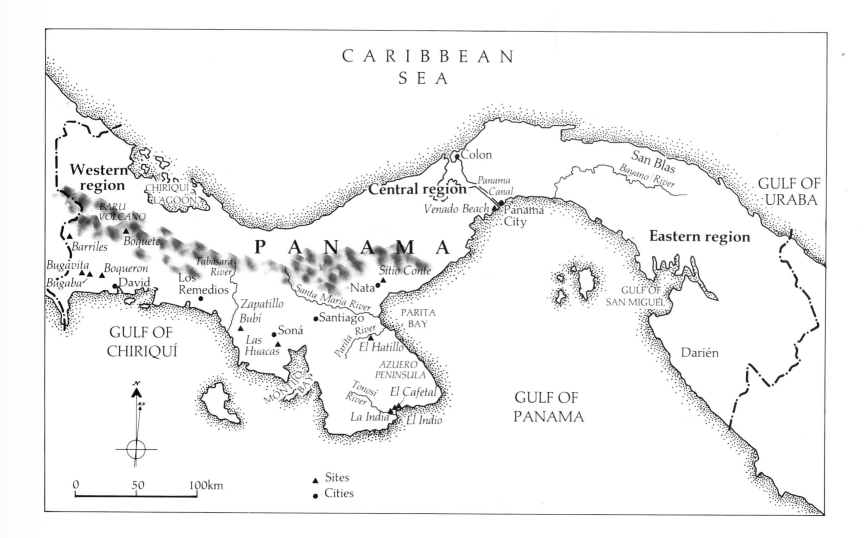

CARIBBEAN
SEA

Western region

CHIRIQUÍ
LAGOON

BARÚ
VOLCANO

Colon

San Blas

Bayano River

Central region

Panama Canal

Venado Beach

Panama
City

GULF OF
URABA

▲
Barriles

▲
Boquete

P A N A M A

Eastern region

Bugavita
▲ ▲ *Boqueron*
Bugaba ● David

Los
Remedios

*Tabasara
River*

Sitio Conte
▲

● Nata

GULF OF
SAN MIGUEL

*Zapatillo
Bubí*

Santa María River

Santiago
●

PARITA
BAY

▲ *Las
Huacas*

● *Soná*

*Parita
River*

GULF OF
CHIRIQUÍ

El Hatillo

*AZUERO
PENINSULA*

Darién

*MONTIJO
BAY*

*Tonosí
River*

El Cafetal

GULF OF
PANAMA

La India

El Indio

N

0   50   100km

▲ Sites
● Cities

The Goldwork of Panama:
An Iconographic and Chronological Perspective

RICHARD G. COOKE and WARWICK BRAY

This essay emphasizes the symbolism and regional stylistic evolution of Panamanian goldwork. Our classificatory system (table 1) is different from that of earlier summaries (e.g., Lothrop 1937, 1950; Emmerich 1965; Roosevelt 1979). Prepared by Bray in 1984 (Bray n.d.), it takes into account the most recent research into cultural geography, archaeological periodization, iconography, and exchange networks (see map; table 2; Helms 1977, 1979; Linares 1977; Linares and Ranere 1980; Cooke 1984a, 1984b).[1]

THE ORIGINS AND SOURCES
OF PANAMANIAN METALWORK

Metal objects appeared on the Isthmus of Panama during the first five hundred years of the Christian era. All lines of evidence point to the Tairona and Quimbaya areas of Colombia as the principal sources of inspiration and to the Gulf of Urabá as the original contact point. The vagueness of the introductory date is due to current uncertainties over the chronology and interrelationships of the pottery styles with which the earliest metal objects have been associated. Although we have included these objects within an 'Initial Group,' they are not primitive. They demonstrate complete control over alloying, hammering, annealing, depletion gilding, open-back casting, and lost-wax casting over a clay core (Bray n.d.).

The Colombian origin of some cast items found in Panama has been apparent since the Sitio Conte excavations (Lothrop 1937: figs. 115i, 137a). Some authors, arguing that early Spanish documents do not describe metal-casting on the Isthmus, have claimed that goldworking in Panama was limited to hammering sheet metal and to gilding already-cast pieces, and that all alloyed lost-wax figurines were imported from Colombia (Sauer 1966; Helms 1979). In the Contact-period chronicles, there are only two reliable references to the melting of gold in Panama. A 1513 letter of Balboa (1913: 135) states that the chief Comogre exchanged cotton cloth and slaves for gold to be 'melted.' Benzoni illustrates Panamanian Indians melting gold to pour into the throats of captive Spaniards (Benzoni 1857: 73). These references do not specifically mention casting, yet Agustín de Ceballos, a Franciscan priest residing in Talamanca (Caribbean Costa Rica) during the early 17th century, describes a casting tradition that must surely be a Precolumbian survival.

'The Indians hereabouts make . . . eagles, lizards, toads, spiders, medals, plates, and many other items of gold, many kinds of which they work by pouring gold into molds after melting it down in clay crucibles . . . their poor skill obliges them to mix copper in order to melt the gold . . . but in the plates, which they only beat and extend without having to mix [copper], the purity of the gold is noteworthy, reaching 22 carats'
(Fernández Guardia 1968: 9–10; RGC's translation)

New archaeological data corroborate the documentary allusions to casting in Panama. Metal residue from the casting process has been found, as well as several badly miscast pieces from Coclé and Veraguas, which would have been useless for exchange (fig. 1). Moreover, in 1951, 8 km. northwest of El Caño (Coclé), the tomb of a goldsmith was discovered, with seven collapsed furnaces, molds, a quantity of river sand with flakes of gold and copper, and painted plates and personal jewelry, including gold-capped ear rods (personal communication to WB from excavator). A basalt chisel from the Azuero Peninsula, with a heavy residue of gold at the tip, has been used as a polishing tool.

Gold and copper are quite abundant in Panama. Placer deposits were widely used for acquiring gold dust and nuggets in Contact times (Anghiera 1912, I: 404; Colón 1959: 241–261; Oviedo 1944–45, 13: 19) and have continued to be exploited by itinerant miners on both coasts (Castillero 1967). Fernando Colón (1959: 252) talks of 'mines' at over a day's walk from the coast in the chiefdom of Urirá, perhaps the River Santiago or Concepción mines, which were productive between 1560 and 1590 (Castillero 1967: 59–60). Modern commercial activities have concentrated on deposits in Veraguas, eastern Chiriquí, and Darién.

The iconography of many cast pieces affirms their Panamanian manufacture. Motifs on many are so similar to those on the polychrome pottery that it would be illogical to assume that the ceramics are local and the gold objects imported (Linares 1977; Cooke 1984a).

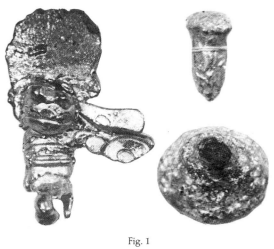

Fig. 1
Miscast figure (left) and casting residue from Central Panama.
The miscast figure is less than 6 cm. high.
Photo: courtesy of Warwick Bray.

THE SOCIAL CONTEXT OF PANAMANIAN METALLURGY

Once introduced, metal objects rapidly became the primary symbols of authority in Isthmian society. Important people bedecked their bodies with gold. They used it to bribe allies and to pay ransoms for captured sons. They stole it from their rivals, and, in times of danger, hoarded it in secret places in large baskets (Acosta 1848: 97; Anghiera 1912: 403–407; Espinosa 1913a: 170, 172, 179; 1913b: 281, 284). Stone statues from Barriles (Chiriquí) show female and male figures with what must be gold anthropomorphic pendants suspended by cords around the neck (Haberland 1973; Linares et al. 1975). A stone male statue from El Caño (Coclé) has a large gold frog hanging down his back (RGC, personal observation).

Gold also accompanied important personages in death. Anghiera (1912: 218) records how golden masks covered the faces of Comogre's ancestors in the mortuary house. In 1519, Gaspar de Espinosa chanced upon funerary rites for a number of important people, including his erstwhile rival, Parita, all of whom had been decked out for burial.

'Each [person] was covered up in a long bundle, the upper cover of hammocks, very fine and very well made . . . tied with fiber cord . . . and underneath [this] another wrap and cover of many very good and brightly painted blankets, tied in the same way with cotton string and, farther inside, another wrap of thinner and finer blankets, tied in the same way with cords made of Indian hair, and inside this the body of the dead person, one of whom they said was chief Parita . . . he was all covered in gold, and on his head [was] a large basin of gold, like a helmet, and around his neck four or five collars made like a gorget, and on his arms gold armor shaped like tubes . . . and on his chest and back many pieces and platters and other pieces made like large piaster coins, and a gold belt, surrounded with gold bells, and on his legs gold armor, too, so that the way the said body of the said chief was arranged, he looked like a suit of armor or an embroidered corset . . . at his head was a dead women, and at his feet another, who also had on many pieces of gold. And in the other two bundles were two other chiefs . . . who were covered with gold in the same way, and, although not so richly or elegantly, in large quantities . . .'
(Espinosa 1913b: 280; RGC's translation)

In life and in death, then, gold was the symbol of rank and prestige. 'Each man attempted to make himself conspicuous to the eye so that his deeds might not be overlooked and the leaders wore some outstanding ornament such as a golden helmet or a huge breast plate. . . .' (Lothrop 1937: 22).

At the same time, it is important to view Panamanian metallurgy within the context of Tropical Forest tribal societies to whom gold pieces conveyed diverse kinds of information about the human social, natural, and supernatural environments (Linares 1977; Helms 1977, 1979). Although the precise meanings are lost, we can attempt some decipherment by identifying the animals and human types represented in the images, by referring to 15th- and 16th-century documents, and by making cautious analogies with the myths, legends, and social behavior of the present-day Chibcha-speaking groups of Panama and Costa Rica (Legast 1980; Cooke 1984b).

Fig. 2
Embossed gold plaque with a split representation of frog/pelicans.
Excavated at Sitio Conte, Cocle province.
After Lothrop 1937: fig. 88.

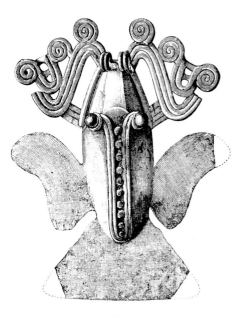

Fig. 3
Tumbaga pendant in frog form
with spread-eagled bird wings and tail.
After Holmes 1888: fig. 40.

ICONOGRAPHY

Zoomorphic Representations Isthmian craftsmen often depicted animals as identifiable taxa (Holmes 1888; Helms 1977; Linares 1977). Some Conte Polychrome pottery effigies, for example, can be identified to the family, genus, and even species level (Cooke 1984b). At times, prominent visual characteristics common to a number of taxa within an order—forked tongues, long crests and plumes, and clawed feet—were intentionally exaggerated, permitting identification only as 'birds,' 'mammals,' 'fish,' and so on. The appendages noted above are also used in combinations quite against the laws of taxonomy, so that composite 'beasts' or 'monsters' are created, with reptilian claws, bird plumes, and insect wings. In these cases, metaphorical significance was presumably more important than taxonomic precision. Linares (1976, 1977) has proposed that certain animal species and characteristics were emphasized to draw attention to the aggressive or warlike attributes of the wearer or that they functioned as insignia of individual warriors in a highly competitive rank society. 'Property marks' were used to brand war captives (Oviedo 1944–45, 7: 305). Helms (1981) has speculated that the animal figures embossed on personal items were, in fact, 'property marks.' The human-animal relationships visible on metal pieces might be related to kinship nomenclature and origin myths (Cooke 1984b); the owners of the gold and pottery wore, or were buried with, only depictions of organisms that identified their clan or other descent group. Bribri myths refer to ancestors brought to earth by giant birds and to parrots and macaws who taught people to speak (Bozzoli 1977, 1979). The first idea may be reflected in the spread-eagled birds that carry human beings, and the second in human faces with psittacid ears and with tongues that have parrot heads on the end; these are commonly represented on Central Region polychromes and metal objects (Cooke 1984b).

Animal motifs are often 'twinned' or joined. Tails have the heads of other animals at their ends. Long, sinewy tongues are often head-bearing. Faces have 'headdresses' or 'frames' shaped like other zoomorphic forms. In goldwork, as in polychrome pottery, 'split representation' is encountered (fig. 2); a single design element represents more than one image (Linares 1976; Cooke 1984b). This device is amenable to the common belief of American Tropical tribes that objects, individuals, and social groupings possess alter egos, a light and a dark side, human and animal in one.

Naturalistic images depicting an identifiable taxon with varying degrees of precision are common on cast figurines and bells found between Yucatán and Colombia. Traditionally identified as Panamanian, particularly 'Veraguas' (Lothrop 1950), they are here classified as belonging mostly to the International Group, not necessarily of Panamanian origin.

The majority of naturalistic images fall into five broad categories: (1) *fish*, usually with sharklike fins and tail; (2) *anurans* with froglike rather than toadlike morphologies; (3) *spread-eagled birds* with long, generally downcurved bills; (4) *felids*—jaguars, ocelots, and/or pumas—often indistinguishable from other Panamanian carnivorous mammals such as the tayra, *Eira barbara*; and (5) *saurians*—lizards, iguanas, and/or crocodilians (see Helms 1977). Many other animals are also utilized realistically. The anteater, armadillo, crab, deer, dog, freshwater shrimp, kinkajou, parrot, Marine Toad, and sea- and river-turtles have been found in archaeological middens in

Fig. 4
Cast pendant of a feline with animal head tail
and a human arm in its mouth.
L. 3 in. (7·5 cm.).
Museum of Fine Arts, Boston; Maria Wharton Wales Fund, 22.306.
Photo: Museum of Fine Arts.

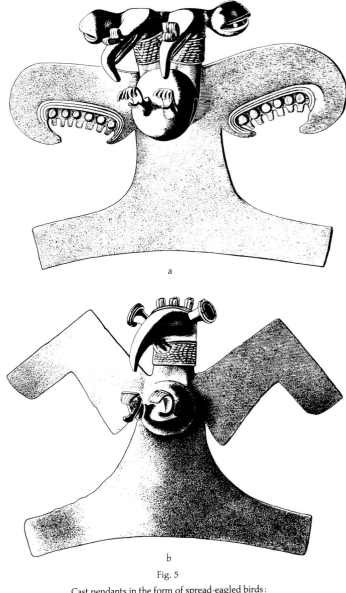

a

b

Fig. 5
Cast pendants in the form of spread-eagled birds:
(a) possibly represents a King Vulture and
(b) a hummingbird.
After Lothrop 1950: fig. 72.

the Santa María drainage and were probably common in Panama (Cooke 1979, 1981, 1984a; Linares and White 1980; Wing 1980). All, including the Marine Toad, were regularly eaten. The abundance of gold frogs, felines, and crocodilians, and their combination with double-headed tongues (fig. 3) and animal-ended tails (fig. 4) implies a less mundane iconographic significance; all over Tropical America, they figure prominently in myths. Felines carrying human arms in their mouths may refer to myths or legends of individual places or tribes.

When Columbus passed along the coast of Bocas del Toro in 1502, his son Fernando saw 'Indians who were as naked as they came from their mothers' wombs. Some wore only a gold mirror at the neck, and others a "*guanín*" eagle' (Colón 1959: 241). Over a century later, Fray Adrián de la Rocha, who worked among the Doraces on the slopes of the Barú Volcano in Chiriquí, talks of pendants 'made like eagles, with open wings and a long and curved beak' (1964: 94–95). Bird pendants with outstretched wings and tail are abundant in Panamanian goldwork, in forms recalling Colombian types (Lothrop 1937: fig. 177). They are usually identified as 'eagles.' Those with beaks sharply curved at the tip and prominent ceres could be King Vultures, *Sarcorhamphus papa* (fig. 5a; Emmerich 1965: figs. 135, 139). Figure 6 shows a realistic owl.

Raptors probably had specific mythical significance. In Bribri myths, culture heroes fend off hawks and King Vultures that swoop down upon unsuspecting mortals (Bozzoli 1977). Human beings grasped in raptor beaks, on gold pectorals, may represent primeval culture heroes being carried down to earth. It is not certain, however, that all such birds are raptors. Many examples have a long, gently curving beak, lacking a cere, and a wing-and-tail pattern that might be interpreted as that of a hummingbird (fig. 5b; Cooke 1984b: fig. 6).

The spread-eagled bird motif, long-lived on painted Panamanian pottery, obeyed the stylistic changes typical of Central Region polychromes, that is, stylized-realistic-exhuberant-geometricized (Cooke 1976b: fig. 2). A similar evolutionary pattern begins to be apparent with the metal bird figurines, although the absence of colors and the techniques of goldworking make this less obvious (cf. fig. 13h [early?] with fig. 5 [late?]).

Zoomorphic figures combining obvious elements of more than one organism are rarer on gold than on ceramics. Lothrop (1950: fig. 102) illustrates a beast with a turtle body and a tapir or anteater head. Figure 3 depicts a Chiriquí frog, with characteristics of two common Neotropical genera, *Leptodactylus* and *Rana*, and spread-eagled bird wings and tail (see also fig. 2).

Cast-metal figurines and embossed plaques commonly combine animal and human characteristics. The most prevalent associations are with bats and saurians. Classifiable under the Conte and Veraguas–Gran Chiriquí groups, their primary centers of manufacture are likely to have been the Central Region and Gran Chiriquí, mostly between AD 700 and the Conquest. These figures have bat and saurian heads; the bodies, and sometimes the hands and feet, are human. They may be dressed as humans and may carry weapons. Customarily referred to as 'gods,' they are more reasonably interpreted as tribal man-animal culture heroes, mythical warriors, eponymous clan markers, or alter egos (Helms 1977).

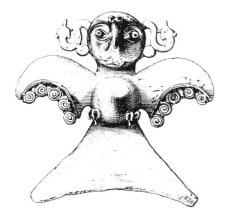

Fig. 6
Spread-eagled bird pendant representing an owl.
After Bollaert 1860: opp. page 32.

Fig. 7
Cast pendant representing twinned bat-human figures
holding paddle-shaped clubs and spear throwers.
Reportedly from Chiriquí province, Panama.
H. 3 in. (7·5 cm.).
*The Metropolitan Museum of Art, New York,
Gift of Meredith Howland, 04.34.8.
Photo: Metropolitan Museum.*

The bat-human figures (fig. 7) have anatomical features of the former: a nose leaf, erect ears, and open mouths showing pointed teeth. Sometimes they have small feet, held in clinging position, and crescent-shaped wings with medial claws. The figures are frequently twinned; occasionally, they have eyes on 'pegs,' as if the artisan were accentuating their ability to see at night. The Bribri believe that the bat exemplifies contrasts, symbolizing the upper world by its ability to fly and the nether world by its nocturnal life and ability to hang upside-down and drag itself along the ground. In one creation myth, a bat flies to the center of the earth to suck the blood of a young girl (Bozzoli 1979: 156). Vampires are common in Panama, and the association of these figures with warlike attributes is logical. Paddle-shaped clubs, brandished by bats, saurians, and naturalistic human beings (figs. 7 and 9c) are probably the wooden *macanas*, or clubs, mentioned in the 16th-century chronicles (e.g., Andagoya 1913: 197; Herrera 1944–47: 325; Oviedo 1944–45, 7: 300). Figure 7 shows twinned bat-humans carrying paddle-shaped clubs and spearthrowers, identifiable by the hooks at one end. A stone spearthrower was found at El Caño (RGC, personal observation), and the chronicles refer to the use of spearthrowers in battle (e.g. Espinosa 1913b: 285)

The second major category of anthropomorphized animals comprises reptiles, which can be variously interpreted as iguanas, basilisk lizards, crocodiles, or caimans (fig. 8). Helms (1977) made a strong case for some figures being iguanas, while those with tricuspid teeth she identifies as basilisk lizards. Iguanas figure prominently in the myths of the Talamancan groups and of the Kuna, although sometimes not quite in the capacity described by Helms. The consumption of iguana meat, associated with warrior elites, had a ritual significance in ancient Panama (Espinosa 1913b: 280 and passim). Crocodiles and caimans are also represented, with long, flat snouts with prominent nostrils, rows of sharp teeth, and, occasionally, skin markings. Although some lacertilian images can be identified to the generic or specific level, many have only generalized saurian traits.

Saurian-human figures are depicted with about equal frequency on embossed plaques (fig. 8) and cast-metal figurines. Some examples so resemble one of the most common motifs of the Macaracas Polychrome pottery (AD 700–1100; fig. 9b) that it is reasonable to assume contemporaneity. The saurian-human has a long history in ceramics, however, demonstrating an internal evolution: Figure 9a, from Grave 32 at Sitio Conte dates, on current evidence, from shortly before AD 500 (Cooke 1976b; Ichon 1980), and the motif continues to the last Precolumbian centuries.

Saurian-humans often wear a belt, fashioned to look like thick, twisted cord. This is also worn by some bat-human, spread-eagled-bird, and realistic human representations; sometimes it is placed in the figure's mouth. At the ends are heads of animals, which may be saurians, snakes, or fish(?). Helms (1977: 95–96) concludes that two Sitio Conte plaques represent a 'priest-chief/hero-deity clad in a belt or sash with long ends falling to [beyond] his feet, which are actually depicted in the form of iguanas. Both the belt, as an aspect of "golden clothing," and the iguanas signify the chief-hero-deity's solar affiliation.' Many counterarguments could be garnered from the ethnographic literature. Since the cord often emanates

Fig. 8
Embossed gold plaque with a saurian-human figure.
H. 10¾ in. (27·7 cm.).
Excavated at Sitio Conte, Coclé province.
The University Museum, Philadelphia, 40-13-26.
Photo: University Museum.

Fig. 9

Saurian-human depictions found on pottery vessels
from Sitio Conte (a, b) and in a cast pendant (c).
The similarity of (b) and (c) suggests contemporaneity, AD 700–1100.
After Lothrop 1940: (a) fig. 227; (b) fig. 148.
Drawing (c): courtesy of Warwick Bray.

from the area of the penis, which is sometimes in the form of a snake or fish(?), it possibly has sexual or procreative significance. The Bribri believe that endogamic incest is punished by death from snake bite (Bozzoli 1979), while human male sexuality is commonly related by Tropical tribes to snakes, toads, and fish (Reichel-Dolmatoff 1971: 90, 102–103). Fray Adrián de Ufeldre (1965: 77), who worked among the Ngawbere-speaking Guaymí in the early 17th century, related a painful story: 'To placate the lightning god . . . they would pierce their foreskins with a fish spine . . . and through the hole . . . would then thread a cotton cord, half a finger thick, whose ends they would tie to two sticks . . . and they would all sing running the cord back and forth until the subject bled heavily. . . .' An Openwork saurian-human has a twisted cord belt and deer antlers (fig. 10). The *cucua* dancers of the Caribbean Coclé use deer masks with antlers for their *'danza de los diablos'* (Torres de Araúz 1972a).

The sideways saurian head, with prominent crocodilian teeth and upturned snout ending in a volute, is used to frame or 'crown' other figures. One spread-eagled bird with a bat or feline head protruding from its stomach, has a double saurian crest (Lothrop 1950: fig. 75). These crests are perhaps best interpreted in terms of zoomorphic duality or 'energy symbols' (Helms 1977: 102).

Conventional Human Figurines There are many realistic human portrayals—both male and female—belonging primarily to the International Group. They illustrate details of dress, music, dance, and warfare. Because they were apparently manufactured over a wide area, however, it is dangerous to assume that they contain information necessarily representative of the cultural patterns of a specific region. There are gold figurines with conical hats, which are also encountered on statues from Barriles and on ceramics from the same general area (Linares et al. 1975). The Ngawbé Guaymí used bark-cloth conical hats during their stick-throwing ceremony, the *balsería* (Johnson 1948: pl. 45; Young 1971, 1976).

A number of cast-gold figurines—usually naked males, sometimes with plumed headdresses—carry small, rattlelike objects in both hands, while others appear to play flutes (fig. 11). They seem to be engaging in an activity that incorporates chanting and dancing. Some of the many rattle shapes look like the traditional gourd rattles used by the Kuna. The present-day Ngawbé play small flutes, made of deer tibiae, throughout the night during the balsería (RGC, personal observation). The objects carried by the man in figure 12b are similar in shape to the flat curing sticks used by the Chocó of eastern Panama; little parrot-shaped rattles also suggest shamanistic or curing activities. Some figures display erections and hold their hands with palms out, as if they were dancing in a trance or a similarly aroused state. The twisted sash of figure 11 might have had a mundane function, for shell penis-sheaths, tied on with strings, are recorded from Caribbean Panama in Contact times (Andagoya 1913: 193).

Realistic human warrior figures are usually twinned. A piece from Grave 5 at Sitio Conte (Lothrop 1937: fig. 150; AD 700–900) shows two men with a headpiece in the form of a tail, recalling de la Rocha's (1964: 93) description of the Doraces of Chiriquí with hair tied with bark-cloth strands to look like a thick canvas hanging a yard or so down the back. The Sitio

Fig. 10
Cast pendant of saurian-human with deer antlers on his head,
an example from the Openwork Group.
H. 3⅛ in. (7·9 cm.).
The Cleveland Museum of Art; Gift of Mrs. Benjamin P. Bole, 46.80.
Photo: Cleveland Museum.

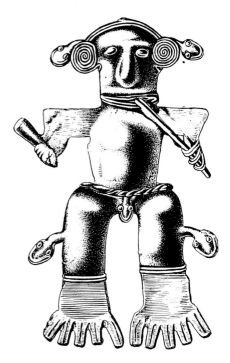

Fig. 11
Cast pendant of male figure possibly playing a flute.
After Lothrop 1950: fig. 107.

Conte figures also wear necklaces, leg bindings, and a small loincloth. Embalmed(?) parrots hang suspended by a cord at the waist. The figures bear flat wooden macanas with human trophy heads dangling from them.

Female figurines are usually nude (fig. 12a); however, they have elaborate hairdos, necklaces, and wear ligatures on their legs. There is little Contact-period information on female attire. Some women wore skirts (Andagoya 1913: 193), and those of high rank wore painted cotton blankets.

STYLE AND CHRONOLOGY

Our classification and chronology concentrate on items that can be associated with known pottery types and radiocarbon dates, emphasizing, for reasons of space, objects from sites not well known in the English literature (Bray n.d.). Five stylistic clusters or metal groups are discernible: Initial Group, Openwork Group, International Group, Conte Group, and Veraguas-Gran Chiriquí Group (table 1). It seems that each group occupies a particular segment of time, with its own development and characteristic spatial distribution. The current periodization for the Central Region pottery styles, to which several pieces are referred, is summarized in table 2.

The Initial Group

This, the oldest metalwork on the Isthmus, is obviously introduced from outside, appearing in Panama as a homogeneous stylistic and technological manifestation, with the Tairona and Quimbaya regions of Colombia the most likely progenitors. Four sites in the Central Region have Initial Group pieces (see map):

Rancho Sancho de la Isla, Coclé (Dade 1960) Three tumbaga chisels were found in Dade's Burial 18. The associated pottery comprises a Conte-style turtle effigy and seven vessels classifiable as Montevideo Group, transitional between Periods IV and V (Cooke 1972: 400–402; Ichon 1980).

El Cafetal, Los Santos (González 1971; Ichon 1980) The pottery from this cemetery belongs to Ichon's El Indio phase (AD 200–500), corresponding to the later part of Period IV. In two graves, metal objects (fig. 13a–e) were associated with Period IV pottery. A radiocarbon date of AD 390 ± 100 (Gif-1641) was recovered from a refuse dump in a context described as transitional between Periods IV and V. González found also a broken armadillo head and a tumbaga plaque.

La India-1, Los Santos (Mitchell and Heidenreich 1965; Ichon 1980) Various kinds of burial were found at this site (Russell Mitchell, personal communication to WB): (1) bundle burials or jumbled bones, with fragments of tumbaga sheet (possibly cuffs), a pendant in the form of three conjoined curly-tailed animals, a spiral nose ring, part of a bell-eyed creature, a conical nose clip, and a large, double, spread-eagled bird (fig. 14); (2) a flexed burial on top of a large, oval metate, associated with a spiral nose ring; (3) a burial inside a Tonosí trichrome urn of Period IV (Mitchell and Heidenreich 1965: pl. 2a), containing a double-animal effigy of tumbaga; and (4) burials in urns of Ichon's La India Rouge type, accompanied by a spread-eagled bird (fig. 13h), two tumbaga discs, a frog effigy (fig. 13j), and a quadruple-bird pendant (fig. 13i).

Fig. 12
Pendants depicting female (a) and male (b) figures were
apparently widely distributed; (b) was found in Yucatán.
After (a) Lothrop 1937, fig. 147; (b) 1940, fig. 395.

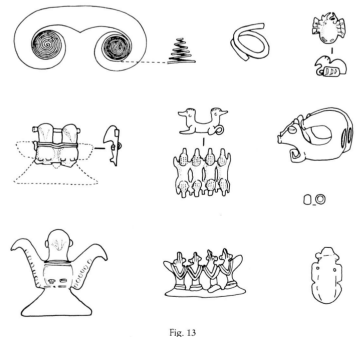

Fig. 13
Initial Group objects from the sites of El Cafetal (a to e),
Las Huacas (f, g) and La India-l (h to j), AD 1–500.
Drawing: courtesy of Warwick Bray, (a, c–e) after Inchon 1980.

Las Huacas, Veraguas (Casimir 1971, 1972, 1973: 131–134)   This cemetery has been extensively excavated, but the material has never been completely studied. Individual shaft-and-chamber tombs were apparently reused in different periods. Metal objects consist of wire rings, spherical and tubular beads (fig. 13g), a pair of conjoined curly-tailed animals in surface-enriched tumbaga (fig. 13f), five necklace elements cast over clay cores, an enigmatic tumbaga object, and a large, double-headed, spread-eagled tumbaga bird, which is fragmented. The one radiocarbon sample from the site (AD 405 ± 100) is associated with Period IV and IV/V pottery.

These four sites indicate that metal objects—tools as well as jewelry—were widely used in Panama before the advent of the four-color Conte polychrome ceramics (AD 500). Stylistically, the objects form a fairly homogeneous group. The presence of spread-eagled bird figures in the Initial Group inventory shows that this motif had a long history in Panamanian iconography, both in ceramics and in metalwork. The existing radiocarbon dates average AD 415 ± 26, suggesting that metallurgy entered Panama at the beginning of the 5th century; but some Period IV gold items are possibly older than this. At Venado Beach, on the Pacific side of the old Canal Zone, some Initial Group conjoined and curly-tailed animal pieces have been found (fig. 15). A tumbaga animal with a recurved tail (Sander et al. 1958: fig. 3) is similar to a pendant from Sitio Conte Grave 32 (Lothrop 1937: fig. 174c), which, on ceramic grounds, dates *c.* AD 400–500 (Cooke 1972, 1976d). Lothrop (1937: fig. 174b) illustrates a set of Initial Group conjoined animals from Río Grande, near Panama City.

Openwork Group

Some of the most outstanding pieces from Venado Beach belong to the Openwork Group (Bray n.d.). Characterized by false-filigree and by open spaces that make attractive diamond, lattice, and scroll patterns, these are usually zoomorphic figurines (Lothrop 1956: figs. 5, 6) or nose clips; an Openwork standing deer-human figurine is illustrated in figure 10. WB believes that the Openwork Group is a local Panamanian tradition, centered in the Eastern Region, and that it might be the 'missing' early style of the Darién, a link between the Initial and Conte Groups and the early Colombian styles. It seems to be early (*c.* AD 500) and fairly short-lived. It also occurs in the Central Region, in the 'correct' stratigraphic position. At Sitio Conte, delicate openwork nose clips were found in Graves 1 and 32 (Lothrop 1937: fig. 121b–d), whose polychrome pottery dates AD 500–700.

International Group

It has been customary to incorporate objects of certain categories, which do not fit easily into any of the Panamanian regional gold styles, within the Conte style, presumably because they occur at Sitio Conte. This attribution is misleading, however, and has obscured the real significance of this quite separate tradition of metalwork. The pieces are international in distribution and content. The basic forms, with local variants, run from Yucatán and, possibly, west Mexico to Colombia. The iconography, stressing simple, realistic animal and human figures, may have been widely acceptable because of its lack of specific imagery or mythology. Its most common

Fig. 14
A double spread-eagled bird pendant from La India-l.
Initial Group, AD 1–500.
*Photo: Museum für Völkerkunde, Hamburg,
courtesy of Wolfgang Haberland.*

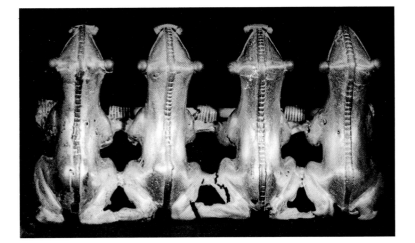

Fig. 15
Pendant of conjoined animals from Venado Beach
belonging to the Initial Group, AD 1–50.
Photo: courtesy of Neville Harte.

forms comprise human figures, bells with cylindrical handles, crocodilians, 'Darién' pendants, and animals with recurved tails. Their temporal distribution seems to be AD 400–900, though in-context radiocarbon-dated finds are needed to confirm this.

Human figurines belong to two basic types: those with uncluttered bodies, heavily lidded eyes, and prominent lips, and those with elongated, fishlike bodies, which sport a headdress with a vertical central element with long, recurved wings (fig. 16b, 17; Falchetti 1976: 85–92). The first type recalls Quimbaya figurines dated to the first millennium AD (Plazas 1978; Bray 1978) and the second, figurines from the Sinú region. The first type has been found in stratigraphic context at Sitio Conte (Lothrop 1937: figs. 147a, 148a, c), where it must date AD 500–900, but it is not common and should not be thought of as typical of a 'Coclé' culture (a term now abandoned). Present distributional evidence indicates that the Atlantic Watershed of Costa Rica was a major center of production, one that probably accounted for the figurines in the Cenote at Chichén Itzá (Bray 1977). The Sinú type has been found at Venado Beach and at Sitio Conte. At the latter site, figures with the characteristic headdress occurred in Lothrop's Grave 32 (1937: fig. 151a; AD 400–500) and in Mason's (1942) excavations in contexts dated AD 700–900. Ceramic associations indicate a life span of at least AD 400–900. An example from the Azuero Peninsula is illustrated in figure 16b. Figurines with bells or rattles with cylindrical handles, and the bells, themselves also belong to the International Group. This type of bell has been found at Río Grande, Panama City (Lothrop 1937: fig. 75c), at Venado Beach, and at Sitio Conte, in Grave 1 (AD 400–500; ibid.: fig. 74f).

Two types of crocodilian can be classified in the International Group, realistic ones (fig. 16a) and those with danglers and with ornamental plaques on the nose. The first type was found at Sitio Conte in Grave 32 (Lothrop 1937: fig. 154) and the second in Grave 15 (AD 500–700; ibid.: fig. 155b). A double caiman (ibid.: frontispiece g) is from Grave 26 (AD 700–900). Human forms and seahorses also occur.

The well-known 'telephone-bell' Darién pendants show a remarkable ability to hybridize with local styles (Falchetti 1979). In Colombia, they have a long life; in some areas, they were being manufactured after AD 1200. In Panama, they have been found at Venado Beach and around Parita Bay.

Animals with thick, recurved tails, usually squared off at the tip, most commonly have bird heads; other forms are monkeys, human beings, and doglike animals. They resemble the multiple conjoined animals of the Initial Group, but usually are modeled as a single piece. At Sitio Conte, they extend into Period VIA (Lothrop 1937: fig. 170a). Although generally attributed to a 'Coclé' culture, the greatest concentration of this style is in Atlantic Costa Rica.

The Conte Group

The Conte Group is characterized by motifs occurring on the Central Region polychromes that date mostly AD 400–1100. Saurian- and bat-human figures are the most prevalent, but there are other zoomorphic and anthropomorphic motifs, such as serpent figures, frog-pelicans (fig. 2), and

Fig. 16

International Group pendants of crocodilian form, AD 400–900
(a) from Sitio Conte (b) from the Azuero Peninsula.
Drawing: courtesy of Warwick Bray.

Fig. 17

Human figure pendant with a recurved headdress,
belonging to the International Group.
Excavated at Sitio Conte, Coclé Province, AD 700–900.
The University Museum, Philadelphia.
Photo: The University Museum.

seahorses. The close iconographic association between goldwork and ceramics suggests that the Conte Group was probably manufactured primarily within the Central Region. Its regular occurrence, however, all along the coast, from Chame to the Bayano River (Torres 1972b: 62–63), implies that this area was also involved in either manufacture or distribution, as was true of painted pottery (Cooke 1976a, 1976b). The group probably continues up to the Conquest, with internal stylistic changes, but its evolution during Period VII is scantily known.

Conte Group pieces datable by pottery associations have been reported from nine sites: Sitio Conte (Lothrop 1937; Mason 1942), Periods IVB-VIA; Sixto Pinilla (Ladd 1964: 206–207), Periods VI and VII; Cerro Zuela (Cooke 1972: 548–549), Periods IV–VI; Potrero San Luís (ibid.: 759–761), Periods VI–VII(?); Potrero Riquelme (Lothrop 1942: fig. 410), Period VIA/B; El Hatillo, or Finca J. Calderón (He-4) (Ladd 1964; Dade 1972), Periods VI–VII; Guararé (Paso Espavé) (Bull n.d.a, n.d.b); El Caño (Doyle 1960; Cooke 1976c; Torres and Velarde 1978), Period VII, and Natá (Cooke 1972: 366–370, 509–511), Period VII.

The Parita Assemblage (AD 700–1520?)   Many fine objects of the Conte Group excavated at sites on the Azuero Peninsula, especially El Hatillo (He-4), are now in museum collections in the United States. They include embossed plaques, flange-footed frogs, Darién pendants, and some splendid bat- and saurian-human figures, often twinned and holding paddle-shaped clubs (Biese 1967). The fact that most of the objects in this 'Parita Assemblage' (Bray n.d.) were excavated without field records is a tragedy to Panamanian archaeology. The polychrome pottery at the El Hatillo site belongs to Periods VI and VII (Ladd 1964), and accurate gold-ceramic associations would have enabled archaeologists to work out the relationships between pottery and metal evolution in a controlled context. At Sitio Conte, similar materials were recovered from Period VIA tombs (Lothrop 1937: figs. 71, 150, 160a; Mason 1942). Dade (1972) reports a direct association between a double-warrior pendant and Period VII polychromes at El Hatillo.

The few metal objects attributed unequivocally to Period VIIB come from El Caño, where they are associated with El Hatillo polychromes and European trade beads (fig. 18; Cooke 1976c; Torres and Velarde 1978). In general, these pieces do not reflect the fully developed Conte Group iconography nor the sumptuous artifacts described at Chief Parita's burial in 1519. The sample is small; apart from noting the prevalence of miniatures as a possible diagnostic of Period VII, we must await the *in situ* recovery of more objects before describing the late development of the Conte Group.

The Veraguas–Gran Chiriquí Group

Just before the Conquest, a unified 'Veraguas–Gran Chiriquí' style, which includes objects described by Holmes (1888), MacCurdy (1911), and Lothrop (1950), was in evidence from the Gulf of Montijo to Diquís. Partially merged with the post-AD 900 Conte Group saurian-, bat-, and other warrior figures, it shows a preference for open-back casting, as opposed to the enclosed forms of the Conte Group, and for the spread-eagled-bird motif, flange-footed frogs, jaguars, crocodilians, and animal-

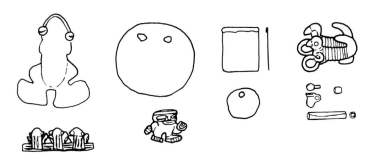

Fig. 18
Metal objects from the site of El Caño in Coclé province
that date to the closing years of the Precolumbian era.
Drawing : courtesy of Warwick Bray.

headed human beings.

The present archaeological distribution of 'Veraguas–Gran Chiriquí' spread-eagled birds and flange-footed frogs suggests that they are more common in western Azuero than in Coclé and Herrera (Bray n.d.). This distribution may, however, reflect the greater intensity of huaquero activities in the western part of the range. The spread-eagled bird certainly has a long history in goldwork, occurring as early as Periods IV and V. 'Eagles' have been found, however, at Venado Beach (Bray n.d.) and at Sitio Conte, where they came from Burial 25 (AD 700–900; Mason 1942 and field notes) and from Lothrop's (1937: fig. 176) trench-digging in late deposits. The spread-eagled-bird motif is also depicted on an embossed cuff (AD 700–900) and on Conte polychrome pottery from the site. Flange-footed frogs have been recovered in Period VI and VII contexts at Guararé (Paso Espavé), El Caño, and El Hatillo, and also in the 'Parita Assemblage' (Doyle 1960; Ladd 1964: 250; Emmerich 1965: fig. 109; Cooke 1976c).

In spite of uncertainties about the spatial and temporal distribution of the 'Veraguas–Gran Chiriquí' Group, there is no justification for thinking that half the metal objects found in Chiriquí were imported from Veraguas (Lothrop 1950: 85; Aguilar 1972a: 20–24) or that objects in this style were not locally made (McGimsey 1968).

CONCLUSION

The technology, stylistic evolution, and subject matter of gold objects are interrelated in multiple, and sometimes unpredictable, ways. In Panama, a metallurgical tradition, introduced from the south, was quickly adapted to the myths, legends, and symbols of the local populations. At the same time, some items were manufactured over a wider area, being used, perhaps, for inter-elite exchange. It is, of course, logical that Costa Rica, Panama, and northern Colombia should have represented a single metallurgical province (Bray n.d.); Chibchan-speaking tribes still live in most of the area today, bound, as were their ancestors, by a common intellectual heritage (Helms 1979) and by similar ecological adaptations and social organization (Linares and Ranere 1980; Cooke n.d.).

Table 1
PANAMANIAN GOLD STYLES WITH THEIR APPROXIMATE TIME SPANS
(after Bray n.d.)

Group name	Approximate date
Initial group	AD 1–500
Openwork group	AD 400–700
International group	AD 400–900
Conte group	AD 400–1100 (*perhaps survives to AD 1520*)
Veraguas/Gran Chiriqui group	AD 900–1520 (*perhaps as early as AD 400*)

Table 2
THE CURRENT PERIODIZATION OF THE PAINTED POTTERY
OF THE CENTRAL REGION OF PANAMA

Period	Date	Stylistic groups
IV	300 BC–AD 500	Aristide (300 BC–AD 500)
		Tonosí (AD 1–500)
		Pre-Sitio Conte
IV/V	Transitional AD 400/500	Montevideo
		First Sitio Conte graves
V	AD 500–700/800	Conte
		Canazas (southern Azuero)
		Burial activities at Sitio Conte
VIA	AD 700/800–900	Macaracas (Higo and Pica-Pica-Pica varieties; Ladd 1964)
		Late graves at Sitio Conte
VIB	AD 900–1100	Macaracas (Cuipo Variety)
		Sitio Conte not used for burials
VIIA	AD 1100–1300	Parita
VIIB	AD 1300–1500	El Hatillo

1. Cooke (hereafter RGC) has been largely responsible for the iconographic information and interpretation, and has provided some chronological details. In addition to preparing the classificatory system, Bray (hereafter WB) has researched the distribution and stylistic development of Panamanian metallurgy and has been instrumental in recovering information on unpublished materials.

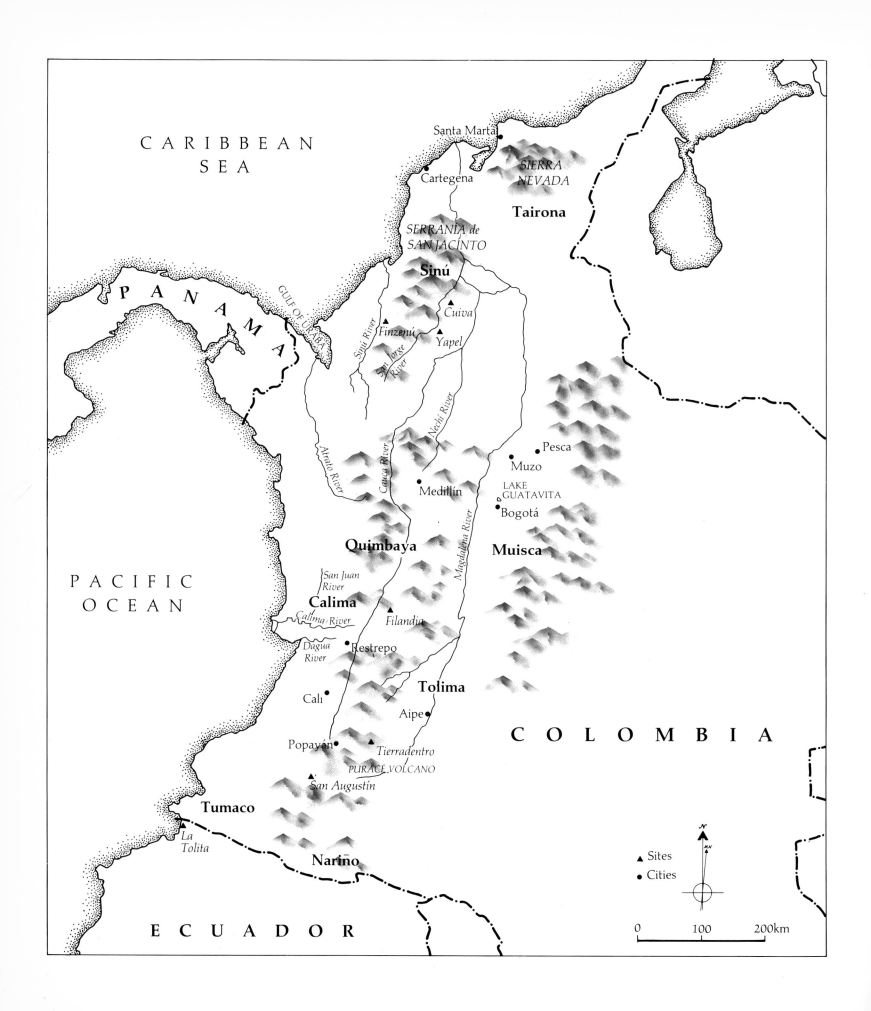

CARIBBEAN
SEA

PANAMA

GULF OF URABÁ

PACIFIC
OCEAN

Santa Marta

Cartegena

SIERRA
NEVADA

Tairona

SERRANÍA de
SAN JACINTO

Sinú

Sinú River

San Jorge River

Finzenú

Cuiva

Yapel

Nechí River

Atrato River

Cauca River

Pesca

Muzo

Medillín

LAKE
GUATAVITA

Bogotá

Quimbaya

Magdalena River

Muisca

San Juan
River

Calima

Calima River

Filandia

Dagua
River

Restrepo

Cali

Tolima

Aipe

COLOMBIA

Popayán

Tierradentro

PURACÉ VOLCANO

San Augustín

Tumaco

La
Tolita

Nariño

ECUADOR

▲ Sites

● Cities

N

0   100   200km

Cultural Patterns in the
Prehispanic Goldwork of Colombia

CLEMENCIA PLAZAS and ANA MARÍA FALCHETTI

Beyond the initial astonishment at the technical excellence and the variety of the subject matter of prehispanic Colombian goldwork, there has been, in previous studies, a tendency to view the gold objects as products of cultures unique and isolated from each other. It is possible, however, to observe common traits among some of the different styles, even though each cultural region had its own expression.

To assimilate the information contained in Precolumbian metal artifacts, it is necessary to go beyond the eye-catching details, to seek the artisan who made the piece, and to discover the broader cultural traditions that shaped his attitude toward the metals. Observing cultural change in different areas through time—reflected in the modification of techniques of working and decorating objects and in the variation of their forms and uses—we can appreciate the cultural dynamic behind the multiple expressions of man as a social being. Associating the objects with their cultural context allows us to see beyond the objects themselves. Information on population density and man's relation to his environment can be obtained from habitation sites. Systems of roads, irrigation, and drainage give evidence of community labor, while differences in the forms of tombs and the richness of their grave goods reveal social hierarchies. If we expect to interpret Precolumbian goldwork correctly, we must try to understand the processes of cultural development and change.

THE GOLD OF SOUTHWESTERN COLOMBIA

The traditional classification by archaeological zones (Quimbaya, Calima, etc.) is a spatial division that takes into account neither the interaction between cultural zones nor changes over time. From a broader perspective, we can see how southwestern Colombia formed, before the 10th century AD, a single metallurgical tradition with technological and stylistic characteristics that contrasted with those of the central and northern areas of the country. This shared cultural substratum did not obscure distinctive regional developments in the zones known as Tumaco, Calima, San Agustín, Tierradentro, Nariño, Tolima, and Quimbaya. Each zone had its own way of assimilating external influences into its own strong tradition, thus maintaining a recognizable identity.

During this stage of great metallurgical development, southwestern Colombia was influenced by the Chorrera culture of the Ecuadorian coast; it is by no means certain, however, that the contact was direct. The ceramic complexes of Tumaco, Calima, and Chorrera share a similar sculptural realism, although each style has distinct decorative elements. The Chorrera culture (1200–300 BC), the culmination of a long process of cultural development in the Ecuadorian lowlands,[1] made its influence felt from the north of Peru to the Calima and Cauca River valleys in Colombia.

The peoples who inhabited southwestern Colombia during this time had a complex socio-political organization, which permitted a specialization of labor that is manifest in their metallurgy. They surely had social hierarchies, with a political and religious elite group that used the sculptural and goldworking arts to affirm its position and record its privileges, and sought to perpetuate its status by means of its tombs and grave goods; this is indicated by the remains of the burials. These groups were relatively large, judging from the skeletal material. They inhabited the slopes of the valleys, utilizing different environmental niches and constructing irrigation channels to support an agricultural complex with various products, notably maize. Throughout the piedmont, houses were built on terraces in groups of varying sizes, with easy access to the rivers that sustained both the people and their crops. The gold objects that were produced served to express the close relationship between man and nature, for they represent mediating mythical animals that justified the existence of man and his powers; jaguars, serpents, avian raptors, monkeys, armadillos, and coatimundis reveal a symbolic structure that is still not fully understood.

Gold artifacts from the southwestern part of Colombia are, for the most part, of a purer gold than those of the rest of the country; this is due, in part, to the relative richness of raw gold sources. In the metallurgy of Nariño and Tumaco (fig. 1), gold was sometimes combined with platinum and silver, metals that are found mixed with alluvial gold. The abundance of these metals does not entirely explain their use, however; another, very important factor is the symbolism of gold. Gold was the 'sweat of the sun' in many southern cultures, and the sun itself was considered to be a masculine, generative principle. Silver represented the tears of the moon, a feminine entity. The color and consistency of both metals caused them to be associated in legend with the most important celestial bodies.

Technologically, southwestern goldwork emphasizes direct working of the metal. Hammering, the most common technique, requires great skill and a knowledge of the physical properties of the metal, as one observes in the large embossed pectorals of the Calima region. Small, oval hammers of meteoric iron were used to beat out plates of gold to an even thinness on cylindrical stone anvils. A design was then drawn on the plate, and, working over a soft surface—thick leather or a sack of fine sand—the goldworker traced it with varying degrees of relief, using chisels, engraving tools, and punches of metal, stone, or bone.

To make three-dimensional objects, the goldworkers of the southwest joined gold sheets with gold 'nails' (fig. 2) or folded metal tabs. Gold foil was also used to sheath objects—sea shells and wooden figurines and staffs, whose cores have now mostly disappeared.

In the construction of delicate pieces incorporating wires and sheets of gold, diffusion bonding was employed. To join two elements of high-carat gold, a drop of copper acetate (obtained by dissolving copper in vinegar) was placed on the spot to be soldered. When a flame is applied in an oxygen-free atmosphere, the organic fraction burns away and the copper forms a molecular alloy with the gold at the point of the union. Welding requires high temperatures, only some 25°C below the melting point of the metal (800–1100°C), and the slightest error results in the destruction of the piece. If achieved, however, such a union is strong and almost indiscernible (fig. 3).

The various cultures of southwestern Colombia shared many forms in their metalwork, while maintaining their regional styles. In the Calima zone and in the region of San Agustín and Tierradentro, a general uniformity of goldwork prevails. There we find diadems in the shape of an H, large pectorals of sheet gold, hollow ear spools, and masks. The last two also appear in Tumaco, along with spherical, tubular, and disc beads, depilatory tweezers, and figurines assembled from separate parts. Diffusion bonding is relatively common throughout the area.

The Quimbaya and Tolima zones, in the middle valleys of the Cauca and Magdalena Rivers, exhibit a similar repertoire. There we see pectorals of embossed sheet gold, beads with squared-off ends, depilatory tweezers, pins, and solid anthropomorphic pendants; diadems, masks, and hollow ear spools are absent, however. These zones received strong cultural influences from the northern part of the country, and the middle valley of the Cauca River seems to have been a region characterized by much experimentation in metallurgy. It was here that alloy compositions and casting techniques were perfected. Lost-wax casting of solid and hollow forms (the latter require a separate core) reached its zenith here. This technology spread to the upper Calima region, and eventually even to Central America, far to the north (Falchetti 1979).

Tumaco Tumaco, a region sharing cultural traits with La Tolita, in northern Ecuador, has yielded the oldest prehispanic gold in Colombia, dating to 325 BC (Bouchard 1979). Associated ceramics show similarities to Chorrera pottery from the Ecuadorian coast. The goldsmiths of Tumaco created giant masks of sheet gold, portraying jaguar jaws; they also made pectorals, pendants, and ear ornaments, and assembled human figurines with cranial deformation like that seen in the clay effigies typical of the region. A great quantity of miniature objects—nose ornaments, nuggets, and wires—no doubt adorned human figurines of gold and of clay. Sometimes gold was combined with silver or platinum to produce goldwork that was stylistically unique, yet shared technological traits with the rest of southwestern Colombia.

Calima Recent research in the Calima region has established several periods of occupation. Goldworking reached its apogee in the so-called Yotoco period—from the 3rd to the 10th centuries AD, a time of great population expansion—but an earlier metallurgy cannot be ruled out.[2]

Complex and handsome attire, dominated ostentatiously by a great quantity of gold—diadems, nose and ear ornaments, pectorals, bracelets, and large anklets—must have left little of the wearer's body exposed (fig. 4). Inexpressive funerary masks; lime flasks in the form of fruit, human beings,

Fig. 1
Frontal of a two-part ear ornament.
The condor's beak is of platinum. Tumaco zone (?).
H. 2 in. (5 cm.), W. 3¼ in. (8·4 cm.).
Museo del Oro, Bogotá (29.253).
Photo: Jorge Mario Múnera.

Fig. 2
Spool-shaped ear ornaments of sheet gold
joined together by small gold nails. Calima zone.
Diam. 2¼ in. (5·8 cm.).
Museo del Oro, Bogotá (29.385, 29.386).
Photo: Jorge Mario Múnera.

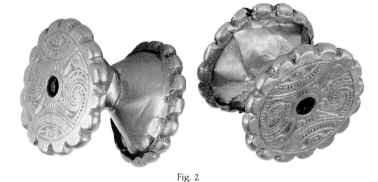

Fig. 3
Small granules of gold fused together form the beads of this necklace. Calima zone.
L. of each bead ¼ in. (0·7 cm.), W. of each bead ⅛ in. (0·3 cm.).
Museo del Oro, Bogotá (26.752).
Photo: Jorge Mario Múnera.

and animals; spoons, and vessels—these are some of the types of objects that accompanied these gold-covered bodies in their tombs. Mask faces of unidentifiable personages wearing a nose ornament on which the same face appears give a disquieting sense of infinite repetition. Sheet-gold pieces festooned with pendant plaques produce a tinkling sound when moved. The only cast pieces—which are technically well made—are pendants, portraying ornately dressed men, or pins crowned with birds, monkeys, or masked human figures similar to those represented on San Agustín stone sculpture (fig. 5).

Quimbaya   Research carried out in the middle Cauca River valley revealed occupations postdating the 10th century AD; these are known as Middle Cauca and Caldas (Bruhns 1976). It can be determined that the simplest goldwork is associated with these later occupations, while the so-called Quimbaya gold—perhaps the zenith of lost-wax casting, with its anthropomorphic vessels of striking realism, its lime flasks in plant forms, and its embossed gold helmets—was shown to be earlier, before AD 1000. Stylistically associated with it is a dark, polished pottery, sometimes decorated with human figures showing the same realistic, serene face seen in the gold pieces.

Repeated finds with confirmed associations, especially the 'Treasure of the Quimbaya' (Plazas 1978), allow the placing of several other artifact types in the same time range: cast pins with Calima-like motifs, hollow ear spools, and stylized anthropomorphic pendants. This category of pieces shows regional variations: pins from the Cauca tend to be made in several castings with elements of different gold-copper alloys, which give the object a vivid, multicolored aspect.

Ear spools of this region are always small, have closed ends, and are cast, while Calima examples are large, hammered, and open-ended. The emphasis on casting and the use of different alloys of gold and copper in the same piece characterize the metallurgy of the middle Cauca River valley, where gold was less abundant than on the Pacific slopes; here lost-wax casting was developed with unequalled mastery.

Tolima   The middle Magdalena River valley has yielded Calima-style goldwork, including laminated pectorals decorated with faces in relief and assembled figurines; objects typical of the Magdalena zone, such as pendants and necklace beads with squared-off ends, have been found in the Calima and Quimbaya regions. These stylistic and technological similarities suggest ancient trade relationships that can be confirmed only by controlled excavations (fig. 7).[3]

Tolima goldwork includes large cast and hammered pectorals in the form of stylized winged men, ear ornaments in bat shapes, and cast pendants depicting humans, felines, or fantastic insects (fig. 6).

San Agustín and Tierradentro   In this region of the Colombian highlands, less emphasis was placed on goldwork than in other regions of the south-west. There was, nevertheless, a local metallurgical production of objects that belong technically and formally to this tradition (fig. 8). Noteworthy objects include diadems, masks, bracelets, and large pectorals with

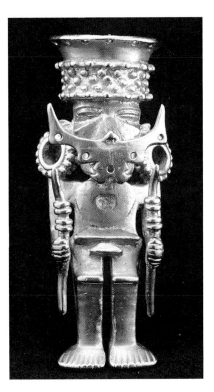

Fig. 4
Pendant in the shape of a figure wearing ornaments characteristic of the Calima zone. Calima zone.
H. 2⅜ in. (5·9 cm.), W. 1 in. (2·5 cm.).
Museo del Oro, Bogotá (26.632).
Photo: Jorge Mario Múnera.

Fig. 5
Top of a pin with a masked figure similar to those found on certain San Agustín sculpture.
Calima zone.
Total H. of pin 11¾ in. (30 cm.), W. of figure ⅞ in. (2·2 cm.).
Museo del Oro, Bogotá (26).
Photo: Jorge Mario Múnera.

Fig. 6

Rock carvings at Aipe in the department of Huila,
show the distinctive designs of Tolima pectorals.

Fig. 7

Figure pendant found in the Cauca River Valley
that is stylized in the characteristic Tolima manner.
H. 9¼ in. (23·4 cm.), W. 10¼ in. (25·7 cm.).
Museo del Oro, Bogotá (6.029).
Photo: Jorge Mario Múnera.

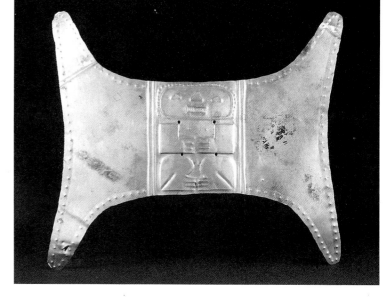

Fig. 8

Headdress ornament of sheet gold in the shape of an H,
a common shape in the goldwork of the southwest.
The repoussé figure on this example from San Agustín exhibits
traits similar to those on the statues of the zone.
H. 7¼ in. (18·3 cm.)., W. 8¼ in. (21 cm.).
Museo del Oro, Bogotá (5.975).
Photo: Jorge Mario Múnera.

embossed jaguars that display the crossed fangs so typical of the stone sculpture of the region. Tiny cast beads in the shapes of men, eagles, and pottery vessels are also seen.

A gold-bearing funerary mound in the Alto de los Idolos yielded a radiocarbon date of 40 BC (Duque and Cubillos 1979), the oldest for San Agustín goldwork. The find included geometric sheets and laminated beads of high-carat gold. During this epoch, goldworking was part of a cultural complex that included funerary shrines, sculpture, and monolithic sarcophagi in tombs with closed entryways faced with flagstones, all characteristic of a regional florescence in San Agustín, the first manifestations of which can be traced back as far as 800 BC (Luis Duque Gómez, personal communication).

It is possible that there were contacts between San Agustín and neighboring Tierradentro near the end of this period.[4] Goldwork from Tierradentro (fig. 9) displays iconography very similar to that of San Agustín stone sculpture, and there is a general correspondence in the pottery and sculpture of the two regions. Tierradentro is famous for its large chambered tombs cut into bedrock, painted inside with red and black geometric motifs; these tombs contained funerary urns and other ceramic offerings. Primary and secondary burials of a humbler type are also known (Cháves and Puerta 1973–79, 1980). None of the tombs excavated by archaeologists has yielded goldwork, which, as local stories have it, is found only in simple pit burials along with crude, undecorated pottery.[5]

Nariño   The highland region of Nariño presents unusual metallurgical evidence. Of the two goldworking complexes recognized there, that known as Capulí shares formal and technological traits with other regions in the southwestern tradition, while the other complex, known as Piartal-Tuza, cannot be assigned to any known metallurgical tradition in the country (Plazas 1977–78). The radiocarbon dates that place the Capulí development between the 7th and 12th centuries AD (Uribe 1977–78) are late in comparison with other complexes of the southwestern tradition.

The hammering and soldering of high-carat gold are techniques diagnostic of Capulí metal artifacts (fig. 10). Goldwork includes circular ear ornaments with embossed human (fig. 11) and jaguar heads, or semicircular examples with geometric motifs to which monkeys and other zoomorphic forms have been soldered. Nipple ornaments, beads, and pendants in bird shapes are also characteristic of this style.

Capulí goldwork is closely related to late metallurgical complexes on the Ecuadorian coast—Milagro, Quevedo, and Manta—where similar gold ear ornaments, in the shapes of jaguars, are found. Interaction between the Ecuadorian coast and the Nariño altiplano, via the valley of the Guayas River, seems to have been maintained throughout history.

The complex known as Piartal-Tuza, which was apparently contemporary with Capulí, has a unique metallurgy that emphasizes tumbaga of high copper content, often capped by a thin layer of surface gold. With sheets of this metal, diadems with featherlike motifs were made; while the 'feathers' are not realistically rendered, they reveal a sure artistic hand and a firm concept of design. Also characteristic of this goldwork are ornaments of sheet gold, made to be sewn on cloth, and nose ornaments of rectangular

Fig. 9
Mask from Tierradentro, that is exceptional for its realism and expressiveness. Masks are often found in the goldwork of southwest Colombia.
H. 3¾ in. (8·7 cm.), W. 5 in. (12·7 cm.).
Museo del Oro, Bogotá (28.918).
Photo: Jorge Mario Múnera.

Fig. 10
Ear ornaments made of elements that were hammered separately and then soldered together. Nariño zone.
H. 3¾ in. (8·5 cm.), W. 4¼ in. (10·9 cm.).
Museo del Oro, Bogotá (25.405, 25.406).
Photo: Jorge Mario Múnera.

Fig. 11
Pendant discs for Nariño ear ornaments.
Nariño zone.
Diam. 3⅞ in. (10 cm.).
Museo del Oro, Bogotá (22.041, 22.042).
Photo: Jorge Mario Múnera.

Fig. 12
Rotating disc on which radial polish and different colors
and textures have been used for surface elaboration. Nariño zone.
Diam. 6½ in. (16·5 cm.).
Museo del Oro, Bogotá (25·191).
Photo: Jorge Mario Múnera.

Fig. 13
Nose ornaments of complex design changed the facial expression of those who wore them.
Nariño zone.
H. 2⅜ in. (5·9 cm.), W. 7⅛ in. (18·1 cm.).
Museo del Oro, Bogotá (21·560).
Photo: Jorge Mario Múnera.

(fig. 13) and other forms, with decoration that serves to change the facial expression of the wearer. Perhaps the most striking metallurgy, however, is seen in rotating discs, in which gold, copper, and symmetrical decoration on both sides produced special effects when a disc revolved. These discs are unique in the history of Colombian metallurgy (fig. 12).

Late Goldwork After AD 600–900, a new cultural tradition spread throughout southwestern Colombia; its goldwork, characterized by the extensive use of tumbaga and certain techniques of casting and mise-en-couleur gilding, contrasts radically with that of the previous regional developments. The forms are simple and standardized. Typical pieces include half-moon and circular nose and neck ornaments of gold wire, spiral and hollow ear ornaments, pendants in the form of toads, other reptiles, and snail shells, and cast heart-shaped pectorals. In the middle Cauca River valley, simple circular pectorals, some with geometric or zoomorphic motifs (fig. 14), became popular, along with gold objects to be inserted in the skin.

Pérez de Barradas (1966) characterized this late goldwork as 'invasionist,' associating it with Carib-speaking peoples from Amazonia, who first populated the Caribbean islands and coasts and later moved inland to the Magdalena and Cauca River valleys. More recently, archaeological research has shown that southwestern Colombia was occupied by groups who shared a common culture, very similar in its various facets to that observed by 16th-century conquistadors. They lived in large, circular thatched structures, grouped in villages, and they buried their dead in shaft- and chamber-tombs.

Although varied, their pottery emphasized resist decoration, anthropomorphic vessels, cups, and similar forms. The late occupations of the Calima and Dagua River valleys (AD 1200–1600)[6] are characterized by a simple metallurgical tradition with little variation: it includes twisted nose ornaments, spiral ear ornaments, and pieces to be implanted in the skin. Controlled archaeological data, with radiocarbon dates, has allowed placement of this late occupation between the 11th and 17th centuries AD.[7]

In the San Agustín region, we see a break with older regional traditions and the arrival of cultural traditions that come possibly from Amazonia.[8] This assumption is supported by the presence of heart-shaped pectorals, and neck and nose ornaments of tumbaga.

In the upper reaches of the Cauca River, between Tierradentro, Popayán, and Puracé, a late local complex developed, of whose origin we know nothing. The style has been called Cauca or Popayán (fig. 15); the pieces include primarily nose and chest ornaments and tumbaga pendants in the shape of birds (*águilas*). The late appearance of pieces like the heart-shaped pectorals in the upper and middle valleys of the Cauca and Magdalena shows the closeness of the two regions; in the Magdalena, this metallurgy is associated with urns and polychrome vessels that occur after the 11th century AD (Cardale 1976; Falchetti 1978).

Thus, the data from different regions reinforces the hypothesis of a cultural tradition that extended throughout southwestern Colombia *c.* 500 BC–AD 700. This contrasts with the situation in the same zone and in the northern and central parts of the country after the 11th century AD. In the latter regions at this time, there was an emphasis on the use of

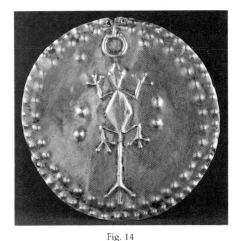

Fig. 14
Pectoral disc with embossed decoration.
Such discs become common along the Cauca River valley after the 10th century AD.
Quimbaya zone.
Diam. 3⅞ in. (9·9 cm.).
Museo del Oro, Bogotá (6.112).
Photo: Jorge Mario Múnera.

Fig. 15
Pendant of a winged figure, which wears a particular kind of twisted nose ornament, is the type found in the environs of Popayán. Cauca zone.
H. 9⅞ in. (24 cm.), W. 6½ in. (16·5 cm.).
Museo del Oro, Bogotá (3.038).
Photo: Jorge Mario Múnera.

tumbaga, casting, and mise-en-couleur, techniques that had been perfected earlier in the Cauca River valley and diffused toward the north to be integrated into different goldworking traditions of Colombia and Central America.

THE GOLD OF THE NORTH

In northern and central Colombia, a similar technology links the different metallurgical traditions developed by peoples of diverse cultural extraction with different approaches to the metals. In the Caribbean lowlands, the Zenú culture marked the zenith of development during the first few centuries after Christ; in the mountainous north-central zone, the Tairona and Muisca peoples (both of the Chibcha language group) reached their highest degree of social and political consolidation in the final centuries before the Spanish conquest.

Sinú   Here, as in other lowland tropical regions in the Americas, an increasingly, efficient exploitation of the varied natural resources found in the riverine, lacustrine, and tropical forest biotopes, along with an emphasis on root and other tropical crops, produced mixed and stable economies, which permitted the establishment of complex societies. These developments, perhaps merged with external influences, reached their climax with the culture of Zenú, which, in the 16th century, when the Spanish conquerors explored the Caribbean lowlands, still survived along the Sinú and San Jorge Rivers, where Finzenú and Yapel were the major economic and political centers.

These two centers, according to indigenous legend, were the surviving chiefdoms of a large socio-political system that reached its climax many centuries before; at that time, the territory of Gran Zenú was divided into three provinces ruled by related caciques. The major province was Zenufana, located near the principal sources of raw gold, the lower Cauca and Nechí Rivers; next in importance was Finzenú, on the Sinú River and then Panzenú, extending throughout the San Jorge valley.[9]

The Spanish were impressed by the agricultural and fishing resources of Yapel, as well as by its efficient economic system, all consolidated centuries before, when dense populations inhabited Panzenú.

Archaeological research has shown that these populations, between the 2nd century BC and 10th century AD, occupied the San Jorge depression; now this lowland zone is less than 25 m. above sea level, receiving a tremendous quantity of water and sediments from the Cauca and Magdalena Rivers before they empty into the Caribbean. Today the zone is sparsely inhabited and flooded for eight months of the year, but in prehistoric times, it was drained by man-made canals covering 500,000 hectares; the fertile flood plains were then a cornucopia of riverine and agricultural resources. The abundant ancient population, with a strong rural orientation, was distributed along the river courses, in isolated hamlets and small villages of up to 600 occupants; the living sites were built on artificial platforms, which also contained the tombs of the dead.[10]

After AD 1000, the flood zone was gradually abandoned,[11] marking the beginning of the decline of Gran Zenú. Nevertheless, some Zenú people continued to live in the savannas, maintaining regional economic control from strategically located sites, like Finzenú, which controlled commerce on the Sinú River.

As late as the 16th century in the Sinú River valley, groups of specialized artisans were to be found in certain communities; their works were widely traded. A group of goldworkers lived in Finzenú. They, and others like them, produced objects very similar in style and technique to those found in funerary mounds dispersed throughout the territory of Gran Zenú.[12]

A prodigious amount of gold was worked, judging by the abundance of pieces made from high-quality metal that was hammered into plates or sheets, then embossed from both sides to accentuate whatever motif was used. With this technique, spectacular mammiform pectorals and laminated skirts were made, as well as a variety of ear ornaments in circular, half-moon, and U-shapes, conical nipple ornaments, small beads, and numerous other simpler adornments.

The metalsmiths of this region also cast gold, sometimes mixed with small amounts of copper; these tumbaga pieces were then gilded. The cast objects are solid, heavy, and often of considerable size. Examples include staff heads with human or animal shapes (fig. 16), anthropomorphic pendants, bells, and many kinds of zoomorphic effigy beads. Most pieces are decorated with threads, braids, spirals, and circles of false filigree (fig. 17); the same technique, diagnostic of Zenú gold, was used to produce semicircular ear ornaments decorated with thick rings and figure-eight motifs.

The typical fauna of the lowland plains and swamps was represented with considerable realism. Deer, peccaries, and anteaters are seen, as well as crocodiles, snails, and jaguars. The aggressive traits of the animals are not emphasized. Showy species predominate; for example, birds with beautiful plumage emphasized by openwork false filigree and crests of cast wires. Sometimes the apparent desire to express that which was beautiful or symbolic in the animal diminishes the realism of the work. In general, this style of metallurgy plays up the brilliance and the varied tonalities of the gold. Gold ornaments reinforced the prestige of the governing elite, who ostentatiously displayed them during their lives and hoarded quantities for their tombs.

The Spanish chronicles speak of an elite cemetery in Finzenú that was reserved for priests, chiefs, and headmen of the three Zenú provinces. It was ordained that they be buried there, or, at least, that they inter part of their gold as a tribute to that necropolis. The burial mounds, constructed communally during regional festivals, varied in size according to the importance of the deceased. Ritual ceramic pieces, and probably gold items, too, were made for the event. The human effigies found in such tombs are of interest: they show musicians, with rattle and trumpet, seated in backed chairs, along with women in two-pronged headdresses and carrying gourds in their hands. Music and drink, two themes seen repeatedly in the iconography of gold, also appear in the elaborate pottery sculptures of Betancí,[13] ancient Finzenú.

Archaelogical investigations have also revealed important cemeteries in the San Jorge valley. At Cuiva, Ayapel, and Montelíbano, there are mounds up to 6 m. in height, which contain multiple burials, abundant ceramic offerings, and spectacular gold pieces. Less elaborate cemeteries nearby have

Fig. 16
Staff head adorned with a heron, the type of showy plumaged bird
that appears on Zenú objects. Sinú zone.
H. 5⅝ in. (14·2 cm.), W. 6⅛ in. (15·5 cm.).
Museo del Oro, Bogotá (29.806).
Photo: Jorge Mario Múnera.

Fig. 17
Ornament from the Zenú where human representations are both realistic and much adorned.
Sinú zone. H. 2¾ in. (7 cm.), W. 3¾ in. (9·6 cm.).
Museo del Oro, Bogotá (6.403).
Photo: Jorge Mario Múnera.

Fig. 18
Staff head of tumbaga representing a jaguar attacking a cayman; such animal scenes
are common in the goldwork of the Serranía de San Jacinto. Sinú zone.
H. 2 in. (5 cm.), L. 3⅜ in. (8·7 cm.).
Museo del Oro, Bogotá (24.291).
Photo: Jorge Mario Múnera.

small mounds and humbler grave goods—a few pieces of gold and ceramics—indicating social differentiation in mortuary practices. At the ceremonial center of Finzenú, there was a large temple containing twenty-four wooden idols covered with sheets of gold, where the populace left offerings; the walls were hung with gold pendants and even the trees around the temple were festooned with golden bells. Gold, as emblematic adornment, and as religious and funerary offering, played a fundamental role in the ceremonial activity that helped to maintain the social cohesion of the peoples of Gran Zenú, reaffirming the prestige of the chieftains and priests, privileged individuals who dominated the union between the sacred and the social in this society, in which political, economic, and religious power were closely linked. For this reason, these individuals had the primary right to gold. Gran Zenú chiefdoms had a theocratic orientation, and an interesting absence of militarism is apparent in their nonagressive iconography, in which warriors, trophy heads, and other threatening emblems are not used.

Part of the production of Finzenú goldsmiths was destined for commerce, however; according to the chronicles, it made its way to distant regions such as Urabá and the Antioqueño highlands. Simple, laminated pieces produced in great quantities were probably made for export.

Zenú influence was felt as far as the Serranía de San Jacinto, the mountain chain that separates the lowlands from the coast. There, in the 16th century, lived a large indigenous population that buried its dead in ceramic urns and produced goldwork that reflects certain Zenú influence.[14] Many staff heads decorated with men and animals are found, along with musicians, men with gourds in their hands, and various zoomorphic representations (fig. 18), including fauna from both the high, mountainous and low, swampy zones. False filigree was used to decorate many pieces and to form ear ornaments (fig. 21), although it differed from the Zenú type, for the cast thread is finer and the motifs more various; zigzags, circles, spirals, braids, and stylized ducks or herons were combined to form ear ornaments of many shapes and sizes.

The metalwork of the mountain zone displays distinctive technology, forms, iconography, and functions. Technologically, it stressed the use of tumbaga with a low gold content, casting, and gilding. The notable versatility in the way human and animal effigies are represented ranges from the considerable realism of the staff heads to the extreme schematism of the anthropomorphic figurines. Great quantities of small, roughly made adornments were made and used.

While forming a distinctly local style, the highland metalwork does show various external influences, notably from the Tairona area. Tumbaga nose ornaments with divergent prongs, stylized stone plaques depicting bats, and cornelian beads are the most common objects in the Tairona area, but they were also made in the highlands. In iconography, both zones stress the association of man with eagles, jaguars, and frogs.

Tairona and Muisca Many of the gold artifacts that astonished the Spaniards in the 16th century were made by indigenous peoples a thousand years before, during a time of cultural florescence. This gold came to light through the feverish looting of tombs along the Sinú and Calima Rivers,

Fig. 19
Living platforms in the central plaza of Buritaca 200,
one of the largest urban centers of the Tairona, 14th century.
Sierra Nevada de Santa Marta.
Photo: Loraine Vollmer.

among others. Yet, at the time of the Conquest, in the Sierra Nevada of Santa Marta and the altiplano of Cundinamarca and Boyacá, a lively metallurgical tradition still existed among the Chibcha-speaking Tairona and Muisca peoples. Inhabitants of the mountainous zones belonging to the same linguistic families were united by a common cultural substratum, in spite of the differences that appeared in many aspects of its socio-political organization and its material culture.

The Tairona began their process of consolidation as a social and political entity in the first centuries after Christ, reaching their maximum development after AD 1000,[15] when dense populations were grouped in many urban centers (fig. 19). Today, more than 200 Tairona sites are known, ranging from the coastal lowlands up to an altitude of 2000 m. (Cadavid and Turbay 1977). Settlements of different sizes reflect a hierarchical political order; several large centers controlled numerous smaller ones, through a chiefly and priestly elite. Tairona goldwork, represented by thousands of ornaments, both baroque and stylized, shows men and animals combined in a complex iconography.

The Muisca, people with a more rural orientation, occupied the highlands of Cundinamarca and Boyacá after the 7th century AD, according to available dates.[16] A dispersed agricultural population, along with the inhabitants of small villages, was controlled by local chiefs who in turn paid allegiance to more powerful leaders. Two of the latter, Zipa and Zaque, aspired to the complete domination of the southern and northern parts of Muisca territory, respectively, in a period of expansion and consolidation that continued into the 16th century. Muisca gold pieces are very crude and are found in great quantities, suggesting mass production and popular use as religious offerings.

Both the Muisca and Tairona peoples had a similar attitude toward gold, although each ascribed different functions to it. Similarities and differences can be inferred from the style of the pieces themselves, their context and associations when found, and the techniques used in their manufacture. The generalized use of tumbaga, with more copper than gold, indicates the scarcity of the latter in both regions. In fact, raw gold sources are not found in the altiplano and are few and far between in the mountain ranges. Commerce with lowland peoples supplied gold to both groups.

Muisca goldwork appears throughout the highlands of Cundinamarca and Boyacá, and down the watershed of the mountains to the Magdalena River. Although, in the 16th century, this region was dominated by the Muzos, a people of Carib origin, traditionally it had belonged to the Muisca. Spanish chronicles relate how Muisca people entered surreptitiously into the then-Muzo domain to leave offerings at the hilltop sanctuary called La Furatena. For the Muisca, objects of gold were closely related to the religious cult; the majority of objects found in the altiplano are offerings, crude little figures representing men, women, children, miniature ornaments, and scenes from social and political life.

Since Muisca metal objects were fundamentally votive offerings, there was no reason to conceal their high copper content. Almost immediately after being made, they were deposited as offerings, and thus were not gilded, as the pieces of the Tairona and other traditions usually were. Most Muisca metal objects are flat, made without a core. They were lost-wax

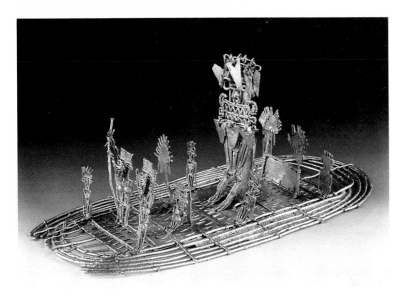

Fig. 20
Offering object depicting the investiture of a cacique.
The ceremony is taking place on a raft presumably on the waters of a lake.
Muisca zone.
H. 4 in. (10·2 cm), L. 7⅝ in. (19·5 cm.).
Museo del Oro, Bogotá (11.373).
Photo: Jorge Mario Múnera.

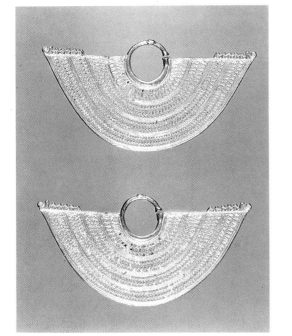

Fig. 21
Left
Semicircular ear ornaments of false filigree, frequently found
in the Serranía de San Jacinto. Sinú zone.
H. 1¾ in. (4·3 cm.), W. 3¼ in. (8.2 cm.).
Museo del Oro, Bogotá (13.834, 13.835).
Photo: Jorge Mario Múnera.

Fig. 22
Right
Female figure with a child, a popular offering object
among the Muiscas of the central Colombian plateau. Muisca zone.
H. 3¼ in. (8·4 cm.), W. 1 in. (2·5 cm.).
Museo del Oro, Bogotá (4.678).
Photo: Jorge Mario Múnera.

cast, and sometimes series of the same figure were made, frequently representing required images.

The casting technique involved the use of a stone matrix, to avoid the necessity of designing a separate mold each time. Pieces of soft stone were used to carve designs in high relief, often several motifs to a stone. These were then impressed into soft clay, producing a negative imprint which, when dry, was coated with a layer of beeswax. The wax was stamped again with the same stone piece. The result was a wax model stamped on both sides, which served for the casting of a quantity of the required objects. With this procedure, necklace beads and, occasionally, ornaments for pectorals and other objects of larger size would be fabricated.

The human figurines known as *tunjos* were usually not polished or otherwise finished after casting; they show overflows of metal, and the funnel and conduits through which the molten metal was poured. The rough surfaces of these pieces were caused by slow cooling in the molds, resulting in a dendritic surface texture. The coarse appearance and simple, childlike design typical of such pieces remind us that their symbolic function was more important than a technically sophisticated finish. Their triangular shape, tapering towards the base, was suitable for sticking in the ground or fitting into the small-mouthed clay vessels designed for this use.

Among the Muisca, there were highly specialized goldsmiths as well as the numerous, humbler artisans. Some of the former, like those from Guatavita, travelled throughout the territory offering their services, while others were established in metalworking centers. One such center seems to have been located in Pasca, where gold arrived through trade with Magdalena River valley people. Numerous stone matrixes and objects utilized in casting have been found there, along with polished flat stones used in preparing wax and ceramic blowpipes for heating casting fires, as well as pieces notable for their fine finish. Besides these major metallurgical centers, there were other smaller ones in the vicinity of the shrines, where metalsmiths used the carved stone matrixes in less careful casting to produce quantities of votive offerings available to those who visited the sanctuaries. At the time of a trip made by Diego Hidalgo de Montemayor, in 1577, to inspect and destroy 250 indigenous shrines, local goldworkers cast pieces for offerings in the attempt to save some of the sanctuaries.

The 'office' of goldworker may have been hereditary. Upon visiting the village of Lenguazaque, in 1595, the Spaniards found that '. . . in the house of Pablo . . . Indian of this town, goldsmith, were found molds in the forms of discs, frogs, and other figures . . . and having shown them that they were molds of black stone, he said it was true that the stones were his and that he had inherited them from his father . . .' (Caciques e Indios n.d.).

The Muisca shrines and sanctuaries were located in isolated, almost inaccessible situations—peaks, caves, lakes, places of great natural beauty. There the people deposited their offerings, either personal or communal, always through the local priest (shaman), the mediator between the people and their gods. The lakes were the most important shrines (fig. 20), sites of large group ceremonies like those carried out annually at Guatavita. Other sanctuaries were to be found near the villages, small conical structures with thatched roofs, dark and gloomy, with doorways so low that a person was obliged to enter on hands and knees. Inside were found figurines of

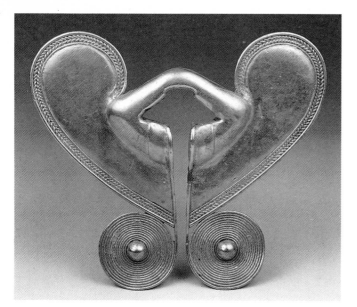

Fig. 23
Nose ornament of cast gold.
Most Tairona objects were utilized as personal adornments.
Tairona zone.
H. 2½ in. (6·4 cm.), W. 3 in. (7·5 cm.).
Museo del Oro, Bogotá (26.128).
Photo: Jorge Mario Múnera.

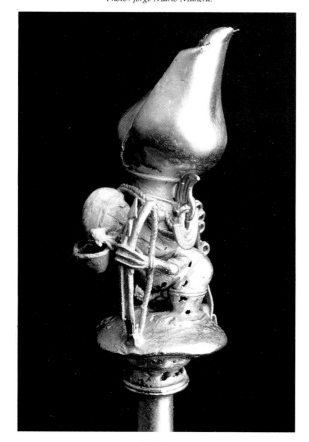

Fig. 24
Staff head presenting an armed bird-man.
The figure wears the ear ornaments characteristic of the Serranía de San Jacinto,
indicative of interchange with the Tairona zone.
Tairona zone.
H. 3 in. (7·6 cm.), W. 1⅛ in. (2·7 cm.).
Museo del Oro, Bogotá (20.064).
Photo: Jorge Mario Múnera.

gold, copper, wood, or cotton, adorned with emeralds and feathers, then wrapped in cotton and placed in ceramic vessels or hollow gourds. These were put in a twined mesh bag hung in the center of the shrine or buried in the floor. The finds of votive offerings that have made their way to museums consist of a varying number of metal figurines—between five and thirty—usually placed in a ceramic vessel and deposited beneath stone slabs in open sites or in caves; they are almost never found in living or cemetery sites.

When we observe carefully the tunjos and other figures, a semiotic system can be discerned, based on certain set graphic conventions. Masculine figures with costumes that signify different ranks, warriors, personages with paraphernalia for taking coca and other drugs, women with children (fig. 22), miniature adornments of various kinds, condors, serpents, and jaguars, all indicate a specific offering to obtain a special request.

The 'language' of the votive offerings is necessarily multisymbolic: a warrior, a woman with a child, or an animal signifies more than it literally depicts; an ornament may symbolically represent the wearer; a part may stand for the whole. Precise knowledge of the customs and conceptual system of the Muisca is required to interpret the small depictions correctly. Although the votive custom is universal, the meaning of the offering is comprehensible only through the symbolic code established by the religion in question.

Among Muisca peoples, different classes of offerings were determined according to the material from which they were made. Gold was associated with wood and cotton. We know for certain that an offering of gold implied the same request as one of cotton; the difference in material reflects the difference in social rank of the supplicants. The technology employed in metalworking, the imagery of the objects, the context of the finds, and the information contained in the Spanish chronicles and other historical documents, all help to establish the basic characteristics of Muisca religion, as well as other social institutions.

We know that certain persons specialized in making offerings and that offerings were given on a massive scale. A religious practice of this kind required a priestly caste charged with overseeing the procedure. The chroniclers relate that these individuals had to undergo many years of training and celibacy to carry out their functions. They were in charge of the shrines and collected the offerings after fasting with the supplicants. Their priestly function was linked to the political system; certain 'captains,' men who controlled small groups of people, but who, in turn, paid fealty to regional chiefs, took part in many kinds of religious and other ceremonies, and knew where most shrines were located and what they contained. The Spaniards made use of this knowledge to loot the shrines.

Votive offerings found throughout Muisca territory are very much of a kind. The stone matrixes studied by Long (1967) do not show significant variability from one site to another. This pattern is confirmed by an analysis of some 400 pieces of different provenance, belonging to the collection of the Museo del Oro (Plazas 1975). This homogeneity reflects the cultural unity of the highlands of Cundinamarca and Boyacá.

Tairona metalwork differs from its Muisca counterpart in technology, forms, iconography, and function. The Tairona used lost-wax casting, but the pieces were not made in repetitive series; each mold was individual and very elaborate. The pieces had volume, and, upon removal from the mold, they were cleansed of residues, gilded, polished, and given a superb finish. Tairona gold pieces were made for long-term use: diadems, nose ornaments, and necklaces often show signs of wear and abrasion, while the suspension rings of other pieces have been worn almost completely through by use.

Many Tairona pendants, known as 'caciques,' represent human figures with animal attributes; these bat-men, jaguar-men, and bird-men may symbolize a belief that certain individuals, incorporating the traits of these animals, could thereby control them. Nose, ear, head or other gold ornaments sometimes served to exaggerate or deform the facial features of the wearer, simulating the traits of a certain animal. The bat-man acquired his diagnostic aspect through tubular ornaments that lengthened the nose upward, and by diadems representing the ears of that animal (Legast 1982). Some masks include prominent animal teeth. The 'butterfly' or 'whiskered' nose ornaments so common in this region alter the face and make the mouth area a different shape and color, possibly signifying the jaguar-man (fig. 23).

In some gold pieces, the central figure is accompanied by other animal effigies. Thus, the bat-man frequently has birds on his head or wears a belt in the form of a two-headed serpent with bifid tongue, elements seen also on pectorals, lipplugs, and ear ornaments. The overloaded designs of Tairona pieces conform to this emblematic tendency. The complex man-animal

symbolism may identify special social groups with a mythic and ancestral relationship to certain animals (fig. 24). The motifs tend to be baroque. In this, they contrast with the simple designs of Muisca pieces, which were made quickly and simply as votive offerings, so that symbolic elaboration was unnecessary.

The Tairona and Muisca societies utilized gold in different ways, but the function of Tairona ornaments as motifs charged with symbolism and the Muisca pieces as offerings are really two manifestations of the same belief system. We can see this unity in the mythology and world-view of Chibcha-speaking groups living today in Colombia, among them the Kogi and Ijka of the Sierra Nevada de Santa Marta, descendants of the Tairona. The Kogi do not value gold, other metals, and gems as indicators of wealth and personal prestige. For them, gold is a symbol of potential fertility belonging to all members of their society. The sun, the masculine, procreating force *par excellence*, transmits its power to gold. For this reason, Kogi priests expose their archaeological, inherited gold pieces to the rays of the sun to recharge them (Reichel-Dolmatoff 1981).

The priests also explain the reasons for giving offerings. Among the Ijka, communal and personal offerings are made through the priest, who deposits them in special places—lakes, for example. These places are always located near rocky points or peaks, which represent the ancestral spirits, transformed into stone by the coming of the sun. The high lakes, where the offerings are made, symbolize the womb of the mother earth, fertilized by the sun and by gold offerings (Tayler 1974).

This paper was translated from the Spanish by Michael J. Snarskis.

1. Lathrap (1980) says that 'many of the elements that reached their zenith in Chorrera have roots in the Machalilla and Valdivia cultures,' 1500 and 3000 BC respectively.

2. Traditionally, Calima gold has been associated with Ilama-period pottery, dated 1500–90 BC, although these dates are considered tentative (Bray et al. 1981). A recent radiocarbon date of AD 210 for the wooden core of a hammered-gold trumpet and a detailed study of objects associated with it affirm that this gold is found with material of the Yotoco period (Warwick Bray, personal communication).

3. Artifacts of this high-quality gold have been excavated only once with clearly recorded associations, by Julio Cesar Cubillos (1954) in Río Blanco. They were found with simple red-slipped ceramics decorated with appliqué or incising, apparently unrelated to the later polychrome traditions of the region.

4. San Agustín's developmental period continued until at least AD 570, when mortuary mounds with sculpture and chambered tombs decorated with painted motifs were still being produced at the Alto de los Idolos (Duque and Cubillos 1979). Part of this long sequence (AD 40–330) has been called the Isnos period by Reichel-Dolmatoff (1975a).

5. A tomb in Río Chiquito, for example, contained a rough anthropomorphic vessel, a gold ear spool, and other metal artifacts.

6. This late occupation corresponds to the so-called Sonso period (Bray et al. 1981).

7. In this zone, there are persistent reports of the association of late pottery with plain gold helmets, circular pectorals (plain and embossed), small tumbaga animals, and other relatively non-ornate metal objects.

8. This period is called Upper Mesitas or Recent by Duque (1964) and Sombrerillos by Reichel-Dolmatoff (1975a).

9. The three provinces had different and complementary economic roles: Panzenú was the major food producer, Zenufana provided gold for working, and Finzenú supplied specialized artisans (Plazas and Falchetti 1981).

10. Along the Carate, Rabón, and Viloría canals, pottery of the Modeled and Painted tradition is found in living sites and burials, associated with a population expansion (ibid.).

11. We have no radiocarbon dates later than AD 1000. The Spanish accounts of their incursions into this zone in the 1500s reveal hardships because of intense flooding and the scarcity of population and foodstuffs.

12. Objects of this goldworking tradition have been found in the San Jorge and Sinú River valleys, as well as in the lower Cauca and Nechí.

13. The excavations of Reichel-Dolmatoff and Dussán (1958) in the middle reaches of the Sinú allowed them to identify the 'Betanci complex,' the last cultural development in the zone, which survived as late as the 16th century. This period is characterized by the construction of living platforms and funerary mounds, and by a style of ceramics closely related to the Modeled and Painted tradition of the San Jorge valley, though with local idiosyncrasies. This pottery is most nearly like that of Ayapel and Montelíbano, sites which represent the last developmental stage of that tradition in the San Jorge plains (Plazas and Falchetti 1981).

14. Repeated finds of this gold with glass beads and Spanish iron artifacts in indigenous tombs attest to the persistence of the tradition into historic times.

15. A pre-Tairona Nahuanje phase (AD 500–1000) has been established by the work of Bischof (1969). Radiocarbon dates associated with urban centers are few and after AD 1300 (Groot 1980).

16. The oldest radiocarbon date associated with Muisca goldwork is AD 840 $\pm$ 60 (Duque 1970).

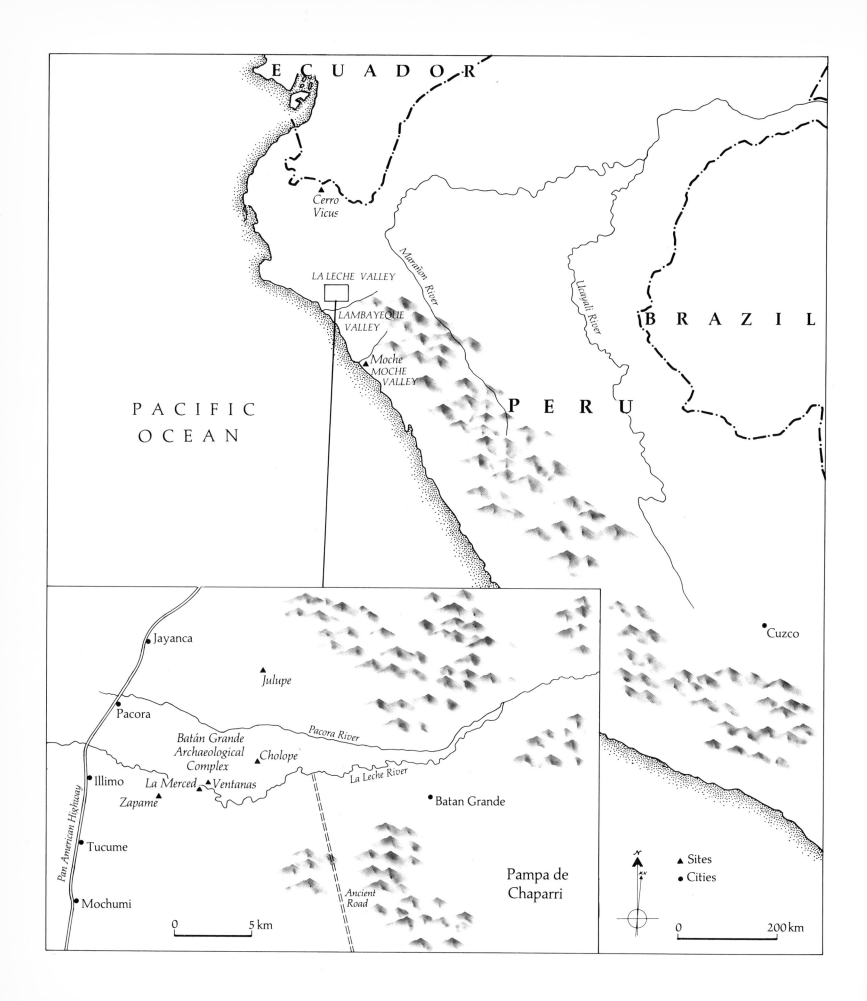

ECUADOR

▲ Cerro
Vicus

LA LECHE VALLEY

LAMBAYEQUE
VALLEY

Marañón River

Ucayali River

BRAZIL

▲ Moche
MOCHE
VALLEY

PERU

PACIFIC
OCEAN

• Cuzco

• Jayanca

▲ Julupe

• Pacora

Pacora River

Batán Grande
Archaeological
Complex

▲ Cholope

Illimo •

La Merced ▲ Ventanas

La Leche River

Zapame ▲

• Batan Grande

Pan American Highway

Tucume •

Pampa de
Chaparri

Ancient
Road

Mochumi •

▲ Sites
• Cities

0   5 km

0   200 km

Behind the Golden Mask:
Sicán Gold Artifacts from Batán Grande, Peru

PALOMA CARCEDO MURO and IZUMI SHIMADA

INTRODUCTION

The Batán Grande Archaeological Complex (*c.* 55 km. square), in the central La Leche Valley, near the north coast of Peru (see map), spans over 3000 years of prehistory, beginning *c.* 1500 BC. Today, it presents a picture that contrasts with the typical lush, green, irrigated fields seen in river valleys along the Peruvian coast to the south. This unique appearance is due, in part, to the ubiquitous evidence of grave-looting at some 50 archaeological sites within the complex. Many of these sites (with pyramids nearly or over 40 m. high) protrude out of the extensive, dense, subtropical, thorny forest that provides home for many indigenous fauna no longer seen elsewhere on the coast.[1] Their appearance is somewhat reminiscent of the lowland Maya landscape on the Yucatán Peninsula.

The long tradition, magnitude, intensity, and areal extent of grave-looting (known locally as *huaquería*) in the complex, which was a major funerary and religious center for much of its prehistory (Shimada 1981, 1982, n.d. a, n.d. b, n.d. c; Shimada et al. 1981, 1982), have been known for many years. Modern, generalized, local, individual looting probably dates back to the 1920s. The epoch of specialized, large-scale, labor-intensive looting spanned *c.* 1936–1960. In 1936 and 1937, sensational discoveries of Middle Sicán tombs with impressive grave lots that included numerous gold artifacts[2] were made at Huacas La Merced and Las Ventanas (Valcárcel 1937), including the famous '*Tumi* Knife of Illimo'.[3] Tello (1937a, 1937b) attempted a largely unsuccessful salvage operation at Huaca Las Ventanas shortly after the discoveries. Looting fervor, fanned by the lure of gold artifacts, continued at an intense pace until *c.* 1972, when the area was incorporated into the Agrarian Cooperative Pucalá. In fact, the decade of the 1960s saw the introduction of heavy earth-moving equipment for looting. It is said that a bulldozer and crew looted for as many as five continuous years, four days a week, throughout the archaeological complex. Today, we can still see hundreds of bulldozer tracks. Examination of 1949, 1968, 1969, and 1975 air photos clearly documents the escalation in scale and extent of looting activities. In the central area of the archaeological complex alone, one can count about 20,000 looters' pits, many of them precise squares, 5 to 10 m. to a side. We suspect that the total number of pits in the complex and immediately adjoining areas reaches 100,000.

It is not our intent to chronicle or comment on these destructive activities; rather, we offer a tentative characterization of artistic and technical features of Middle Sicán gold objects looted from Batán Grande and housed in numerous public and private collections throughout the world, and an elucidation of their temporal, spatial, and cultural contexts in order to assess properly their behavioral and cultural significance. Their artistic and technical dimensions have been described, and analyzed (e.g., Bray 1972; Easby

1955b; Lechtman 1973, 1979, 1984a; Tushingham 1976; Tushingham et al. 1979); but too often the objects under study have been treated individually, in isolation from their broader cultural setting, and given inappropriate, if not incorrect, temporal and cultural identification. Until our study, they have not been systematically described or analyzed within their proper cultural contexts (grave lot, tomb, site, and culture).

In this study, we combine data from two levels of concurrent analyses; more narrowly focused artistic and technical study of Sicán gold artifacts by Carcedo and more generalized archaeological investigation of the Sicán Funerary-Religious Precinct (fig. 1), which includes large-scale surveys and excavations directed by Shimada. Our focus here is not on individual artifacts but on groups of artifacts that represent substantial parts of, or entire grave lots from, the Sicán precinct. The grave lots provide contemporaneous, localized, and unified cultural contexts. This approach allows us to focus on the behavioral and cultural significance (including the symbolic dimension) of variation observable among artifacts. The common archaeological problem of inadequate chronological control is thus minimized. In order to gain an adequate picture of the original artifactural composition and organization of grave lots, we have utilized various lines of evidence: published documents; photos of grave lots taken immediately following their looting; data from a series of independent interviews (1978–1983) with eyewitnesses, collectors, and looters, which were cross-checked against each other; and our independent surveys and excavations carried out prior to, and subsequent to, the interviews. The last served to cross-check the interview data. We have examined Sicán gold artifacts in various private and public museums in Peru, the United States, and West Germany. Some museums have acquired a majority of the pieces in a grave lot, thus facilitating our study. It should be clearly noted that we feel that our data base is still inadequate and, at times, tenuous.

This paper presents a brief synthesis of the broader cultural, chronological, and physical contexts of the Sicán gold artifacts, followed by a tentative characterization of their artistic and technical features. We end the paper with a discussion of some of the behavioral and cultural issues raised in the preceding sections. The new perspective presented here also allows us to correct various misunderstandings and misconceptions about Middle Sicán gold artifacts.

SICÁN CULTURE: A TENTATIVE CHARACTERIZATION

Our understanding of the long and complex history and dynamics of the Sicán culture is still fragmentary. Around AD 700, domination of the region by the intrusive Mochica[4] culture came to an end. Little is known of the local culture during the succeeding 150 years, when ceramics were heavily influenced by Wari and/or Pachacamac, as well as Cajamarca, styles. Concurrent with these new ceramics, we see a major change in funerary practices, perhaps reflecting adoption of a new religion and ideology. In the preceding period, the deceased had been buried in an extended position, often within rectangular adobe chambers; now there were cross-legged, seated burials in cylindrical pits. In general, we have not identified any population center, architecture, or other physical manifestation of corporate undertaking, political centralization, or complex social hierarchy for this period. Tentatively, this poorly known post-Moche V culture has been designated as Early Sicán, after the indigenous Muchik (extinct language) name for Batán Grande, Sicán (or Sicani, Cani, Çicán), signifying the house or temple of the moon (Brüning 1922–23; Kosok 1965; Rondón 1965–66; Shimada n.d. a, n.d. c).

During the brief span of c. AD 850–900, we see rapid formalization of a set of material, organizational, and ideological features with far-reaching impact, which distinguishes the florescent period of the Sicán culture, the Middle Sicán (AD 850–1050). There are four major interrelated features, all of which, in some significant aspects, have antecedents in the preceding Early Sicán or Mochica cultures. These can be described as innovations only in the sense that selected extant or old ideas and material traits were integrated into a new configuration with new overall cultural significance. The rapid formalization process may be seen as part of a 'revitalization movement' similar to that suggested for prehistoric cultural changes on the south coast of Peru or historically documented for Tupac Amaru (Lyon 1966; Menzel 1960). The hypothesis that the inferred charismatic leader of the movement corresponds to the legendary Ñaymlap is discussed elsewhere (Shimada n.d. a).

One of the principal features is the resurgence—and the importance—of monumental religious architecture employing the chamber-and-fill construction technique (which first emerged during the Moche V phase) and marked adobe bricks (which first appeared in Mochica pyramidal constructions). Rectangular adobe chambers were filled with loose rubble or refuse to build up rapidly the cores of pyramids or platform mounds, which elsewhere on the North Coast were replaced by 'secular' constructions that culminate in the gigantic *ciudadelas* at Chan Chan.

The most notable concentration of Middle Sicán monumental religious architecture at Batán Grande is found in the T-shaped (1600 m. east–west by 1000 m. north–south) Sicán Funerary-Religious Precinct (fig. 1), the inferred physical and symbolic center of the Middle Sicán culture. Here, at least seventeen major constructions were placed in various alignments and surrounded by a variety of auxiliary constructions, including many large shaft tombs, multiroom enclosures, roofed terraces with colonnades, and adobe–limestone, flagstone floors (Shimada 1981, 1982, n.d. a, n.d. b).

Our computer-assisted analysis of the distribution and qualitative and quantitative characteristics of adobe bricks with primarily geometric marks (Cavallaro 1982; Cavallaro and Shimada n.d.; Shimada n.d. a, n.d. c; Shimada et al. 1981) supports the hypothesis that different marks represent sponsors of given religious constructions. The sponsor hypothesis posits that powerful or resourceful individuals or groups commanded or contracted various adobe-makers to produce adobe bricks bearing the sponsor's distinctive mark(s). The sponsor thus might have gained social prestige or religious favor, such as the privilege of being interred close to the monuments that he helped to erect.

The second feature is the complex of unprecedented funerary practices, distinguished by large shaft tombs, some of which were 14 m. square at the top and over 20 m. deep (Huaca Menor), human and camelid sacrifices, and impressive quantities of gold and other metal funerary objects (see Pedersen 1976; Shimada 1981, 1982, n.d. a, n.d. c; Shimada et al. 1981; Tello 1937a, 1937b; Valcárcel 1937). In addition, grave lots of elite tombs typically contained fine blackware effigy jars, wooden objects, and exotic precious and semiprecious stone ornaments. In the modern looting history of Batán Grande, there were at least three particularly 'rich' tombs. One was looted from the end of 1936 through the beginning of 1937 at Huaca Las Ventanas, and its grave lot contents were reported by Valcárcel (1938). The inventory of gold artifacts includes: three tumis, or 'knives,' resembling an inverted T in shape, with rectangular 'handles' or 'shafts' and semicircular or crescent 'blades,' including the 'Tumi knife of Illimo'; 'several' masks; 'hojas' (gold foil) for 'túnicas y edificios' (tunics and buildings); beakers of various sizes, with or without inlaid semiprecious or precious stones; embossed plates; discs; necklaces; pendants; *tupus*, or hairpins; and other small items.

Another major grave lot was looted in the final years of the 1950s (probably 1959–1960, at Huaca El Corte), and the rare historic photographs illustrated here (fig. 2a, b) shows much of the grave lot shortly after its looting. Apparently, the grave lot contained over 200 gold and silver objects. The photographs show some 189 objects, 176 of which are beakers. The remaining objects are: one bag with approximately 1000 gold beads; a box with some 20 necklaces; a tumi showing a 'winged' seated Sicán Lord figure (see below); two tubes or 'staffs'; one Type A mask (discussed below); an unidentifiable rectangular object; and four vessels depicting a bird (two are dovelike and two condorlike). By far the major portion of these objects are of gold, although some silver and gold-silver objects were also identified. In addition to the above, the grave lot contained precious and semiprecious stones such as emeralds, lapis lazuli, and pearls (grey and white). Only a few ceramic vessels were found.

In the early 1960s (probably 1961), yet another great grave lot was found, which was similar in composition to the preceding ones and also characterized by a large number of objects. The three grave lots noted here are distinguished for the quantity and quality of the gold objects each contained.[5]

We cannot ignore other tombs, however. For example, Pedersen (1976) reports that a looted Huaca Menor shaft tomb contained seventeen human bodies, mostly sacrificial; mantles of *Spondylus princeps*,[6] lapis lazuli, and cinnabar; wood scepters and arrow shafts; great quantities of gold foil; an estimated 500 kg. of copper[7] artifacts such as 'spear points'; one quartz necklace; at least one blackware effigy jar; and many stacks of *naipes*.[8] A largely looted Middle Sicán tomb—at the west base of the principal pyramid of Huaca La Merced—that was salvaged in 1983 contained a 'diadem' with an embossed Sicán Lord representation fashioned out of gold sheet metal, a double-spouted blackware jar covered with badly oxidized

Fig. 1
Architectural features of the Sicán Funerary-Religious Precinct.

b

a

Fig. 2
Grave lot from a major Middle Sicán tomb,
probably looted from Huaca El Corte between 1959 and 1960.
Photos: courtesy of Junius B. Bird.

copper sheet metal, and various stacks of—as well as loose—naipes of different sizes and shapes (Elera 1984). There are also reports of elite tombs that contained more tumis (up to four) than the three major grave lots described above, although with fewer gold objects, and of funerary bundles with masks but hardly anything else. Overall, there seems to be considerable variation in the composition and quantity of grave lots looted or salvaged from the Sicán Precinct.

The preceding descriptions provide a glimpse of the elite Middle Sicán tombs that are, in many ways, unparalleled on the prehistoric Peruvian coast, perhaps with the exception of Chimú royal burials. Consider the labor and material investment necessary to produce the 500 kg. of copper artifacts interred in the Huaca Menor tomb. Most, if not the overwhelming majority, of these artifacts, show no evidence of use. Many are also poorly crafted (Shimada n.d. a, n.d. c; see also Lechtman 1981), and it seems likely that they were made rapidly for the exclusive purpose of interment as offerings.

Various lines of evidence attest that the entire Sicán Precinct is a gigantic cemetery. The most important burial grounds seem to be the areas immediately adjoining and enclosed by U-shaped religious architectural complexes such as those at Huacas El Corte and Las Ventanas. In fact, we suspect that much of the Batán Grande Archaeological Complex is fundamentally a cemetery—possibly the largest in the New World.

Perhaps the most notable feature of the Middle Sicán is its distinct art style and iconography, with highly homogeneous and ubiquitous representations of the Sicán Lord, the principal deity, who has been variously described as 'tin-woodsman' (Scheele and Patterson 1966), 'bird-man' (Carrion 1940), 'Naymlap' (Kauffmann 1973), or 'rotund figure' (Kroeber 1944). Strong genetic linkage can be seen between the style and iconography of Middle Sicán and those of the Mochica, on one hand, and of Wari and/or Pachacamac, on the other. Menzel (1977: 61) argues that similarities between mythical beings of the Mochica and Wari religions 'provided the basis for the rapid but selective syncretism.' The Sicán Lord is invariably represented by a roughly rectangular face with rounded jaw and elaborate headdress, comma- or almond-shaped eyes, vertical lines below the eyes, and conventionalized ears with pointed tips and large circular ornaments in the lobes. The Sicán Lord face may have been elaborated originally in gold masks; it also appears in textiles, ceramics, murals, and wood artifacts. Additional details of Middle Sicán iconography are described elsewhere (Shimada n.d. a, n.d. c).

The fourth feature of the Middle Sicán culture is its sophisticated metallurgical production. Middle Sicán metallurgy is distinguished by: local, large-scale smelting and diversified use of arsenical copper; goldsmithing that produced objects of previously unseen technical complexity and size; and unprecedented accumulation of 'gold' objects by individuals.

In regard to the use of arsenical copper, earlier Mochica metallurgists already knew of this particular alloy and, presumably, its smelting technology, for limited quantities of primarily small personal ornaments have been recovered from Mochica burials (Lechtman 1979). It appears, however, that the large scale, permanent shift from copper to arsenical copper on the north coast of Peru coincides with the onset and florescence of the Middle Sicán culture.

Fig. 3a
View of the 1983 excavation at Huaca del Pueblo Batán Grande, showing three of five rows of Middle Sicán smelting furnace sets. Furnaces appear as dark triangular pits. Looking north.
Photo: Izumi Shimada.

Fig. 3b
Three sets of superimposed smelting furnaces found at 4–4.5m below surface in the 1983 excavation. Those in back are the earliest. Note the offerings near the mouths of two of the furnaces in front.
Photo: Izumi Shimada.

Excavations at Huaca del Pueblo Batán Grande, a small mound in the center of the modern village of Batán Grande, have clearly documented a gradual evolution of arsenical-copper smelting technology, beginning c. AD 800–850. The 1983 excavation, for example, revealed four well-preserved sets of smelting furnaces and part of a fifth (a total of fifteen furnaces) in five superimposed Middle Sicán floors approximately 4–4·5 m. below the surface (Shimada n.d. a, n.d. c; figs. 3a, b). Remains of charcoal fuel inside the bowl-shaped furnace chambers and associated troughs have been radiocarbon-dated to c. AD 900–1050. The three earliest furnaces, with their hemispherical basins, were placed side by side along an east-west axis. Later, rows of three, four, and five (the last, originally, perhaps six) furnaces were oriented north-south or east-west and organized along narrow troughs. Smelting areas were only partially delimited by wattle-and-daub type walls, probably for ease of movement and ventilation of heat and noxious gases. Inside and outside of these furnaces, we found slag lumps; jet-black, brittle ground slag; ore fragments (primarily copper oxides and iron-rich minerals that probably served as 'flux'); and whole and broken ceramic blowtube tips, called tuyères. Overall, evidence from Huaca del Pueblo Batán Grande suggests that the wide range and large quantities of arsenical copper artifacts—such as tumi knives, naipes, 'spear points,' and 'hoe blades'—found in Middle Sicán tombs were locally produced.

The widespread interment of arsenical-copper artifacts implies symbolic importance. This impression is reinforced by the discovery of offerings carefully placed at or near the mouths of some Middle Sicán smelting furnaces at Huaca del Pueblo Batán Grande (fig. 3b). The offerings consist of smudged short-necked jars, perhaps once containing perishable food, with their mouths covered by inverted plates with ring bases. Construction of the Middle Sicán furnaces and their intensive use were also immediately preceded by elaborate 'ritual' activities that included sacrificing at least fourteen fetal/neonatal camelids (Shimada and Shimada n.d.) and additional short-neck jars with plate covers. Smelting is a 'creative act' involving metamorphosis of naturally occurring substances such as varied ores and fuels through human manipulation. The products (metals) are intrinsically and extrinsically different from the ingredients. The creation of new valued substances through investment of much time, effort, and skill is likely to have been imbued with considerable symbolic importance.

In regard to the second aspect of metallurgy, the Middle Sicán goldsmiths were not technological innovators; their work was based on innovations achieved by Mochica metallurgists and metalworkers. The Sicán goldsmiths retained the emphasis on copper-gold alloys, or tumbaga, and sheet metal. These alloys were well-suited for sheet metal working, for they could be hardened by hammering, while remaining malleable. Lechtman (1979, 1984a, 1984b) emphasizes the fact that copper-gold alloys could be surface-treated to produce 'goldness.' Still, Middle Sicán gold objects fashioned out of sheet metal show a wide range of fabrication techniques: templates for cutting; dies for stamping; embossing for rigidity and surface ornamentation; raising; mechanical joining such as lacing, stapling, crimping, and use of tabs and wiring; and metallurgical joining such as welding and soldering (see Lechtman 1973; Tushingham et al. 1979: 10–25). What distinguishes Sicán gold objects is the implementation of the above-listed

techniques, particularly in the scale and complexity discussed later.

The third aspect concerns the overall character of the socio-political and economic organization and is described in depth elsewhere (Shimada n.d. a, n.d. c).

The preceding summary, along with discussion and data presented elsewhere, gives a picture of a culture with a dynamic economy based on large-scale irrigation agriculture, interregional (coast-highlands and maritime) exchange—and perhaps some form of trade—and unprecedented metallurgical production. Its stratified socio-political organization allowed differential and impressive accumulation of material wealth. Its territorial control seems to have covered all of the northern north coast of Peru (Jequetepeque to La Leche Valleys), and its products reached as far south as Ancón and Pachacamac and as far north as Isla La Plata, coastal Ecuador. Clearly, the organized religion, with its ideology embodied in a distinct iconography expressed in varied media, particularly gold, played a (if not the) dominant role in Middle Sicán culture, leading us to characterize its polity as a politically active Vatican-like religious state. With this general picture in mind, let us now turn to a detailed examination of the Middle Sicán gold artifacts.

ARTISTIC AND TECHNICAL FEATURES OF SICÁN GOLD FUNERARY ARTIFACTS
Masks

Many of the Middle Sicán elite funerary bundles looted from the Sicán Funerary-Religious Precinct (fig. 1) were found with as many as five gold masks, only one of which covered the face. The others were placed at the base of the bundles. These masks have been widely exhibited, illustrated, and even used as logos by corporations. Commonly, features such as size, brilliant gold color, two-dimensionality of sheet-metal construction, and relatively invariant iconography have been emphasized. Our study of over 20 gold masks, however, shows that most masks are, on close observation, characterized by three-dimensionality and colorfulness. This significant discrepancy stems from the facts that: only a few 'impressive' masks in accessible public collections (e.g., Museo de Oro del Perú, in Lima, Museo Arqueológico Regional Brüning, in Lambayeque)[9] have been publicized; in many cases, the semiprecious and precious stones and metal ornaments that originally decorated the masks have been removed or lost; and, in misguided efforts to emphasize the gold color and composition of the masks, the surviving traces of original paint and feathers have often been removed during cleaning and restoration stages.

Figure 4 serves to illustrate our points. On most masks, part of the face—except around the nose, eyes, and ears and below the mouth—was painted red (with a thick coat of cinnabar) or other color(s). Mask MOP-3076 (fig. 5) still retains green and white paint on the eyes, below the nose and on the ears. Mask MOP-1229 (fig. 4c) also shows traces of white and green paint. At times, the unpainted areas of masks show traces of carefully pasted, tiny feathers of varied colors that once formed colorful mosaics. Also, miniscule feathers were individually pasted onto pieces of leather, which were fastened to the lateral projections of the mask corresponding to the ears and ear ornaments. If the Middle Sicán murals found at Huaca El Corte,

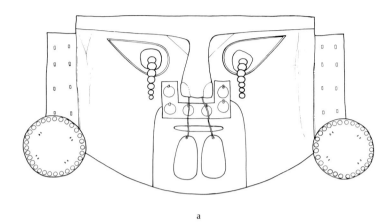

a

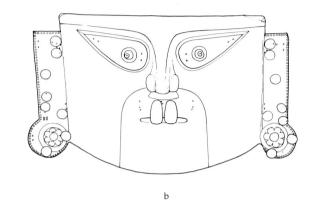

b

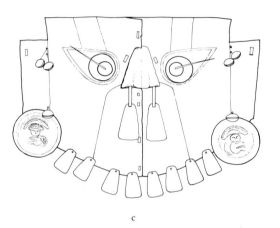

c

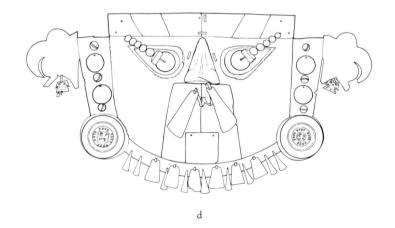

d

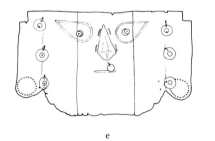

e

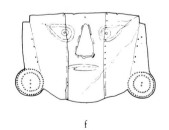

f

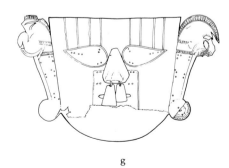

g

Fig. 4
Variation found among Middle Sicán masks:
a) MOP-1624, H. 31·7 cm., W. 63·5 cm.; b) MOP-2060, H. 28·5 cm., W. 48·3 cm.;
c) MOP-1229, H. 32·5 cm., W. 44·6 cm.; d) MOP-s/n V.29, H. 32·2 cm., W. 61·9 cm.;
e) MOP-1230, H. 18·5 cm., W. 31·7 cm.; f) MOP-1130, H. 16·3 cm., W. 25·4 cm.;
g) MOP-1132, H. 22·6 cm., W. 36·2 cm.
Drawing: Izumi Shimada.

in the Sicán Precinct (fig. 9; see also the murals at Huaca del Oro [Kosok 1965: 165] and at Ucupe [Alva 1984]), are any indication of feather decoration on the masks, there were probably at least six colors: red, yellow, greenish-blue, black, white, and orange (Shimada 1981, n.d. a). The murals show that it is quite likely that many masks originally had elaborate feather-work attached to the upper edges. One gets a similar impression from the embossed figures found on numerous gold beakers with flaring sides and flat bases. Also informative are the details found on 20 miniature wooden figures standing inside the six major portals or 'temples' that decorate the so-called 'Chimu Litter'[10] (figs. 7, 8). Each figure has a masklike face, much of which is painted red. Some of the different headdresses among them are decorated with tiny feathers of varied colors (Carcedo n.d.).

The bright colors and three-dimensionality of the masks effectively complement each other. Consider, for example, the elaborate mask MOP-1624 (fig. 4a), which has a circular ornament representing each pupil, covered with the vestiges of tiny feathers. A gold wire runs straight out from the center of each pupil ornament to pierce seven spherical emeralds, graduated in diameter from 5 cm. to 1 cm., as if to represent a series of teardrops. Other elaborate masks have similar wire projections with pierced lapis lazuli or 'gold' (hollow) spheroids. Mask MOP-1229 (fig. 4c) has eyes of carved shell with 'copper' pupils and projecting wires. In addition, it is decorated with disc-shaped ear ornaments with pendant bells, and trapezoidal spangles hang from the nostrils. Combined with the traces of green and white paint noted earlier, the mask presents a colorful, three-dimensional image. Perhaps we are emphasizing unduly the 'goldness' of the masks and other objects treated in this paper (see Lechtman 1984a, 1984b). Rosshandler (1976: 19; see also Shimada n.d. c) points out this difference in etic and emic perceptions of 'gold.' He observes that 'Precious as it was, gold was often subordinated to painted decoration' and that 'gold did not have the absolute intrinsic value in the eyes of the ancient Peruvians that it has for us.' The symbolic importance of surface paint and feather decoration and their relationship to the underlying gold of Middle Sicán artifacts remain a major research issue.

The base of the nose on elaborate masks is often decorated with crescent or U-shaped copper or gold ornaments, e.g. MOP-1624 (fig. 4a) and MMA 1974.271.35 (fig. 6), that bear traces of feathers or hemispherical metal ornaments (usually six or seven). On many masks, the nose ornament is no longer there, although perforations in the area attest to its former presence. In the case of mask MOP-1624, a teardrop-shaped gold pendant hangs at the end of a square wire projecting from each nostril. Figures on the 'Chimu Litter' (figs. 7, 8) have the same sort of nose ornaments.

'Chinstraps' are rarely found; two good examples are MB/144 and another in a private collection in the U.S. However, perforations found along the chin on some masks suggest that 'chinstraps' or other hanging ornaments are more common than we realize (see fig. 4). Figures on the 'Chimu Litter' (fig. 8) have leather 'chinstraps.'

A casual glance at these masks belies their original polychrome, three-dimensional character. Various hanging ornaments could have added mobility and acoustic effects. When seen in this light, the variation in thickness of sheet metal used for masks may be related not only to overall size

Fig. 5
Mask with vestiges of green and white paint
on the eyes, below the nose, and on the ear ornaments.
The pupils of eyes are gold hemispheres from which thin gold tubes protrude.
Spangles hang from the ears and nose.
MOP-3076, H. 20·4 cm., W. 38·8 cm.
Photo: courtesy the Royal Ontario Museum.

Fig. 6
Single-sheet Middle Sicán mask with numerous trapezoidal spangles.
The pupils of the eyes are hemispheres from which tapering gold tubes protrude.
Originally the tubes may have held graduated, pierced precious stones or gold beads.
H. 29·2 cm., W. 49·5 cm.
Metropolitan Museum of Art, Gift and Bequest of Alice K. Bache, 1974.271.35.
Photo: Thomas A. Brown.

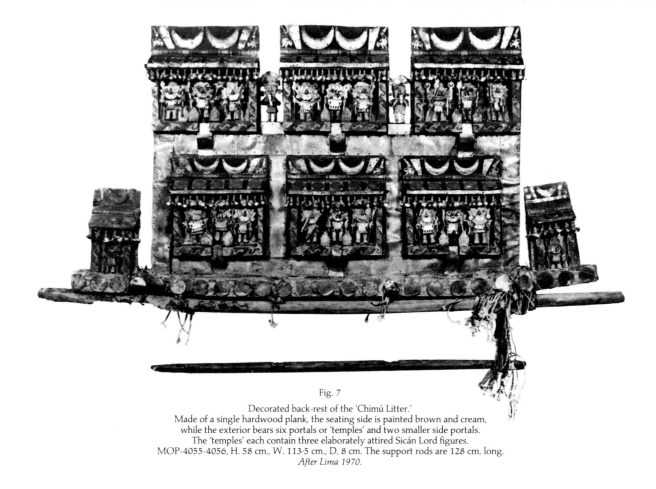

Fig. 7
Decorated back-rest of the 'Chimú Litter.'
Made of a single hardwood plank, the seating side is painted brown and cream,
while the exterior bears six portals or 'temples' and two smaller side portals.
The 'temples' each contain three elaborately attired Sicán Lord figures.
MOP-4055-4056, H. 58 cm., W. 113·5 cm., D. 8 cm. The support rods are 128 cm. long.
After Lima 1970.

but also to the weight of the sheet metal itself and of the various added ornaments. Our thickness measurements of masks (edges and, to the extent that the caliper or micrometer reaches, interiors) agree well with those taken by Tushingham, Franklin, and Toogood (1979). Commonly, ingots or blanks destined for masks were hammered down to a thickness of 0.10–0.25 mm. Tushingham et al. (1979: 6) marvel that 'Thickness varies so slightly within one sample of sheet that it compares very favourably with the standards achieved with modern machine tools.' The single-sheet mask with elaborate ornamentation, commonly made of relatively thick sheets, occupies the 'large' end of the overall size-variation range. Mask MOP-1229 (fig. 4c) is peculiar in that plain-weave cotton cloth is glued to the back. It is not clear whether the cotton cloth represents original backing, an effort to anchor the mask more firmly to the funerary bundle, or an as yet unknown purpose.

Figure 4 effectively illustrates the range of technical, stylistic, and icono-graphic variation found among Middle Sicán funerary masks. Primarily on the basis of observed stylistic variation—and keeping in mind the small sample size—we have established a tentative typology.

Type A masks seem to be most common. Their distinguishing feature is the pair of circular ear ornaments that project out beyond the vertical, or nearly vertical, line that defines the outer margins of the conventionalized ears. Thus, the maximum width of Type A masks is that between the extreme points of the earplugs or earlobes. Most of the masks of this type are fashioned out of single, relatively thick sheets with facial features and ornaments chiefly formed by embossing, perhaps using wood templates, e.g., MB/52; MOP-1624 (fig. 4a), 1898, 2060 (fig. 4b), 3076 (fig. 5).

There are a few made of two (one for the face and the other for the nose; e.g., MB-145) or three sheets. Mask MOP-1229 (fig. 4c) is composed of two sheets mechanically joined in the center of the mask, with a small third sheet forming the nose. Masks MB/57 and MOP-1130 (fig. 4f) are formed by three roughly equal-sized, but quite thin, sheets joined by series of staples. The last two could be considered a subtype.

Type B masks, on the other hand, are those whose ears and ear ornaments form straight lines, such as MOP-1131 and 1230 (fig. 4e) so that the overall shape approximates a rectangle. Type B masks are often made of three mechanically joined sheets, which are quite thin. One such composite mask in a private collection, micrometer-measured by Merkel and Shimada, has a thickness range of 0.11–0.18 mm. On the other hand, the impressive mask at the Metropolitan Museum of Art (fig. 6) is fashioned out of a single, relatively thick sheet. The mask in the John Wise Collection at the Dallas Museum of Art is made of two thick sheets (one for the face and one for the nose). Type A and B masks vary considerably in size; those we have measured range from 100 to 30 cm. in width.

Type C masks have projecting ornaments atop, or along the upper edge of, the conventionalized ears. The ornaments are usually representations of human figures or faces, or of animal heads with feline and serpentine characteristics. Combined with the slanting edges of ears, these ornaments give Type C masks a trapezoidal overall shape. The face is made of a single sheet, with nose and ear-top ornaments fashioned out of separate sheets in the cases of masks MB-114, MB-115, MOP-1132 (fig. 4g), and s/n V. 29 (fig. 4d). Mask MB-116, however, is made out of a single sheet. In general, Type C masks are made from relatively thin sheets.

Fig. 8

Detail of one of the six 'temples' on the back-rest of the 'Chimú Litter.'
Three richly attired Sicán Lord figures stand inside it,
the central figure is slightly recessed and more elaborate than the others.
Figures 8 cm. high; interior dimensions of the 'temples': H. 11 cm., W. 18·5 cm.
Photo: Paloma Carcedo.

Fig. 9

Detail from a polychrome mural on an exterior perimeter wall
surrounding the main funerary-architectural zone of Huaca El Corte.
Drawing: Izumi Shimada.

We find that the same range of techniques is used for all types. In other words, observed technical variation does not directly affect or correlate with stylistic variation.

The relevance of the typology above for the present analysis of Sicán gold objects is evident in the covariance seen between masks of different types, on one hand, and their typical size, gold content, and associated objects, on the other. One also notes the differential distribution of different type masks. In general, masks of Type C are the smallest and are made out of the thinnest sheets. The great grave lots described earlier as having numerous large gold objects contained masks of Types A or B, while Type C masks are found elsewhere, typically with small, primarily 'personal' objects such as necklaces, tupus, and ear ornaments, as well as tiny gold figurines and ceramics. Most Type A and B masks were found in major tombs at Huacas Las Ventanas, La Merced, and El Corte, whereas at least some Type C masks are known to have been looted from Huaca Facho, an extensive site with numerous small platform mounds and one bisected, truncated pyramid about 2.5 km. north of the Sicán Precinct. Three Type C masks at the Brüning Museum in Lambayeque (MB/115, 116, and 117), however, are attributed to Huaca La Merced. These observations require further archaeological verification. The cultural significance of spatial, stylistic, and technical variation and clustering among the masks will be considered later, together with other components of major Middle Sicán grave lots and tombs.

Tumis

As in the case of funerary masks, the tumi was elaborated by Middle Sicán metallurgists, using sheet metals, to a point previously and subsequently unseen. Unlike the masks, the knife is found in living, as well as in funerary, contexts. In general, however, tumis found in habitational areas are made of copper, small in size (easily used with one hand), and undecorated. The tumi (of copper or other metals) is commonly found in adult burials of all ranks in the Middle Sicán and later cultures in Batán Grande. Lower-class burials have only one copper tumi, wrapped in coarse cotton cloth. Some major elite tombs contain packages of dozens of copper tumis, grouped by size, tied together as bundles with cords, and wrapped with coarse cotton cloth. Middle Sicán tumis, whether found individually or in groups, whether made of copper or gold, all have the same basic form. The blade is perfectly semicircular and the handle or shaft is rectangular, with overall dimensions at times exceeding 30 cm. in length and 13–14 cm. in diameter of the blade. In other words, the upper edge of the blade and the handle edge approximate a 90-degree angle. Gradually over time, this angle decreases; i.e., the handle width increases toward the top (proximal) end. The tumi shape, thus, is an important chronological indicator, but has rarely been used as such.

Elaborate Middle Sicán ('ceremonial') tumis, made of gold or silver or both, and found in elite tombs, are decorated with a partial or full-body representation of the Sicán Lord or of animals, e.g., those resembling deer (fig. 10), at the proximal end of the handle. Here, those with Sicán Lord representations will be examined in depth, for they exhibit technical mastery of goldsmithing (partly because of their small size) and unparalleled details

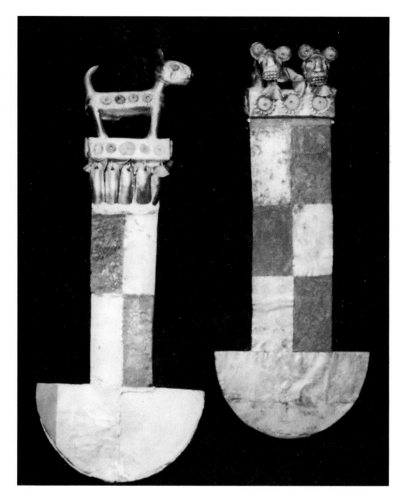

Fig. 10

Two 'ceremonial' tumis with animals on the finial end.
The animals, which most closely resemble deer, are inset
with turquoise and *Spondylus* shell inlays and have checkerboard pattern blades.
MOP-3058; MOP-3059, H. 27·5 cm.
Photo: courtesy Library Services Department, American Museum of Natural History.

allows us to posit the following typology of tumis with full-figure representation of the Sicán Lord (Class I):

Type 1: Standing figure with no 'wings,' partially flexed arms, each hand holding half of an unidentified spherical object, and feet shown in plane view (e.g., MOP-2707).

Type 2: Standing figure with 'wings,' holding a cup with both hands at waist level, and feet shown in plane view (e.g., MNAA-BG/39).

Type 3 A and B: Standing figure with (A) or without (B) 'wings,' holding at waist height a cup, and with feet in profile (e.g., MOP-3131; tumi at the Art Institute of Chicago; two tumis in the John Wise Collection at Dallas Museum of Art).

Type 4: 'Winged' figure seated cross-legged (left leg over right), holding an unknown circular object in the right hand and a tumi in the left, both at waist height.

In addition, there is one known example (MOP-2444) of a tumi with only the bust of the Sicán Lord holding a vase at waist level (Class II). It does not have the typical semicircular cap decoration; instead, the decoration has the form of 'feathers,' with their terminal portions representing three *Spondylus*, or thorny oyster, shells.

The last major class (III) of 'ceremonial' tumis are those with only the head of the Sicán Lord, at the proximal end of the handle. Class III includes most of the tumis with bimetallic, checkerboard-pattern decoration on the handle and blade. For example, MOP-2708 (fig. 12) has a handle and blade of silver with alternating rectangular sections overlaid with gold foil. Above this checkerboard pattern is the head of the Sicán Lord, with turquoise-bead eyes, ears decorated with turquoise, and gold-turquoise pendant earrings. The elaborate headdress consists of a cap with inset turquoise roundels and red *Spondylus* shell, and a semicircular filigree crest with a gold bird hanging from either end, inlaid with turquoise and holding a lapis lazuli bead on a gold ring in its beak (Tushingham 1976: 126, no. 227). The same pattern of a silver base with alternating rectangles of gold foil is seen in MOP-3130, while MOP-3075 shows a copper base with alternating gold foil.

The close relationship between gold and silver noted above is also seen in other classes of funerary-ritual objects, such as beakers with flaring sides and the 'Chimu Litter.' When we examine the whole spectrum of Sicán tombs and grave goods, we find copper to be the metal of the populace, while gold and silver are reserved for the elite; this is much the same as the later Inca differentiation. The combination and differentiation of the latter two metals seem to have been much more than an aesthetic-stylistic consideration. In the 'Chimu Litter,' we see clearly differentiated use of gold and silver (figs. 7, 8). The roofs of the 'temples' are alternately decorated with gold and silver, just as the Sicán Lord figures inside the temples show a matching pattern of alternating gold and silver dress. Also, a nearly identical pair of gold (MOP-2443) and silver (MOP-3132) tumis shows the winged Sicán Lord seated in a typical Mochica cross-legged position with left leg over right, left hand holding a tumi and right hand a circular object. The front of tumi MOP-3131 is made of elaborately embossed gold sheet with precious stone insets, while the back is fashioned out of silver sheet. Various scholars (e.g., Carrión 1940; Kauffmann 1973) have argued that

of Middle Sicán ceremonial costumes and iconography. Among tumis, we find the total range of goldsmithing techniques. The following discussion distinguishes the technical, stylistic, and iconographic variation observable on the front and the back sides of tumis.

Seen from the front, the characteristic Sicán Lord figure on tumis shows (fig. 11): a cap or helmet, with or without inset semiprecious stones, typically turquoise or lapis lazuli; a semicircular decoration (usually filigree, at times with small hanging birds or teardrop-shaped pendants) at the crest of the cap; a stylized face with round ear ornaments that often have inset precious or semiprecious stones; a knee-length tunic; at times, sandals or knee decorations; and a podium or pillow upon which the figure stands or is seated. Iconographic variation among these components, in turn,

Fig. 11
'Ceremonial' tumi with a seated Sicàn Lord at the finial end of the handle.
He holds an unidentified circular object in the right hand and a tumi in the left.
MOP-2443, H. 33·6 cm., W. 13·5 cm.
Photo: courtesy of the Royal Ontario Museum.

Fig. 12
Middle Sicán 'ceremonial' tumi with silver blade and handle,
alternating sections of which are overlaid with gold foil to create a checkerboard effect.
The finial is an elaborately decorated Sicán Lord head.
MOP-2708, H. 27·7 cm., W. 10·3 cm.
Photo: courtesy the Royal Ontario Museum.

the Sicán Lord is the personification of the moon. Menzel (1977) and Shimada (1983, n.d. a) have also suggested that Middle Sicán iconography combines various elements and themes pertaining to the sky and planets. Although we may speculate some linkage with Sicán cosmology, archaeological verification will be difficult.

Let us now examine the backs of these tumis (fig. 13). Although the back shows the same degree of technical mastery and iconographic detail as the front, it has rarely been described or illustrated. The Sicán Lord is always shown in front view; however, the cultural significance of the tumis cannot be fully appreciated without examining them in totality.

Fundamentally, the back is composed of the same five parts as the front. From the top, we find: the uppermost portion of the back sheet, which, together with the corresponding portion of the front sheet, serves to anchor a semicircular (typically filigree), separately made ornament; a rosette or roundel (typically 5–6 cm. in diameter), in the center of which is an inset semiprecious stone surrounded by varied embossed decoration; a rectangular area that contains a central raised trapezoidal part with two horizontal bands and fringelike embossed ornamentation at the bottom; three or four files of embossed trapezoidal 'spangles' or circular ornaments; and a row of triangular ornaments that may represent a short skirt or the bottom of a tunic.

Fig. 13
Variation found on the backs of Sicán Lord figures of Middle Sicán tumis.
From left to right: MOP-2444, H. 35·4 cm., W. 12·5 cm.; MOP-2443, H. 33·6 cm., W. 13·5 cm.;
MOP-3131, H. 33·5 cm., W. 14 cm.; MOP-2707, H. 39·5 cm., W. 20·3 cm.
Photo: Paloma Carcedo.

Fig. 14
Beaker with flaring sides embossed with three standing Sicán Lord figures holding staffs.
The figures, decorated with inlays, are framed at the top and
sides with a border of crow-step designs.
MOP-4584, H. 18·2 cm.
Photo: Paloma Carcedo.

Fig. 15
Two Middle Sicán gold beakers with embossed, stylized bird designs.
MOP-4524, H. 11·3 cm.; MOP-4523, H. 11·7 cm.
Photo: Paloma Carcedo.

The morphological and stylistic variability contrasts with technical uniformity. Both Classes I and III show four basic technical principals: (1) the figures or faces of the Sicán Lord are made out of two sheets, one on the front and another on the back, the edge of the front sheet overlying that of the back (as if to encase it) and pressure-joined, so that, viewed from the front, the figures or faces seem a solid, round, gold mass, instead of a hollow piece; (2) the handle and blade are a single thick sheet, sandwiched between the front and back sheets that form the figure or face; (3) the semicircular upper portion of the headdress is a separate piece, which, like the handle, is held between the front and back sheets; and (4) the 'wings' are separate components that are individually soldered to the front or back sheet. Overall, the manufacture of these 'ceremonial' tumis was a very complex task that required the utmost skill and care, and was most likely left to master goldsmiths. In Middle Sicán tumis from Batán Grande, we find nearly the total range of goldsmithing techniques developed in the prehispanic Andes.

Although the principles listed above assured certain technical homogeneity, we can discern some differences in the specific ways in which they were implemented, perhaps reflecting the idiosyncracies of master goldsmiths. These differences, which have no detectable effect on overall technical or artistic quality, can be seen in details on the back and filigree of the headdress. In the case of masks, idiosyncracies can be noted, particularly on their backs, in details of the specific ways sheets are joined or stone or metal ornaments are hung or supported.

Flaring beakers
The last major category of gold objects to be treated here comprises numerous beakers with flaring sides and flat bases, typically decorated with the embossed face or figure of the Sicán Lord. We must remember that, as seen in figure 2, an impressive number of varied beakers are found nested to form tall stacks in individual graves. Nearly 200 beakers have been found stacked or scattered in a single grave. Each stack typically consists of about ten beakers of seemingly similar size, shape, iconography, and weight. Scattered beakers are of different size and/or shape. Statistical analysis, using beakers from a single grave lot, is currently under way to test our hypothesis that, in fact, there are certain set size-shape categories, as is the case for tumis and naipes. In other words, variation is largely limited to that of molds/templates and ingots/blanks. Figure 2a, b shows 176 gold beakers from a single grave lot. Among them we have identified nineteen different iconographic elements and themes, composed of stylized animals, Sicán Lord figures and heads, auxiliary 'fillers,' 'scenery,' and four types of plain designs in clearly defined decorative zones and areas. The nineteen elements and themes are as follows: isolated Sicán Lord figures (two or more), standing with feet in plane view and holding a 'staff' in each hand as in MOP-4584 (fig. 14); the same figures in profile; frontal view of Sicán Lord heads; profile view of anthropomorphic heads (Sicán Lord?); the same profile heads, but looking down toward the bottom of the vessel; a single Sicán Lord head, with face on one side and hair and simple headdress on the other side of the vessel; an individual or row of stylized birds (fig. 15); stylized toads or frogs; rows of shells (*Spondylus*?); a row of 'staffs'; step-

Fig. 16
Tall 'rattle' beaker with double bottom and flaring sides
is embossed with a wave pattern and a series of stylized birds (?) on the body.
A row of turquoise inlays with beaded borders is between them.
MOP-4608, H. 13·2 cm.
Photo: courtesy the Royal Ontario Museum.

Fig. 17
Inverted Middle Sicán beaker with flaring sides,
the round shape of which is used to represent a head.
The back shows hair and a simple headdress.
MOP-4624 H.18·8 cm.
Photo: Paloma Carcedo.

spiral border designs; and 'scenery,' composed of various combinations of the preceding, covering three-quarters of or the entire circumference of the vessel. Major themes such as a standing Sicán Lord and 'scenery' are not found on ceramics but seem limited to murals and precious metal objects. Middle Sicán ceramic effigy vessels invariably show the Sicán Lord head accompanied by varied combinations of stylized birds, toads or frogs, monkeys, and other animals.

The preceding list is by no means complete. The grave lot also included tall 'gold' beakers with precious or semiprecious stone plaques and elaborate embossing. Many of them have a double bottom with small stones inside that serve as 'rattles' (fig. 16). Most of these special beakers were found in small numbers in tombs containing 'ceremonial' tumis. They may have been used together in special contexts such as funerary rites before the interment.

In addition to 'standardized' beakers and rare rattle-beakers, we must briefly consider 'face' beakers (*vasos retratos*, fig. 17), which present the impression of a full-round sculpture of the Sicán Lord head. One side shows the face (right-side-up or upside-down) with zigzag teeth (fangs are not delineated; see the mural at Huaca El Corte, fig. 9), while the other side displays a headdress that varies among vessels. Apparently, this class of beaker varies considerably in size, from about 25 cm. to over 100 cm. in height. (Beakers of other classes may be as small as 13–14 cm. in height.) Most of the huge beakers—for example, those looted from a large grave at the west base of the principal pyramid of Huaca La Merced—seem to have been melted down to produce gold ingots.[11]

DISCUSSION

With the preceding information and observations in mind, let us address some issues pertaining to Middle Sicán funerary customs and objects, and their broader implications for the culture as a whole.

First, we must address a terminological problem commonly found in the literature. Too often, Middle Sicán artifacts are incorrectly identified as 'Chimú.' In his 1938 description of grave goods looted from Middle Sicán tombs at Huacas La Merced and Las Ventanas, when hardly anything was known of the archaeology of Batán Grande and the broader region of Lambayeque Valley, Valcárcel described them as belonging to a North Chimú culture. Somewhat later, Kroeber (1944), in discussing ceramic collections in the Lambayeque region, employed the same designation. This designation, over time, came to be equated with a northern variant of the culture of the Kingdom of Chimú (Ravines 1980). Both the Middle Sicán culture and that of the Kingdom of Chimú share a similar set of motifs and blackware ceramics. It is now apparent, however, that the Middle Sicán culture is independent of the latter, which was centered at Chan Chan, in the Moche Valley, some 300 km. to the south. The designation Chimú is appropriate only if used as a generic term, as Menzel (1977: 62) uses it, encompassing the broad cultural tradition of the entire north coast that resulted from the merger of the Mochica and Wari cultural traditions, long before the time of the Kingdom of Chimú. If the latter is to be used, it should be specified as such to avoid confusion.

We also prefer the term Sicán over another common designation, the

Lambayeque culture, for the latter is used with various chronological and cultural connotations (e.g., Kauffman 1973; Kosok 1959, 1965; Nolan 1980; Zevallos 1971). In addition, the varied definitions are all based only on brief surface surveys, funerary goods, and/or historical documents, without long-term, sustained research involving excavations and analyses of varied artifacts from both funerary and habitational contexts. The equation of the Sicán Lord with the legendary Ñaymlap is, for the moment, an assumption, rather than an empirically proven fact (Shimada n.d. a). We employ the term 'Lambayeque' to designate the long cultural tradition of the Lambayeque region, including the more specific Sicán Culture.

The chronological significance of the observed technical, stylistic, and iconographic variation is yet to be determined. If the diagnostics of the Middle Sicán style, defined by ceramics recovered from secure stratigraphic contexts (particularly at Huaca del Pueblo Batán Grande) and dated by a set of internally consistent radiocarbon assays, are applicable to metal objects (as we believe they are), all the gold artifacts discussed and illustrated here are Middle Sicán in style and date. In ceramics, over the roughly 200-year span of the Middle Sicán, we see gradual stylistic and iconographic elaboration, as expected (fig. 18). By Late Sicán, however, we find that the ceramic Sicán Lord representations, although similar in overall configuration, have lost many details. We do not see a parallel change among the gold artifacts examined here. Murals and gold artifacts are clearly the most important media of Sicán iconographic expression; the most elaborate and varied expressions appear in them. The prestige of gold artifacts is apparent, not only in terms of iconographic content and differential access, but also in their imitation in other media. Rondón (1965–66) points out that some Middle Sicán blackware effigy vessels faithfully imitate the manufacturing technique and appearance of similarly shaped gold vessels. The relationship between gold objects, on the one hand, and textiles and wood artifacts, on the other, remains to be determined, but examples of the latter are very rare. Murals were essentially public in nature, and we must ask whether gold objects that were also iconographically important had a similar public function.

Typically, Middle Sicán gold artifacts have been implicitly or explicitly described as funerary in character. Whether their 'life history' was exclusively limited to funerary contexts is a debatable matter, however. We must consider the distinct possibility that these objects were used in ritual contexts during the lives of important personages who were interred with them. Rattle-beakers could well have been used in ceremonial dances, and the more common beakers used in key feasts. Masks are no exception to this idea of funerary-living dual functions. The narrow top of the T-shaped principal mound of Huaca El Corte had a colonnade of 48 painted square columns supporting a solid roof, a back wall with polychrome murals, and an elaborately constructed 'duct,' which may have been used for ritual libations (Shimada 1981, n.d. a, n.d. b). There was just enough space for a small number of people to stand. The overall construction resembles 'temples' depicted on the 'Chimú Litter'. We suggest that the mound top was the setting for the public display of key Sicán idols and icons. Masks could well have decorated the faces of such idols, just as they covered funerary bundles. Gold artifacts richly endowed with the iconography used in public

contexts would have served to disseminate its symbolic messages. According to this view, on the death of a given ruler who was regarded as the personification of the Sicán Lord, the varied gold artifacts, used until then in courts and temples, would have been gathered (and perhaps painted red to symbolize death) and then interred. Otherwise, we must postulate a tremendous material and manpower investment to produce over 200 gold beakers and other objects within the short period during which the tomb was being prepared. Even with the use of molds/templates and blanks, which facilitate production of standardized objects, the quantity and variability of objects in this tomb would argue for a substantial quantity of readily available gold and a number of skillful goldsmiths. Logically, we must then ask what became of this pool of skilled labour when there was no such pressing production demand. And was there always enough gold available for these goldsmiths to engage in their craft?

Overall, it is clear that discussion regarding the gold artifacts derived from grave lots is in danger of overemphasizing their exclusive funerary importance.

The general technical and stylistic homogeneity of the gold objects and the differential access to them suggest tightly controlled production and distribution[12]. If the productive organization of arsenical-copper smelting and metalworking is any indication (Epstein and Shimada n.d.; Shimada n.d. a, n.d. b), the time-and-labor-efficient 'mass-production' format that characterizes modern industry is unlikely; rather, we are probably dealing with a labor-intensive setup of a group of compartmentalized workshops, each headed by a master goldsmith. Spatial differentiation of mask types, quantitative and qualitative differences in gold objects, and variation in iconographic details further suggest that different sectors of the elite had their own access to the services of goldsmiths. The emerging picture of the production of gold artifacts is, in fact, quite similar to the organization of labor independently deduced from the analyses of marked adobe bricks, described earlier.

This paper should be regarded as a progress report on our study of Middle Sicán gold artifacts. Although some cultural insights have emerged, the paper also serves to highlight problematical views and unresolved issues, many of which are tied to the small sample size and the tenuous contextual data of the gold objects. Additional excavation research is needed.

ACKNOWLEDGEMENTS

During the course of our research, we received generous cooperation and hospitality, as well as valuable critiques and encouragement, from many colleagues and institutions in Peru, the United States, Spain, and the Federal Republic of Germany. We note our sincere gratitude to the following people and institutions: members of the Sicán Archaeological Project (formerly known as the Batán Grande–La Leche Archaeological Project), the Hon. Miguel Mujica Gallo, Alvaro Roca Rey, and other staff members of the Museo de Oro del Perú, in Lima; Walter and Susana Alva and the staff of the Museo Arqueológico Regional Brüning, in Lambayeque; the late Junius Bird, Peggy Bird, and other members of the Department of Anthropology, American Museum of Natural History; the staff in charge

Fig. 18
Tentative seriation of Sicán effigy jars with Sicán Lord representations.
The left vessel represents early Middle Sicán,
while the specimen at the right dates to Late Sicán.
Drawing: Izumi Shimada.

of metal artifacts at the Museo Nacional de Antropología y Arqueología, Lima; members of the Aurich family, particularly Oswaldo Aurich and his family; the Maeda family in Batán Grande; the Agrarian Cooperative Pucalá and its annex, Batán Grande; Heather Lechtman, of the Massachussetts Institute of Technology; José Alcína and Manuel Ballestero-Gaibrois, of the Universidad de Madrid; Richard P. Schaedel, of the University of Texas, Austin; and Dieter Eisleb and Richard Haas of the Museum für Völkerkunde, Berlin. The research was made possible by generous grants from the National Geographic Society. Supplementary funds were provided by the National Science Foundation, the Princeton University Latin American Studies Committee, and the Ministry of Culture, Spain. Finally our thanks to Elizabeth Benson and Melody Shimada for editorial assistance.

[1] The forest supports a wide range of indigenous animals, some of which have largely disappeared elsewhere on the Peruvian coast, such as puma, deer, fox, anteater, squirrel, iguana (some reaching over 1 m. in length), boa-constrictor, skunk, large and small parrots, and numerous other birds with plumage of varied colors.

[2] Gold artifacts discussed in this paper are usually of tumbaga, or copper-gold or copper-silver-gold alloy that had been depletion-gilded to produce the appearance of pure gold. The alloys and the depletion-gilding technique are described in detail in the various publications by Lechtman cited in the text. Concentrations of the constituent metals cannot be readily determined without careful compositional analysis.

[3] In order to avoid drawing unwanted attention, the discoverers of this tumi attributed it to Illimo, a community adjoining the Sicán Precinct, although it was looted from a grave in the South Sector of Huaca Las Ventanas.

[4] The term Mochica is used to describe the prehistoric culture of north-coast Peru that flourished during the first seven centuries of our era, while the term Moche is employed to describe its first capital and its chronological division.

[5] We have been able to determine that much of the Huaca del Corte grave lot was acquired by a museum in the United States, while a substantial portion of the third major grave lot is now at the Museo de Oro del Perú, in Lima. They provide us with a glimpse of original grave-lot composition.

[6] A bright reddish-pink to orange-colored spiny oyster found in warm coastal Ecuadorian waters.

[7] Most of the Middle Sicán copper artifacts we have analyzed thus far are arsenical copper and not pure copper, as often thought.

[8] The term refers to double-T-shaped artifacts cut from hammered arsenical-copper sheets commonly found in Middle Sicán graves. Although they are usually discarded by looters as worthless, and corroded specimens soon disappear from the surface, they were clearly valued and differentially accumulated by Middle Sicán people. Large elite graves contain hundreds of naipes carefully wrapped and tied together in packages. Apparently, they were set sizes (and perhaps weights), and their similarities to the 'copper-axe money' found in coastal Ecuador, together with historical documentation of a long-distance maritime exchange network linking coastal Ecuador and Peru, suggest their possible use in such a network (see Shimada n.d. c). Naipes were probably manufactured in Batán Grande, and the control of production and distribution may have been a key factor in the accumulation of wealth found in Middle Sicán elite tombs.

[9] Hereafter, MOP refers to the Museo de Oro del Perú (Gold of Peru Museum), while MB corresponds to the Museo Brüning Regional Archaeological Museum); MNAA refers to the Museo Nacional de Antropología y Arqueología (National Museum of Anthropology and Archaeology); and MMA designates the Metropolitan Museum of Art. The numbers that follow these designations correspond to the catalogue or accession numbers of the objects under discussion.

[10] The exact provenance of this litter is not known, but it has traditionally been attributed to Chan Chan, capital of the Kingdom of Chimú. Stylistically and iconographically, it belongs to the Middle Sicán.

[11] We cannot even guess the number of looted gold artifacts that was melted. We know, however, that a foundry was established not far from the looting sites to melt these artifacts and produce pure gold ingots.

[12] A better understanding of the distribution of gold and other valued artifacts may eventually support our suspicion of a considerable degree of social mobility within Middle Sicán society.

Ancient American Metallurgy: Five Hundred Years of Study

WARWICK BRAY

When Columbus sailed westward to find a new sea route to Japan and China, he took with him a letter of introduction to the Great Khan and a Book of Privileges which set out his titles as Admiral of the Ocean Sea, and Viceroy and Governor of the islands and of the mainland. The document also granted him one-tenth of the profits from any precious metals or gems he might obtain (Morison 1942).

It was gold, rather than land or a desire to convert the native population to Christianity, that drew European conquistadors to Central and South America, their hopes summed up by Hernando Cortés in his reply to an official who offered him lands and a settled life in Hispaniola. 'But I came to get gold,' declared Cortés, 'not to till the land like a peasant' (Fisher 1976:59). The early voyages of discovery along the coasts of Venezuela, Colombia, and the Isthmus were soon followed by the conquest of Mexico in 1519–21, and of Peru a decade later. By the middle of the 16th century, the major gold-producing regions of the New World were in Spanish hands, and huge quantities of Indian artifacts were melted down into bullion for shipment to Europe.

Having stripped the living Indians of their wealth, the conquistadors turned their attention to the tombs and monuments of the dead. Figueroa's expedition to conquer the Zapotecs of Mexico is typical of its period. As Bernal Díaz described it: 'He determined to undertake the excavation of the graves and burial places of the Caciques of those provinces, for he found in them a quantity of golden jewels which it was the custom in olden days to bury with the chieftains of those pueblos, and he attained such dexterity that he took out from them over five thousand pesos de oro ... So he determined to abandon the conquest' (Díaz 1905–16, 5:132). In the Sinú region of northern Colombia, the robbing of burial mounds became the main occupation of the first Spanish settlers, so that by 1535 there were complaints that the area was already worked out (Bray 1978:12–13).

Before the end of the 16th century, 'mining companies' were carrying out this work on a large scale, and archaeological sites were ransacked for gold, initiating a sad tale of destruction which has continued until the present. Some of the most famous sites were among the first to be attacked. At Chan Chan, the Chimú capital on the north coast of Peru, a certain García Gutiérrez de Toledo excavated a cemetery in the year 1566 and was able to send more than 5,000 *castellanos* of gold to the Spanish king. The nearby Pyramid of the Sun, a great adobe platform in the former Moche capital, fared even worse. In the late 1500s, the monument was divided into 23 parts and sold off to treasure hunters. Each purchaser of a share gained the right to excavate in the mound, with a grant of Indian laborers to do the heavy work (Pozorski 1980:23). In 1602 another consortium

of looters diverted the Moche River against the mound to expose its center. They destroyed nearly two-thirds of the main platform and were rewarded with 2788 kilos of gold (Lothrop 1952:106).

COLONIAL ACCOUNTS OF INDIAN METALLURGY

Given the gold-fever of the time, it is not surprising that Colonial documents contain a mass of technical detail about native metalworking. Some early writers had a professional knowledge of the subject, and their accounts have the freshness of first-hand observation. Spanish interest was financial rather than aesthetic. The 'heathen idols' offended Christian sensibilities and did not appeal to European taste. Moreover, for accounting purposes it was more convenient to convert the mass of artifacts into ingots and coins. Everything went into the melting pot. The Inca Atahualpa's ransom alone kept nine forges occupied for four months in 1533, and yielded 13,420 pounds of gold and 26,000 pounds of silver. From this Colonial activity hardly a metal object has survived.

The main concerns of the European conquerors were practical ones. Where was gold to be found? What was the composition and bullion value of native jewelry? Did Indian goldsmiths know any technical tricks which the Spaniards might find useful? In the anonymous notes written for the guidance of Sir Walter Ralegh, as he prepared to set out for Virginia in 1585, was this piece of advice: 'An alcamist is not Impertinent, to trye the metaylls that maybe discouerd ...' (Fisher 1976:63). Ralegh found no gold in Virginia, but he did collect gold ornaments during his expedition to Guyana in 1595 in search of the 'great and Golden Citie of Manoa.' He had a trial made of one of these ornaments and found that it was composed of copper with about 30% gold (Ralegh 1848:xii). Columbus had a similar disappointing experience; analysis of an item he brought back from Hispaniola proved to contain 18 parts of gold, 6 of silver, and 8 of copper (Rivet and Arsandaux 1946:60).

This gold-copper alloy, known as *tumbaga*, or *guanín* gold, is described in early chronicles from Mexico, the Isthmus, and the northern Andes. In these regions the silver was not added intentionally but was present (usually around 5% to 10% of the total weight) as a natural impurity in the gold. Farther south, in Ecuador, Peru, and Bolivia, where silver production has always outstripped that of gold, intentional silver-based alloys were in common use. These ternary alloys, which form the basis of north Peruvian jewelry, consist primarily of copper and silver, and may have only a small percentage of gold. Because copper is an essential component of so many alloys, the study of New World jewelry must include copper metallurgy as well as that of gold and silver.

Ralegh (1848:96) noted that the Guyana Indians 'put to [the gold] a

Fig. 1

Mexican metalsmith casting an axe.
He is using a blowpipe to raise the temperature of the brazier;
the molten metal flows into an open mold made of clay or stone.
After Sahagún 1963 : ill. 796.

Fig. 2

Sixteenth-century Indian metalsmiths.
Two are using blowpipes and a crucible to melt the metal,
while the third uses a hand-held stone hammer to produce sheet-metal items.
After Benzoni 1857 : 251.

part of copper, otherwise they coulde not worke it, and they vsed a great earthen potte with holes round about it, and when they had mingled the gold and copper together, they fastned canes to the holes, and so with the breath of men they increased the fire till the mettell ran, and then they cast it into moulds of stone and clay.' This excellent introduction to native metallurgical technology includes all the basic elements: the braziers and blowpipes of hollow canes, the alloying of copper and gold, and the use of casting molds. The same details are illustrated in Sahagún's great work on 16th-century Mexico (fig. 1).

Laboratory analyses have disproved Ralegh's statement that the Indians could not cast gold without first adding copper, though he was right in pointing out the advantages of tumbaga. Not only is it easier to cast than either of its constituent metals alone, it is harder than pure gold and reproduces decorative detail more accurately. The melting point depends on composition, but the alloy containing 20% copper to 80% gold melts at 911°C, well below the figure for pure gold (1064°C) or copper (1084°C). Open molds are suitable for manufacturing axes and utilitarian tools, and they have been found archaeologically from Mexico to Chile and Argentina. Casting in the round, with closed, multipiece molds, is much less common. The finest archaeological examples are Peruvian, and the technique seems to have been confined to South America in Precolumbian times.

In general, the more complicated jewelry was cast by the *cire perdue* (lost-wax) process. This, too, is described by Sahagún (1959:74–75). For hollow objects, the goldsmith first prepared a core of clay and powdered charcoal, sometimes adding a little sand. A mixture of this kind withstands the temperature of molten metal without distortion, is elastic enough to allow for shrinkage of the metal during cooling, is porous enough to take up some of the gases formed during the casting process, and is easily broken up for removal afterwards.

The core was carved with the rough shape of the object to be reproduced in metal, and was dried in the sun for two days to drive out all the moisture and to minimize the risk of explosion during casting. The goldsmith then mixed molten beeswax with copal resin (a hardening agent) and rolled this compound out into a thin sheet, which was pressed over the core, following the shape exactly; final incised or appliqué details were added to the model at this stage.

To achieve greater sharpness of casting, a 'mold wash' (a suspension of finely powdered charcoal in water or in liquid clay) was brushed over the wax. Further layers of semiliquid clay were then brushed on, and the whole model was finally enveloped in a thick and porous casing of clay mixed with coarsely ground charcoal (fig. 3). The internal core was held in place by chaplets, pegs that passed through the wax and into the casing, leaving small circular holes in the metal object. These holes were afterwards plugged and burnished, but their position can still be seen on the finished items (fig. 4). For large and complex castings, vent holes were made in the outer casing to allow the escape of gases and to prevent the formation of bubbles in the metal.

The whole was then heated to melt out the wax and to leave a space between core and casing. While the mold was still hot, molten metal was poured in to take the place of the wax (fig. 5). After cooling, the outer casing was broken open to extract the finished article, an exact copy of the wax original.

The accuracy of Sahagún's description has been confirmed by the examination of cast artifacts from Mexico and Colombia (Easby 1955a, 1956, 1969) and by replication experiments in the laboratory, where Long (1964), following Sahagún's instructions, made precise copies of Mexican copper bells.

Another Spanish friar, Toribio de Motolinía (1950:241, 242), commented that Mexican goldsmiths could cast animals with movable parts, and items 'half in gold and half in silver.' A few bimetallic objects have survived. Most of them, including spectacular sheet-metal ornaments from northern Peru, were made by welding together the gold and silver portions (Tushingham et al. 1979), but in Mexico the technique of 'casting on' was also employed. López de Gómara (Cortés's secretary) noted that bimetallic pieces were made in such a way that the metals were 'not soldered together, but joined in the casting' (López de Gómara 1964:161). This technique, confirmed by archaeological finds in Mexico (Easby 1961:40, 1969:370), is based on the different melting points of the two metals. The gold portion was cast first, since this metal has the higher melting point, and the craftsman then built onto it a wax model of the silver portion. The model was encased in clay once more, and, as in ordinary lost-wax casting, the wax was melted out, and the silver poured in to take its place. The gold remained solid while the silver, at a lower casting temperature, flowed against it. At the interface, some alloying took place and a strong join was formed.

Some items (Plazas and Falchetti, this volume, fig. 21) seem at first glance to have been made by the filigree technique from fine wires soldered together, but closer examination shows that these specimens were cast in a single operation by the lost-wax method from an original model made of fine wax threads. This same false-filigree method was used for the wirelike spirals that are a feature of Colombian and Isthmian goldwork. Elsewhere in Colombia, the Muisca goldsmiths of the high tableland were making mass-produced items with the aid of stone matrices (fig. 6).

Spanish chronicles also refer to the manufacture of sheet-metal objects. One of the best 16th-century accounts for the Andean region is by Garcilaso de la Vega, son of a Spanish father and an Inca mother.

'They used hard stones of a color between green and yellow as anvils. . . . They could not make hammers with wooden handles. They worked with instruments of copper and brass mixed together. They were shaped like dice with rounded corners. Some are as large as the hand can grip for heavy work; others are middle-sized, others small, and others elongated to hammer in a concave shape. They hold these hammers in the hand and strike with them like cobblestones. They had no files or graving tools, nor bellows for founding. Their founding they did by blowing down copper tubes half an ell or less in length. . . . It might be necessary to use eight, ten, or twelve at once, according to the furnace. . . . Nor had they tongs for getting the metal out of the fire'
(Garcilaso de la Vega 1966:130–131)

This is the scene illustrated by Benzoni in 1565 (fig. 2).

It is not surprising to find melting and hammering discussed together, since sheet-metal objects were made from ingots of melted (and often

Fig. 3
Broken lost-wax casting mold from the Ruíz Site, northwest Pacific coast of Costa Rica, AD 1200. The mold seems to have been cracked open to remove the metal cast of a frog pendant. In the photograph, the mold is shown upside down to illustrate the frog in the position as worn. The conical cavity below the feet of the frog is part of the reservoir into which the molten metal was poured during the casting process (cf. fig. 5). *Photo: Frederick W. Lange.*

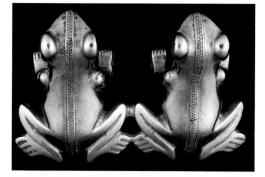

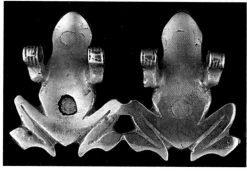

Fig. 4
Panamanian double-frog pendant of surface-enriched tumbaga, cast over a core by the lost-wax process. Four chaplet holes are visible on the underside, two at the head and two at the belly. One plug has been removed to show the internal core. The interior face of this plug still has the red color of the tumbaga alloy, indicating that the plugs were in place when the gilding was carried out. *Photo: Stuart Laidlaw, London University Institute of Archaeology.*

alloyed) metal. Pure gold is soft and presents no problems, but repeated hammering of the alloys causes the metal to become brittle and difficult to work. To restore malleability, the sheet must be annealed (put back into the fire and brought to red heat), a process that can be identified by examining the microstructure of archaeological specimens. The practice of hammering, annealing, and water-quenching is described in a document of 1555 from Caribbean Colombia (Tamalameque 1555). To make a bracelet, the Indians placed it in the fire, 'taking it out and putting it in water, and hammering it on an anvil with the stone described, they worked until they increased its size many times.'

By alternate hammering and annealing, the craftsmen of northern Peru could manufacture metal sheet without hammer marks, and as smooth and even as today's machine-made product (Tushingham et al. 1979). Hammered sheet gives a large surface area, with maximum show and glitter, for a relatively small weight of precious metal. For ornamental purposes, and to give added strength to flimsy metal, embossed or repoussé designs were added, with the object resting on some firm but resilient material. The West Indian version of this technique is described in a letter by Dr Chanca, physician to Columbus's fleet in 1493–6: 'The Indians beat their gold into very thin sheet ... setting it into bitumen which they prepare for the purpose. They could not make their masks without it!' (Jane 1929: 56). Elsewhere, sheet metal was probably worked over a piece of thick leather or pressed into or over preshaped forms.

Colonial accounts from Costa Rica suggest that the Indians were fully aware of the properties of different metals and alloys. In 1587 Don Diego de Sojo commented that the people of the Caribbean coast made hammered plaques out of pure, unalloyed gold (MacCurdy 1911:190; Helms 1979:147), and Fray Agustín de Zevallos said the same of the Talamancans in 1610: 'Their slight skill obliged them to alloy it [gold] with copper in order to be able to cast it; but in their pectoral discs, which had only to be beaten out and extended without any need for alloying, one can see the fineness of the gold which exceeds 22 carats' (Helms 1979:149–150, 200).

These statements are corroborated by analyses from Panama and the Maya zone (Lothrop 1937, 1952). The repoussé helmets and the elaborately decorated discs from the Sitio Conte cemetery are of almost pure gold, as are the well-known plaques with scenes of battles and human sacrifices from the cenote at Chichén Itzá. In contrast, more than half of the cast figurines are made from tumbaga of very variable composition.

The Spaniards found, to their disappointment, that many objects which appeared to be of pure gold were, in fact, of low-grade tumbaga, treated by a process of pickling, or depletion gilding, using acid substances to remove the copper from the outer surfaces and leaving a layer of gold that could be compacted by burnishing. This gold surface is almost invulnerable to corrosion in burial soil, but the copper-rich interior is readily attacked. In consequence, the gold surface tends to flake off, and the tumbaga may be reduced to a black powdery substance (Scott 1983b).

Spanish chronicles from Caribbean Colombia describe the use of plant juices for this gilding process: '. . . the herb they brought to give it color was crushed on a stone and, once crushed in this way, they placed [the

Fig. 5
Defective casting from the Sinú region of northern Colombia.
The metal did not flow properly, and the circular ornament is incomplete.
The surplus metal, which marks the position of the reservoir and the pouring channel, has not been removed.
Photo: Museo del Oro, Bogotá.

Fig. 6
Muisca matrix from highland Colombia.
The raised patterns on the stone were used to make sets of identical wax models, which were then cast by the lost-wax process.
Photo: Museum of the American Indian, Heye Foundation.

bracelet] in a small pot . . . and added water and ground white salt and stirred all together' (Tamalameque 1555). The Indians heated and quenched the bracelet in this solution several times 'until it attained the color and finish it should have.' Similar techniques have been recorded all the way from Mexico to Colombia and have been reproduced under laboratory conditions (Evans 1909-10; Stone and Balser 1967; Scott 1983a). By treating only parts of the surface, or by abrading away the gold-rich layer in selected areas to expose the underlying alloy, the Indians of Nariño, in southern Colombia, produced bicolored designs on objects of sheet metal (Scott 1983a).

In Mexico, Sahagún (1959:75) reported a similar method using what he called '"gold medicine" . . . just like yellow earth mixed with a little salt.' Lechtman (1973) has suggested that this yellow earth may be one of the commonly occurring (and highly corrosive) hydrated ferric sulphate minerals, and has experimented with this mixture on the ternary alloys of copper-silver-gold that are characteristic of north Peruvian metallurgy. Organic reagents, such as plant acids, are not effective in producing gold surfaces on these ternary alloys, but the ferric sulphate method works well on all the standard Peruvian alloys, including those high in silver but with very little gold. Laboratory analyses of sheet-metal objects in the Sicán style of Lambayeque (fig. 8) gave results closely similar to those of the modern experimental material.

In general, the basic accuracy of the first European accounts has been demonstrated in the modern laboratory, but we can hardly expect 16th-century adventurers and bureaucrats to give all the information required by a 20th-century archaeologist. The documentary sources are valuable eyewitness descriptions, but they are also biased, ambiguous, and incomplete. Only in the middle of the 19th century did Precolumbian goldwork come to be appreciated for its own sake.

THE FIRST SCIENTIFIC STUDIES, 1850–1940

The gradual change of emphasis was part of a much wider phenomenon— the emergence of archaeology and ethnography as intellectual disciplines (Daniel 1950; Willey and Sabloff 1974; Bernal 1980). The customs and artifacts of 'primitive peoples' attracted popular and professional interest. Diplomats, gentleman travellers, businessmen, and expatriates of all kinds began to send back curios, and eventually systematic collections, to museums in Europe and America.

When the great cemetery of Bugavita, in Panamanian Chiriquí, was discovered in 1858, gold objects from the tombs were illustrated in popular journals, and, although most of the pieces were melted down, a few survive in New York and Hamburg (MacCurdy 1911:192–193). This discovery drew attention to the Isthmus as a source of gold objects, and, during the second half of the 19th century, rich amateurs, such as J. A. McNeil in Panama and Minor Keith in Costa Rica, built up huge collections of metalwork, pottery, and stone artifacts, which made their way to North American museums and formed the basis of the first serious archaeological studies (Holmes 1888; MacCurdy 1911). In a similar way, the Sologuren collection provided most of the material for Saville's classic monograph of 1920, *The Goldsmith's Art in Ancient Mexico.*

Most of these collectors' pieces were bought from looters and only rarely came from excavations carried out with any scientific control. Nevertheless, as a consequence of this collecting activity, a good deal of Precolumbian metalwork became available for study, and the first attempts were made to identify regional styles and to map their distributions, although (before the introduction of radiocarbon dating in the 1950s) these studies were hampered by a lack of precise dates. In Argentina, quantitative analyses of copper and tin-bronze items were published as early as 1904 and 1909 (González 1979:138), and soon afterwards important publications began to appear in France, Denmark, Sweden, and the United States. This work was brought together in 1946 by Rivet and Arsandaux in a volume of synthesis that marks the end of an era and allows one to take stock of what had been achieved by 1940.

Much of this early work falls short of modern standards, but the period produced some outstanding studies. In one of these, C. H. Mathewson (1915) examined the Inca metal objects collected by Hiram Bingham's expedition to Machu Picchu. All the items are illustrated and meticulously described; metallographic analysis was used to show how the objects were made (cast, forged, edge-hardened, etc.), and chemical analysis was employed to study the composition of 33 specimens. The theoretical issues are discussed in full, with a sharp eye for cultural as well as technological problems. Mathewson demonstrated that Inca metalsmiths appreciated the qualities of various copper alloys, adding a high proportion of tin (10–13%) to the metal used for casting ornaments (to take advantage of the superior strength and castability of this alloy), and a lower percentage (about 5% tin) to metal designed to be forged into axes and chisels.

While the laboratory metallurgists were studying particular groups of material, the archaeologists were trying to use the analytical data to answer broader historical questions. The dominant figure in this field is Erland Nordenskiöld, whose book on the *Copper and Bronze Ages of South America* (1921) is a model of clear thinking and careful documentation. Nordenskiöld studied the Colonial descriptions to see what items were in circulation at the time of European contact. Then, turning to the purely archaeological data, he made a distinction between those metal forms that were widespread in South America and those that were purely regional, concluding, quite correctly, that the widespread types belonged to the period of Inca expansion and that many of the regional categories were earlier in date. By testing this developmental scheme against the evidence from metal analyses, he was able to suggest that, in many parts of South America, a 'Copper Age' preceded the use of tin-bronze.

Although he paid little attention to the presence or absence of arsenic, Nordenskiöld demonstrated a preference for arsenical copper on the north coast of Peru in Pre-Incaic times, while farther south, in Bolivia and Argentina, tin-bronze was already common several centuries before the Inca expansion. These themes have recently been taken up by Lechtman (1979, 1980, 1981) at the Massachusetts Institute of Technology, using the full range of modern analytical techniques.

The third great figure of these early years is Paul Bergsøe, who examined a collection of jewelry, workshop scrap, and part-finished items from the region of La Tolita, on the north coast of Ecuador. Bergsøe's two slim volumes (1937, 1938) are classics, ranging over the whole field of manufacturing techniques: melting and alloying, gilding, wire-drawing, soldering, welding, and granulation. He was the first to make a serious study of Prehispanic platinum-working by the peoples of the Ecuador/Colombia coast, and the accuracy of his conclusions has been fully borne out by analyses and replication experiments (Scott and Bray 1980, n.d.). Bergsøe was equally interested in examining the role of metallurgy within the social system and in questions of trade contacts and the economics of production. In these respects he anticipated the more 'anthropological' study of metal technology which is an important feature of modern research.

In the technological sense, too, the Bergsoe era was a time of transition. Before the 1930s, most analyses were carried out by the wet-chemical method, a laborious process which required a large sample and was, naturally, unpopular with museum curators. Around 1930 the technique of optical spectrography was developed, allowing rapid analysis of very small samples and giving results for a wide range of elements, including the trace elements present in minute quantities. Although he made only limited use of this technique, Bergsøe (1938:45) was aware of its potential value. 'By its help we can determine *the quantitative relations between small impurities* and may thus be guided to deductions as to the source of the metal or of one of the constituents of the alloy' (his italics). He hoped not only to recover technological information but also to reconstruct trade patterns and communication routes along which raw metal and finished objects were circulated. At much the same time, Root (in Lothrop 1937:307–309)

employed spectrographic analysis to examine jewelry from Mexico and Panama in an attempt to distinguish, on the basis of composition, between locally made and imported items. The introduction of optical spectrography marks the transition to the modern era of metallurgical studies, characterized by sophisticated analytical techniques, by large numbers of analyses (in quantities suitable for statistical treatment), and by the attempt to use metallurgical information to answer historical or anthropological questions.

METALLURGICAL STUDIES FROM 1940 TO THE PRESENT

The development of optical spectrography was followed, in the 1950s, by X-ray fluorescence analysis, which gives a quick, cheap, and non-destructive determination of surface composition. Other techniques (neutron activation, atomic absorption spectrophotometry, and the use of electron probes and scanning electron microscopes) derive from the high-technology revolution of the last twenty years. Most of these instruments simply provide better, quicker, or less destructive means of carrying out the traditional tasks of the archaeometallurgist: the analysis of the structure of the artifact and of its composition at the sampling point (fig. 7). With most analytical methods there is always a risk that the sample point may not be representative of the specimen as a whole, a problem that has been recently overcome by the development of electron-beam devices, which take a series of spot analyses in a traverse across a polished section of a metal artifact, and can therefore detect changes and inhomogeneities in composition.

The past few years have seen some notable advances in the study of

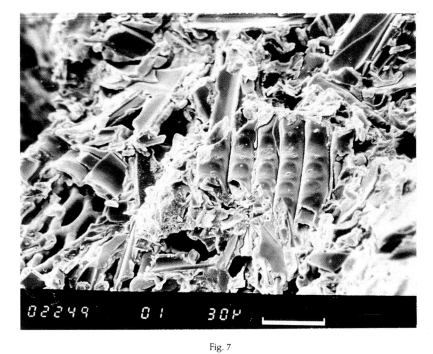

Fig. 7
Scanning electron microscope photograph (at 30 microns) of core material
from a cast necklace ornament from the Tairona region of Caribbean Colombia.
The photograph shows the woody cell structure of the charcoal,
with vestured pits typical of tropical hardwoods.
Photo and information: David Scott.

Precolumbian metallurgy, and some surprises: the discovery of the first tin-bronze in Colombia (Scott 1980) and of a copper alloy with 18% bismuth at Machu Picchu (Gordon and Rutledge 1984), and the revelation that the very thin gilded or silvered surfaces on certain ornaments from Loma Negra, in northern Peru, had been produced by a process of electrochemical deposition (Lechtman et al. 1982).

Some of the most important developments have been in the field of Peruvian copper and bronze metallurgy. Lechtman and her colleagues are currently examining the mechanical properties of copper alloys, attempting to match the metal with ore sources, reconstructing smelting techniques, and carrying out technological studies of both forged and cast objects (Lechtman 1981). It is now clear, as Nordenskiöld hinted, that, in northern Peru and southern Ecuador (Escalera Ureña and Barriuso Pérez 1978), tin-bronze was an Incaic introduction, preceded by several centuries during which arsenic, rather than tin, was added to the copper. This composition implies that the Peruvians could process the sulphide and sulpharsenide ores of the Andes, which have to be roasted with charcoal (to drive off the sulphur and volatile elements, and to oxidize the ore) before being smelted (Caley and Easby 1959; Caley and Shank 1971; Lechtman 1976, 1981). This process releases sulphur and arsenic, though this does not seem to have worried the Andean metalsmiths unduly. As Garcilaso de la Vega (1966:131) remarked: 'They also realized . . . that smoke from any metal was bad for health, and thus they made their foundries . . . in the open air, in yards or spaces, and never under a roof.' This arsenical copper was used as a metal in its own right, and was also alloyed with gold or silver for the jewelry trade.

In spite of the high hopes of the 1930s, it has so far proved impossible to link the finished tools or ornaments with particular ore deposits, or to determine precise centers of production on the basis of metal composition. For copper, the impurity level and trace element composition can vary considerably within a single ore body, and the processes of smelting, alloying, and manufacturing may further alter the pattern. In addition, impurities may segregate as the metal solidifies, so that a single analysis may give an unrepresentative result (Charles 1972). Gold, too, poses problems. The composition of alluvial gold can vary markedly from one place to another in the same stream, and the gold from a tributary stream may be quite different from that of the main river. Since most Precolumbian gold was obtained from river beds, attempts at classification have little significance. Moreover, metal objects were traded over large distances, and scrap metal was recycled, probably several times.

Nor is that the end of the difficulties. As the European experience shows, with more than 30 years of research and some 20,000 analyses from the Copper Age and Early Bronze Age, there are still statistical problems in separating one metal group from another and in coordinating the metallurgical data with the archaeological evidence (Waterbolk and Butler 1965; Butler and van der Waals 1964; Boomert 1975).

It seems best to abandon unrealistic expectations and to concentrate on the broader problems of identifying changes in smelting, alloying, and manufacturing practices, and of defining the number and general nature of the metal sources (rather than the exact ore deposits) in use at any one time. This, in turn, can lead to the definition of 'metal circulation zones,' which reflect political and economic conditions, and of the ways these change with time (Northover 1983).

One consequence of the enthusiasm for high technology is that we now know more about the chemical abilities of Indian metalsmiths than about their manual skills. The studies by Tushingham et al. (1979) of Peruvian jewelry, and by Easby (1969) of the Mexican treasure from Tomb 7 at Monte Albán, show how much information about workshop practices can be obtained by simple visual inspection, with X-ray photographs to show structural details (fig. 8). The study of tool marks can indicate how the goldsmith marked out the design, how he cut, hammered, or embossed the metal sheet, what implements he used, and even how he held his tools. Flaws and defects in cast objects show what problems the jeweller found in getting the metal to flow correctly, and how he patched up his mistakes. Archaeologists still have much to learn from professional jewellers and silversmiths.

In recent years, there has been a revival of interest in the social and economic aspects of the metal industry. Instead of studying the individual artifacts in isolation, archaeologists are now looking for mining, smelting, and processing sites (Lechtman 1976; Shimada et al. 1983) and have carried out excavations in workshops at Pampa Grande (Shimada 1978), Chan Chan (Topic 1982), and other major cities on the north coast of Peru.

The Sicán Archaeological Project at Batán Grande has investigated virtually every phase of copper production in the Leche valley, from the mine to the workshops that produced ingots for export (Shimada et al. 1983). The local oxide ores from the Cerro Blanco mine were carried along a 3-km. road to the furnace site at Cerro Huaringa (also known as Cerro de los Cementerios), where they were mixed with arsenic-bearing sulphide ores possibly brought by llama caravan from Cajamarca, in the highlands some 120 km. away, although local sources may have existed. The processing site has a battery of small furnaces, and the area is littered with ore-crushers, blowpipe fragments, bits of ore, slag-encrusted sherds, and charcoal from furnace cleaning (fig. 9). The furnaces were charged with ore, charcoal and flux, and a forced draft provided by men with blowtubes. The resultant ingots contain arsenic in quantities between 2 and 2.8 percent.

Much of the raw metal was exported to the urban workshops where the manufacture of tools and ornaments was carried out. In these workshops, gold and silver were added to the copper to produce the typical jewelry alloys for casting and hammering. These workshops have yielded crucibles, blowpipes, stone anvils and hammers, ingots, slag, and bits of scrap. Some must also have had furnaces like the one depicted on a Moche pot (fig. 10).

Because of the huge size of these Peruvian coastal cities, and the vast quantities of metalwork looted from their cemeteries, it had been assumed that jewelry and ornaments were mass produced in semi-industrialized factories, perhaps under state control. Instead, excavations in the artisan quarters at Pampa Grande and Chan Chan revealed a much less centralized level of organization, based on small family workshops, each tending to specialize in one or two aspects of manufacturing. This may have been a general rule in ancient America, for Sahagún noted that in Aztec Mexico the casting and beating of gold were regarded as two separate trades.

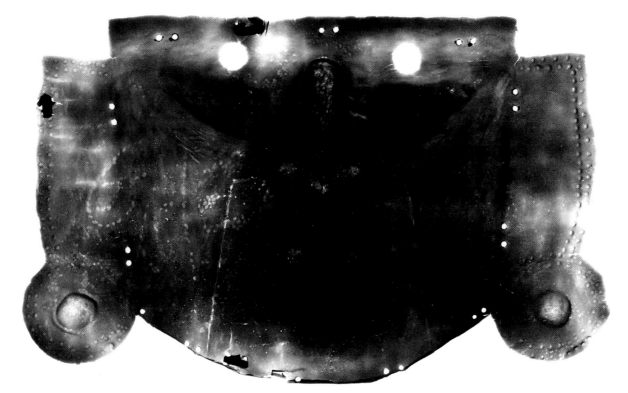

Fig. 8

X-ray photograph of a Sicán mummy mask from northern Peru,
showing the hammer marks, the incisions on either side of the mouth,
and the lacing of cracks with strips of metal.
The mask is made of a silver-copper alloy, with bone eyes.
The surfaces have cinnabar paint and traces of textile impressions.
Photo and information: Margot Wright.

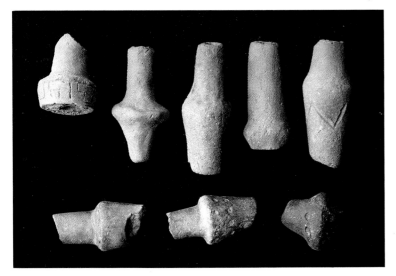

Fig. 9

A selection of whole and partial ceramic blowpipe tips
found by the Sicán Archaeological Project
in association with the smelting furnaces at Huaca del Pueblo Batán Grande.
They were probably inserted into cane shafts perhaps 1 m. to 1·5 m. long
to provide the needed draft into the furnace chamber.
Photo and information: Izumi Shimada.

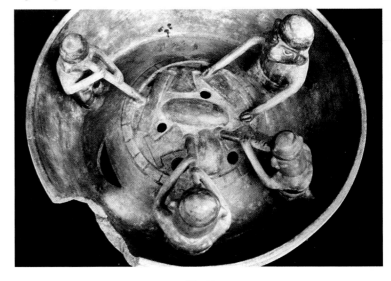

Fig. 10

Moche pot showing a workshop scene of men with blowpipes and a furnace
on which are metal ornaments.
After Donnan 1973: fig. 15.

TECHNOLOGY, STYLE, AND MEANING

One of the most interesting—and long overdue—developments in the last few years has been the realization that native American metallurgy cannot be understood solely in technical terms, without any reference to the belief system of the people who made and used the metal ornaments. Studies of this kind have been few, but have had the value of putting back technological questions where they belong, within the mainstream of anthropology.

Lechtman (1977) has pointed out that in the Andean world precious metals were used primarily for display, by the dead as well as by the living. Alloys were chosen not only for their mechanical properties, but because they gave different colors, were charged with symbolic values, or contained within themselves some essential principle. This is particularly true of the depletion-gilded alloys of gold, copper, and silver, for which a purely technological explanation is inadequate. Why take such metallurgical trouble with a Sicán mummy mask (fig. 8) whose gilded or silvered surface was invisible under layers of paint and feathers? What is the point of making objects from surface-enriched tumbaga? It cannot be to economize on gold, for the gold below the surface is 'wasted,' and a golden appearance could be achieved more cheaply by applying gold foil (Lechtman 1984b). Perhaps, as Lechtman suggests, the 'essence' of the object required it to contain gold throughout, or it may have been the reddish color that was valued, or even the distinctive smell of tumbaga.

In a paper of fundamental importance, Reichel-Dolmatoff (1981) has analyzed the metallurgical symbolism of the Tukanoan tribes of Colombian Amazonia, showing how technological and symbolic qualities are inextricably mingled. According to Desana myth, a stranger 'in the days of Creation' introduced metallurgy to the Tukanoan peoples, including the knowledge of casting in molds and the use of two metals, one white and one yellow.

The natural temptation is to think of silver and gold, but Indian informants explained that 'white' and 'yellow' do not refer to metallic colors but to 'abstract qualities, to an invisible "white" creative force and to a visible and material yellow potential. These two forces met and mingled in different proportions. The basic material state was the visible sun, associated with gold and with human semen, while the "whiteness" was a modifying abstract cosmic force which heightened or diminished the quality of the golden component' (Reichel-Dolmatoff 1981:21). White and yellow are also associated with male potency; red, on the other hand, is a female color.

'In the first place, red is the color of blood, and blood is, according to Desana theories of conception, a basic component of a new life; conception takes place when yellow semen and red uterine blood fuse in the womb. . . . In the second place, red is the color of heat, of fire, of transformation. The process of intrauterine embryonic development is imagined as one of "cooking," of the embryo being transformed in a fiery furnace, a crucible. The color combination yellow/red stands, therefore, for male/female fertility and fecundity' (ibid.:21).

In Tukanoan cosmology, the Sun is a male principle associated with the yellow color range, while the Moon is female.

'Ideally the sun fertilizes a brilliant New Moon which, at First Quarter, proves to be pregnant. Moon then passes through a sequence of yellowish, reddish and copper-colored phases which are compared to the menstrual cycle and the processes of embryonic development. At the same time this process is said to be a model of metallurgical combinations' (ibid.).

Even the smell of copper or tumbaga is significant, resembling that of a certain frog with female and sexual connotations.

At this point in the argument, with so many complementary levels of meaning, the manufacture of a simple tumbaga frog has become simultaneously a technological and a symbolic operation.

The Catalogue

INTRODUCTORY NOTE

The Catalogue that follows is organized geographically, from north to south. The entries begin with Costa Rica and Panama on the Isthmus of Central America, and cover Colombia and Peru in South America. The final entry is from northwestern Argentina, an area as yet little known for its Precolumbian gold. Maps of these regions, with the exception of Argentina, will be found in the appropriate foregoing texts.

The legends with which the individual entries begin include title, style, and date; these assignations are mine. The words used for the stylistic assignations come from many different sources as well as different languages. Originally they may have been personal names, or place names, or culture names, or archaeological phase names. They are seldom the names of ancient New World peoples, but they have come to be attached to visually identifiable and intellectually coherent groups of Precolumbian works of art in gold. It is with this understanding that the stylistic designations are used here.

The illustrations of the catalogued entries are in color. The color of the gold objects they picture will surprise those who are new to Precolumbian art. The color range of American goldwork is wide: it goes from pale white-gold through clear yellow-gold to a notably pink-gold. All of these colors are intentional. The alloying of gold with other metals was an ancient practice in America, and the technical implications of these alloys have long been of interest. The aesthetic implications are equally significant, however, for a range in possible surface color offers another opportunity for meaningful, artistic choice. Ancient American goldsmiths made ample use of this opportunity.

JJ

1

Frog pendant

CHIRIQUÍ, REPORTEDLY FROM PUERTO GONZÁLEZ VÍQUEZ
11TH–MID-16TH CENTURY
H. 4⅛ *in.* | 10·6 *cm.*　　W. 4 *in.* | 10·2 *cm.*

Frogs appear commonly in the goldwork of the Costa Rica–Panama area, a tropical region in which numerous species of small frogs exist. Both tree frogs, which range in length from an inch to 'giants' of five inches, and terrestrial frogs of small size and poisonous skin are known. These frogs are often vibrantly colored; bright-yellow and 'gold-colored' frogs are among them. It is possible that this pendant is the stylized representation of a tree frog; tree frogs have extremely long legs, like those seen projecting from the body here, and equally long feet (the feet here are flattened to rectangles). The frog is sitting, and ethnographic evidence suggests (Snarskis, this volume) that the posture is significant for amphibian imagery on the Isthmus.

Gold objects in Chiriquí style came from both sides of the Costa Rica–Panama border. It was the first Isthmian gold style to be isolated, when burial finds were made not far from the town of David in the Chiriquí province of Panama in the late 1850s. A drawing of a long-legged frog, similar to the present example, appeared in *Harper's Weekly* in the summer of 1859 as part of the announcement of the Panamanian find (Otis 1859). The present frog is said to have been among the gold objects from burials near Puerto González Víquez, Costa Rica, encountered in the early 1960s (Time 1962).

JJ

DESCRIPTION

The frog has a triangular head and a long, rounded body. Thin hind legs project obliquely from the body, and the hind feet are shown as large horizontal rectangles; there are no front feet. The bulbous eyes with central grooves are ringed at the base, and the mouth is outlined by a single, raised molding. Two long streamers, made in false filigree, emerge from the mouth and end in opposing scrolls. In more naturalistic examples, these are double-headed serpents. The streamers are supported by four wirelike attachments joined to the mouth of the frog. A suspension loop appears under either side of the head. The pendant was cast by the lost-wax process; the hole through the left foot is a casting flaw.

HK

EXHIBITED
New York, The Museum of Primitive Art, 1969, no. 136, illustrated.
New York, The Metropolitan Museum of Art, 1972.
Leningrad, 1976, no. 168, illustrated.

PUBLISHED
Emmerich, 1965, facing page 168, plate III.
New York, The Metropolitan Museum of Art, 1972/73, page 71.
Emmerich, 1979, page 99, fig. 6.

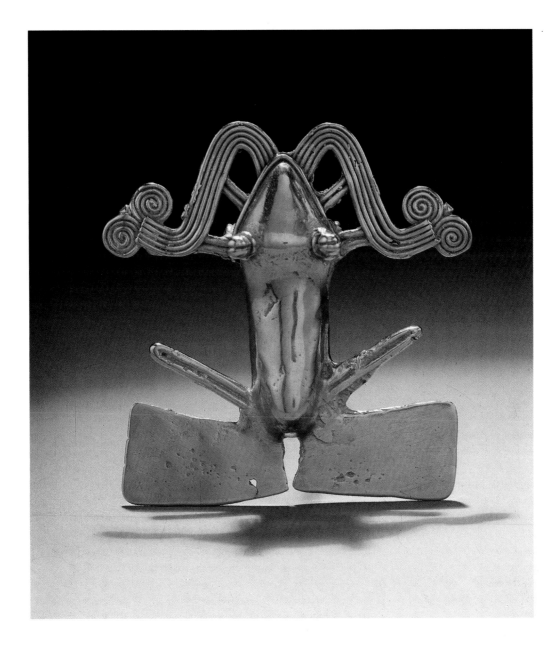

2

Ornamented bell

CHIRIQUÍ

11TH–MID-16TH CENTURY

H. 1¾ *in.* | 4·6 *cm.*   W. 1⅜ *in.* | 3·6 *cm.*

The pendant bells of Costa Rica–Panama are often cast in the shape of animals, or are decorated with zoomorphic representations. Crabs, turtles, birds, and felines are prominent among the many creatures used. The bells are engaging objects, and part of their appeal is the small scale in which they are worked. Some are barely an inch high. The bell here is of good size, and over its top arch two long-necked heads confronting each other. The heads seem to have their origins in deer imagery, with a long snout, open mouth, pointed ears, and antlers. The antlers, however, are twisted into one tall 'horn.'

Not all Isthmian gold bells are elaborated. Plain ones were made, many in the shape of the lower part of this bell.   JJ

DESCRIPTION

This pear-shaped bell, with rounded base and slightly concave sides, has two slender animal heads facing each other on top. The body of the bell is bordered with a triple molding, and a long slit forms the opening on the bottom. The animal heads have long, elegantly curved necks; their spines are marked by a twisted band. Their mouths are open, the noses flattened at the front, and the big, round eyes set into a ring. The pointed ears are erect. The top of their heads is crowned by a raised rim, from which emerge two antlers that wind around each other and curve backwards. A suspension loop is on one side of the bell between the heads, and there is a pellet inside the bell, probably of metal. The object was cast by the lost-wax method.   HK

EXHIBITED

New York, The Museum of Primitive Art, 1969, no. 141.
Leningrad, 1976, no. 160, illustrated.

3

Masked-figure pendant

CHIRIQUÍ, REPORTEDLY FROM PUERTO GONZÁLEZ VÍQUEZ
11TH–MID-16TH CENTURY
H. 4¼ *in.* | 10·8 *cm.*   W. 3¼ *in.* | 8·3 *cm.*

In Isthmian goldwork there are human images that can be interpreted as having various degrees of 'animalness.' In some, it is clear that a human figure is costumed, i.e., wears a mask with the 'face,' and has 'hands' and/or 'feet,' of an animal. Other combinations can be more complex, so that distinction between human and animal aspects is less definite. Illustrated here is a male figure with animal head and feet. The figure stands between two horizontal framing elements, a frequent, if not entirely understood, feature of Isthmian gold. The head appears to be a deer mask; the deer attributes are the large snout with wide nostrils and the short antlers atop the head. The figure has the 'many-fingered' hands characteristic of human representations in the last centuries of the Precolumbian era, but the feet seem to consist of four long toes. They may depict the front feet of a tapir. Ethnographic evidence for some areas of the New World indicates correspondences between certain deer and tapir aspects, and it is possible that there were conceptual links between the two animals in Precolumbian thought.

The pendant is said to be from the Costa Rican find at Puerto González Víquez on the Burica Peninsula, located on the Pacific side of the Isthmus. The gold rich burials at Puerto González Víquez were discovered in the early 1960s.

JJ

DESCRIPTION

The figure of this ornament has a distinctly male body and wears a two-strand belt around his waist and ligatures around the flexed knees; the feet are clawed. A pronounced ridge runs down the middle of the chest. The flattened, outstretched arms project strongly at the sides of the body, and the genitals are depicted. The impressive head of the figure is that of a deer. The well-defined mouth ridge displays four pointed teeth, two up and two down, and a protruding tongue. The head has flaring nostrils and bulging eyes of the dot-and-ring type. There are three horns on either side of the forehead; the two front ones are large and twisted around each other, and there is a short one behind them. The head is flanked by vertical S-shapes, and the figure is framed above and below by two long, curved plaques with prominent hook-shapes at either end. The suspension loop is at the center of the back of the neck. The pendant was cast by the lost-wax technique.

HK

EXHIBITED
New York, The Museum of Primitive Art, 1969, no. 126, illustrated.
Leningrad, 1976, no. 175, illustrated.

PUBLISHED
Von Winning, 1968, page 378, fig. 567.
Emmerich, 1979, page 99, fig. 5.

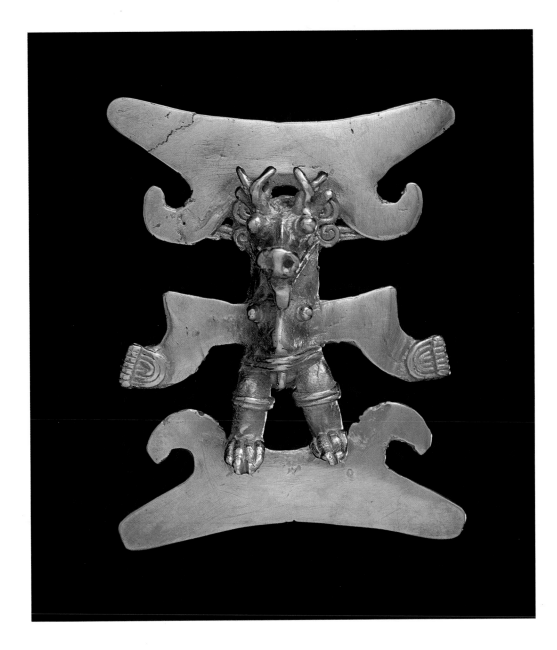

4

Turtle pendant

CHIRIQUÍ (?)

11TH–MID-16TH CENTURY

H. 3¼ *in.* | 8·3 *cm.*   W. 2⅝ *in.* | 6·7 *cm.*

A turtle with a large, bifurcated tail is among the more curious of the gold images of Costa Rica and Panama. It appears, as a rule, on bell pendants, where the turtle is shown with a prominent domed shell, from which four feet, head, and double tail extend. The head here has an impressive beak. The body of the turtle contains the clapper of the bell. The natural enclosing form of a turtle carapace may have suggested the use of the shape for bell-bodies. Details of the turtle pendants differ, in the size and elaboration of the four feet, for instance, but the major variation is in the presence or absence of encircling snakes.

This pendant is of the snakeless-turtle type. The head has been turned so that it faces out over the domed back. Such a front-to-back placement of heads on animal pendants occurs infrequently; it renders the animal in an essentially disjointed fashion. Here, however, the animal seems to be less disjointed than transformed, as the great dome of the back becomes the belly of an upright, beaked turtle, and the bifurcated tail, its legs.

JJ

DESCRIPTION

This bell pendant depicts a turtle with its head turned one hundred and eighty degrees. Four bent legs and a big split tail extend from the sides and end of its shell, respectively. The head has a large, pointed beak and big, bulging eyes, set into rings. The neck is adorned with a four-strand necklace, and the head is flanked by two extended crescents with four simple spirals. There are indications that the front feet were meant to be a series of concentric semicircles bent at the ends to show the toes. A suspension loop is at the back of the neck. Cast by the lost-wax method, the back of the turtle's head is open; the shell, however, is hollow-cast. The plastrum was miscast, and half is now missing.

HK

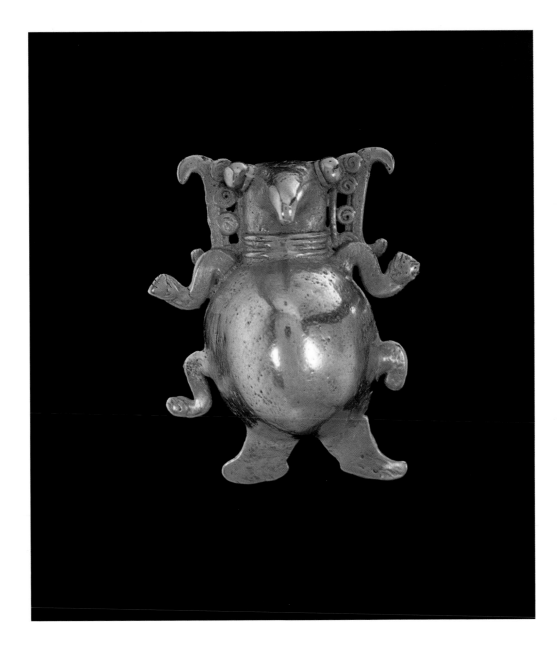

5

Composite pendant

GUANACASTE, REPORTEDLY FROM THE GULF OF DULCE
11TH–MID-16TH CENTURY
H. 4⅜ *in.* | 11·2 *cm.*   W. 3¾ *in.* | 9·5 *cm.*

Both crocodile and human aspects of the so-called Guanacaste pendants are so well worked into the overall configuration that they are hard to isolate. The pendants are unusually integrative, appearing to pull together specific features from other pendant types. In outline, they are related to the bird-form pendants commonly called 'eagles,' but there are salient differences. The vestigial nature of the wings particularly distinguishes the Guanacaste type. The shape of the tail, although more slender-V than triangular plane, is the main point of similarity with the more conventional bird pendants. This pendant has a human torso and head, the latter with a crocodile muzzle. There are paired profile crocodile heads at either side of the neck and tiny profile heads at the ends of the two-part 'wings.' The well-delimited hole in the belly may have been intended for inlay.

The Guanacaste pendants get their name from the northwestern province of Costa Rica, where a number are said to have been found (Aguilar 1972a). Guanacaste, however, is not rich in gold objects. Rather, it is southwestern Costa Rica, from the Diquís Delta south of Panama, that is known for its ancient gold. The present pendant is reported to be from this southern area (Records of the Past 1904).

JJ

DESCRIPTION

This ornament recalls the basic form of Isthmian avian pendants, but it is subjugated to the crocodilian traits of the central figure. The head is that of a crocodile with a projecting snout, upturned nose, two teeth, and bulging eyes. It is flanked on both sides by profile crocodile heads composed of scrolls for nose and ear and a dot for the eye. A triangular crest with rounded corners and a slightly concave top line surmounts the head. The pendant has four lateral extensions, terminating in small crocodile heads made up of an eye and a curled nose. The long tail is bifurcated, with round tips. The bulging stomach has a doubly outlined slit. A suspension ring is at the back of the neck. The object was made by the lost-wax casting technique.   HK

EX. COLL.
George Dissette, Glenville, Ohio.

EXHIBITED
New York, The Museum of Primitive Art, 1969, no. 127, illustrated.
Leningrad, 1976, no. 196, illustrated.

PUBLISHED
Records of the Past, 1904, page 283, bottom, center upper row.

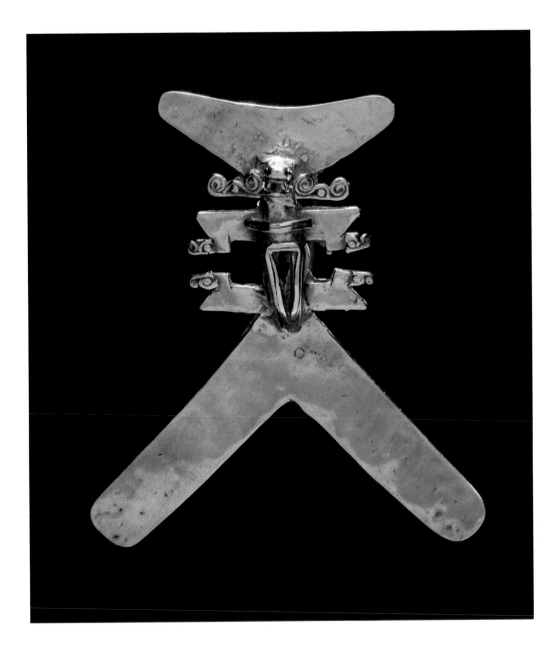

6

Figure pendant

CHIRIQUÍ

11TH–MID-16TH CENTURY

H. 2¾ *in.* | 6·9 *cm.*   W. 2¾ *in.* | 6·9 *cm.*

A crocodile muzzle adorns this human figure, and profile crocodile heads decorate his head-dress. Crocodile symbolism is prominent in Isthmian art of all kinds, and, in objects of cast gold, the long reptilian snout is the identifying feature. The snouts are depicted with an open mouth, frequently showing many teeth, and with nostrils rendered by a wide curl or tubelike element atop the nose. The profile crocodile heads are flat and appear in pairs, usually as secondary elements. They are graphically stylized into an open mouth, with teeth (sometimes only one) and a 'curled' nose. There may or may not be an eye. The profile heads occur not only on headdresses, as might be expected; they also project from ankles, knees, elbows, heads, and the like. The use of paired supplementary crocodile heads is most common in objects in Chiriquí or Diquís style.

The Chiriquí style is named for the Chiriquí province of Panama, where discoveries first brought Precolumbian gold objects to international attention (Bollaert 1860). It is the most vigorous of the Isthmian styles, with the most robust material presence. Its images, while conforming well to Isthmian iconographic patterns, are the least programmatic of them. Chiriquí surfaces tend to be polished to smooth, glassy textures. Such a surface is present in the figure here.   JJ

DESCRIPTION

This male anthropomorphic figure is standing with slightly curved legs and bent knees. He wears a twisted band around his waist, and others around his knees and across the forehead. While the face, body, and legs of the figure are cast in the half-round, the arms are flat; they are large winglike attachments at the sides of the relatively small body. The shoulders are pointed, and the hands are a series of concentric semicircles overlapped at the end to indicate fingers. Samuel Lothrop (1950:69) suggested that this was meant to represent a closed or fisted hand. The genitals are present; no details are on the feet.

The face has a large, projecting mouth with a turned-up nose. The mouth, bordered by a double raised edge, displays seven teeth. The bulging eyes are set into rings, and there are big, single, spiral ear ornaments on either side of the head. The top of the head is rounded, and from it descend two streamers that end in crocodile heads with a curly snout and a pair of teeth. The object was cast by the lost-wax process. There is a suspension loop in the back of the neck.   HK

7

Jaguar pendant

CHIRIQUÍ, REPORTEDLY FROM THE DIQUÍS DELTA
11TH–MID-16TH CENTURY
H. 3⅛ *in.* | 8 *cm.*   W. 1⅜ *in.* | 3·6 *cm.*

Cats, and cat imagery, are significant to Precolumbian art from very early times, and the cat that had the greatest impact in New World myth and art is the jaguar, the most impressive of the large American felines. The average size of a full-grown male jaguar is about eight feet, nose to tail. Jaguars have flat, broad faces, powerful chests, and squat legs. Formidable hunters, they are said to swish their tails in a particularly hypnotic manner while hunting. The jaguar here has a snake head at the end of its tail, perhaps a reference to qualities associated with the feline tail itself. The feline depictions in Isthmian goldwork are usually called jaguars, based more on generalized shape than on specific identifiable features.

A curious aspect of this pendant is the fact that it was made to be worn with the jaguar suspended upside down. The majority of Precolumbian animal-form pendants have the animal facing upward, with suspension loops under or through the front feet. The suspension loops here are under the back feet; there is an additional hole through the left rear foot. With the jaguar facing down, the snake head at the end of its tail is clearly visible. The hole through the left front foot implies that the jaguar might have been worn sideways as well.   JJ

DESCRIPTION

The jaguar is shown standing, his head down, and his tail turned up and ending in a serpent's head. His mouth is half-open, with a well-defined ridge displaying four pointed teeth. His large, oblong eyes are bulging and surrounded by a ring. One ear is in an erect position, the other falls slightly to the side. Under the hind paws are two suspension loops. There are also two holes perforated through the left front and hind legs. The ornament was cast by the lost-wax technique.   HK

EXHIBITED

New York, The Metropolitan Museum of Art, 1970, no. 225, illustrated.
Leningrad, 1976, no. 192, illustrated.

PUBLISHED

Emmerich, 1965, page 104, fig. 128.
Von Winning, 1968, page 378, fig. 569.
Emmerich, 1979, page 96, plate III.

8

Musician pendant

CHIRIQUÍ

11TH–MID-16TH CENTURY

H. 1¾ *in.*|4·5 *cm.*   W. 1⅜ *in.*|3·5 *cm.*

Representations of figures said to be those of musicians are among the Isthmian gold objects. The most common pendant is a male figure holding an end-blown flute in one hand, with either a rattle or a drum in the other hand. End-blown, or vertical, flutes as they are sometimes called, were widely used by the indigenous peoples of the Americas. They are Pre-columbian in origin and continue in use in the present century. In depictions in gold, the flutes may take on zoomorphic aspects, as when, for instance, they end in snake heads. Some authorities believe that snakes are always represented in these depictions (Snarskis, this volume).

Musician pendants of a single figure with flute and rattle were among those discovered in the Chiriquí province of Panama after the 1858–59 gold finds. There was one such pendant each in the De Zeltner (1866) and the McNeil (Holmes 1888) collections, both of which were formed in the years following the discovery of the burial grounds at Bugaba, Bugavita, and Boquete, near the town of David. In the pendant illustrated here, the musician figure has a narrow, looped-up nose, a feature associated with bat imagery.

JJ

DESCRIPTION

A male figure holds a long tube, as a flute, to his mouth with his left hand, while his right hand holds a rattle with an enlarged, rounded top. The body is naked and the genitals are depicted. It is cast in the half-round, whereas the arms are flat and asymmetrical. The facial features are simply crafted. The eyes are of the coffee-bean type, the mouth is a horizontal band, and the nose is a big semicircular loop. Across the flattened forehead is a two-strand, raised band, and the head is flanked by vertical S-shapes. Hands and feet are a series of thread-like elements. The piece was cast by the lost-wax method; the hole through the right knee is a casting flaw. A ring for suspension is behind the neck.

HK

9

Double-musician pendant

DIQUÍS (?)

13TH–MID-16TH CENTURY

H. 2⅞ in.|7·3 cm.   W. 3 in.|7·7 cm.

Dual images, either in the form of paired figures or a single figure with two heads, are associated with musician iconography. The instruments included are the same as those of the single musician pendants—flutes, rattles, and drums. Double figures blowing into conch-shell trumpets also exist. The two figures here appear to carry different types of flutes, only one of which is held to the mouth. Furthermore, the pendant is a bell. The round bodies of the musicians each contain a small clapper that, when moved, as when worn, makes a tinkling sound.

The Diquís style in gold came to recognition in the late 1940s only after the archaeologist Samuel Lothrop worked in Costa Rica's Diquís Delta. During Lothrop's excavations no gold was encountered, but discoveries made in 1956, almost a decade after his work was done, were sufficiently important to be included in the published report (Lothrop 1963). The 1956 gold find was said to consist of three graves, two large and one small. Eighty-seven gold objects were the reported contents of one of the larger graves; thirty-three of the pieces were cast pendants.   JJ

DESCRIPTION

This bell pendant features two male figures standing side by side in a rectangular, braided frame. The figures have splayed trapezoidal feet and naked bodies, with the sexual organs present. Their large heads have outlined eyes, bulbous and oblong; broad noses with flaring nostrils; and mouths displaying a single row of teeth. A band is wound around each head and tied in a square knot. One figure holds a short tube, perhaps a flute, to his mouth with one hand; the other arm is missing. The second figure holds a flute (or baton?) in both hands across his body. Paired, profile crocodile heads extend laterally from behind the knees and heads. The bellies of the figures are hollow and, in back, are partly covered by a tongue. They hold a pellet, probably of metal. There is a slit opening at the bottom. A suspension loop is at the back of the neck of each figure. The pendant was cast by the lost-wax process.   HK

EXHIBITED
Leningrad, 1976, no. 189, illustrated.

PUBLISHED
Von Winning, 1968, page 378, fig. 568.

10

Masked-figure pendant

DIQUÍS

13TH–MID-16TH CENTURY

H. 3¼ *in.* | 8·2 *cm.*   W. 3½ *in.* | 8·8 *cm.*

The masked and winged figure here has a very imposing bird head, with a large curved beak in which a tiny, carefully worked fish is held. The bird-headed figures of Diquís are invariably depicted with distinctive bird wings of constricted-crescent shape. The wings are ornamented along the inside edge in a manner suggestive of the 'feathery' tips of actual bird wings. The Diquís masked-figure pendants, whether crocodile, bat, or bird, are accented, top and bottom, by the wide frame element. By analogy to ethnographic belief, these framing elements may reflect an aspect of the ancient world view (Snarskis, this volume). The figures stand on the lower frame bar and join the upper one at the back of the head. From the heads themselves, paired, profile crocodile heads emanate, and at the ankles a corresponding, reversed pair appears.

Diquís-style cast-gold objects share many iconographic features with Chiriquí objects, but differences of detail, scale, and surface distinguish them. Diquís objects are more tightly, but elaborately, conceived and executed. Areas of surface are frequently left unpolished and have a matte, dry quality. The resulting textures of the gold coordinate well with the complexity and the scale of the designs.

JJ

DESCRIPTION

This pendant, featuring a naked male figure with the head of a raptorial bird, is a symmetrically structured composition, in which the flat areas of the framing plaques and the lateral projections are contrasted with the sculptural, three-dimensional forms of the figure itself. The figure stands with slightly bent knees and ankles; the sexual organs are depicted. The feet are concentric semicircles with bent-over ends. From the sides of the body crescent-shaped wings project. They carry a decorative band on the inner side, consisting of a twisted element framing a row of thirteen dots.

The half-open bird beak projects strongly downward and holds a fish, which has four side fins, a dorsal fin, and a split tail. Its triangular head and eyes are outlined. The bird's eyes are truncated cones, which protrude sideways. A delicate double band encircles each eye and passes under the beak. Between the eyes are two short projections, like brow feathers. The head is flanked by vertical S-shapes. Stylized crocodile heads extend from behind the head of the figure and from the lower legs. A simple horizontal bar across the back of the figure's neck was used to suspend the pendant. It was cast by the lost-wax method.   HK

11

Figure pendant

VERAGUAS (?), REPORTEDLY FROM THE DIQUÍS DELTA
11TH–MID-16TH CENTURY
H. 3⅜ *in.*|8·7 *cm.*   W. 3⅞ *in.*|9·8 *cm.*

A 'presentation' pose, in which a human figure holds two identical objects out to his sides, appears in Precolumbian gold imagery. The presentation figures can be masked, and the objects being held are not always identifiable. Such is the case with the objects displayed by the figure in the pendant here. This figure is not masked, but it wears an impressive headdress which may include crocodilian references. The tail is of the type found on bird pendants.

Among the currently delimited Isthmian gold styles, that of Veraguas is the most difficult to apprehend adequately. Named for the Panamanian province in which objects in the style were physically located, the style is said to occur between those of Chiriquí in the north and Conte in the south, an actual distance of only about ninety miles. Veraguas objects came to light in some quantity during the mid-1930s, when numerous graves were encountered during construction of the Pan-American highway. Few of these gold finds were published at the time, and when they were (Lothrop 1950), no clear image of the Veraguas style emerged, for many Veraguas objects were published in drawings, a method in which stylistic subtleties are lost; other objects of Chiriquí style were included as Veraguas.   JJ

DESCRIPTION

A sexless figure is depicted in frontal view with a triangular tail extending behind the lower body. Flattened arms, squared off at the shoulders, project from the sides. The hands hold V-shaped staffs. The body bulges, the knees are flexed, and the toes and hands are made of threadlike elements. The face has a protruding jaw, a pointed nose, and deep eye sockets with coffee-bean-type eyes. The lips are two straight gold threads. The figure wears a headdress consisting of an axe-shaped element emerging from the flattened top of the head and two lateral extensions with four rows of pointed elements, which might represent crocodilian scales or teeth. Paired spirals are placed next to the head. There are loops for suspension at either side of the back of the neck. The pendant was cast by the lost-wax technique.   HK

EXHIBITED
New York. The Museum of Primitive Art, 1969, no. 133, illustrated.
Leningrad, 1976, no. 184, illustrated.

PUBLISHED
Von Winning, 1968, page 379, fig. 570.

12

Eagle pendant

CHIRIQUÍ, REPORTEDLY FROM THE GULF OF DULCE
11TH–MID-16TH CENTURY
H. 3½ *in.* | 8·8 *cm.*   W. 3½ *in.* | 8·8 *cm.*

Few ancient American gold objects are as well known today as the so-called eagles, bird-form pendants of simplified outline. Basic to the pendant morphology are bird head, wings, and tail; it is the head that varies most in detail. The full fanned-out tail is always prominent; its triangular plane is not decorated. The wings, with either a horizontal or a vertical orientation, can be decorated—usually on the underside—with additional ornamental elements. Eyes and ears, however, and the length and type of beak, and whatever may be held in the beak, are more mutable. Choker-type necklaces can appear or not. The necklace here is a good-sized one. Feet are commonly rendered as bird claws. On the present pendant, human legs and feet appear. Not only are they human legs but they are embellished with ligatures, a most distinctive feature for an Isthmian eagle pendant.

The eagle is said to come from Costa Rica's Gulf of Dulce, where, in the late nineteenth century, heavy rains caused river flooding and 'pottery, carved stone, and gold objects' were washed out of ancient graves. A number of the gold pieces disinterred at the time made their way into a private collection in Glenville, Ohio (Records of the Past 1904).

JJ

DESCRIPTION

The eagle has a spread-out, triangular tail with rounded corners and wings that extend to a vertical position. Along the underside of the wings is a row of seven raised circles enclosed by a double molding. Two bent legs with tripartite ligatures are attached to the round, bulging body. The toes are indicated. At the sides of the bird's head, large spherical eyes, which are solid, are surrounded with a single ring. There is a very long, straight beak, which is half-open and holds a short, spiraled object. A necklace of eight strands of tubular beads adorns the broad neck. Cast by the lost-wax method, the head is hollow. There is a suspension loop at the back of the neck.

HK

EX. COLL.
George Dissette, Glenville, Ohio.

EXHIBITED
New York, The Museum of Primitive Art, 1969, no. 138.

PUBLISHED
Records of the Past, 1904, page 285, center bottom.

13

Eagle pendant

VERAGUAS

11TH–MID-16TH CENTURY

H. 1¾ in. | 4·4 cm.   W. 1½ in. | 3.7 cm.

Precolumbian eagle pendants were crafted in a great many sizes. Tiny ones are not over half-an-inch high, while the largest can reach about six inches in height. Many eagle pendants are wider than high, while some are of roughly equal proportion, height to width. As the pendants were made to be worn—in life and not just in death—there appears to have been something akin to an ideal wearable size, a size also found in pendants of other images. The pendants are presumed to have been strung on a cord or thong—gold chains did not exist on the Isthmus—and worn about the neck.

JJ

DESCRIPTION

A bird with round, protruding belly, raised wings, and spread tail holds a snake's body between projecting curved beak and claws. The body of the snake is a twisted double strand and there is a triangular head at either end. The snake heads are outlined, and the eyes are little spheres. The rounded bird head has bulging eyes and multiscroll 'tufts' to either side. Four scrolls appear on the left, and three on the right, where the fourth is missing. The tail has rounded corners and a slightly concave bottom-line. Cast by the lost-wax method, the ornament has a suspension ring at the back of the neck.

HK

14

Eagle pendant

VERAGUAS

11TH–MID-16TH CENTURY

H. 2⅞ in. | 7·2 cm.   W. 3⅛ in. | 7·9 cm.

DESCRIPTION

A bird pendant with small hemispherical body, extended wings, and splayed tail has a strong, hooked beak that is half-open. Large claws project from the body. A five-strand necklace adorns the elongated neck; it is decorated with a zigzag line. The eyes are ringed globular pellets, and spirals indicate ear ornaments. The elaborate headdress consists of a headband made up of horizontal S-shapes surmounted by twelve stylized feathers. In the back of the neck is a ring for suspension. The object was cast by the lost-wax technique; the wings and tail were further worked by hammering.

HK

EXHIBITED

Leningrad, 1976, no. 146, illustrated.

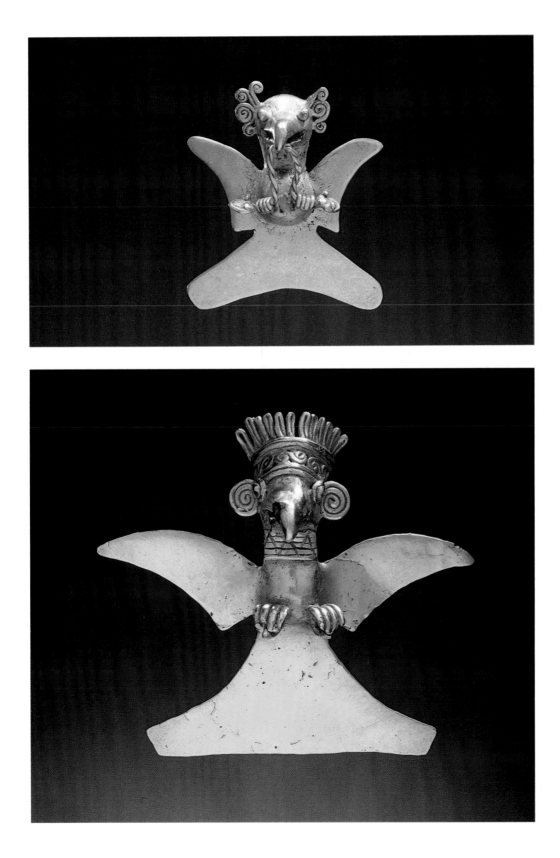

15

Eagle pendant

VERAGUAS

11TH–MID-16TH CENTURY

H. 5½ *in.* | 14·1 *cm.*   W. 6¾ *in.* | 17·1 *cm.*

Isthmian bird-form pendants were first called 'eagles,' *aguilas,* when Christopher Columbus sailed along Caribbean Central America in the early 1500s. Columbus and his men saw the bird pendants being worn about the neck by the peoples of the coast, in the manner of 'an Agnus Dei or other relic' (Colón 1959). They named the pendants *aguilas,* a name they have kept to this day. In the present century, the generalized avian form of the pendants has given rise to much discussion over what type of bird is represented (see Cooke & Bray, this volume). Some authorities believe that the pendants depict birds of prey, thereby endorsing the original Spanish name. The prominence of beaks and claws, and the various items held in the beaks, support such a view. The eagle pendant illustrated here, a large one, has both impressively rendered beak and finely detailed claws, as well as a 'tufted' head.

Precolumbian eagle pendants exist today in some numbers, and many are assigned to the Veraguas style. It is one instance in which stylistic features cohere sufficiently to make the assignation possible. Veraguas eagles are sharp-edged and clean of outline, particularly when compared to those of Chiriquí style with their rounded contours. Wings and tail are worked more laterally, an emphasis that can be seen here where the wing-tail configuration is particularly well resolved, the lunar shapes of the wings carefully balancing the side extensions of the rather severe tail. Veraguas eagles are also often more elaborated around the head and hold fewer things in their beaks.

JJ

DESCRIPTION

A bird pendant with flat, extended wings and tail, has a head, neck, and body that are rendered three-dimensionally. The bird wears a broad, multistring necklace with a diamond pattern in front; the beak has a caruncle atop, and the eyes, surrounded by rings, protrude in a rather gogglelike manner. A headband is made up of a single row of dots, and a pair of looped ridges runs from the front to the back of the head above it. The head is flanked by five scrolls of graduated length with a hook motif at the bottom. A suspension loop is in the middle of the back of the neck. The ornament was cast by the lost-wax process. The surface has been visibly abraded, perhaps in modern times.

HK

EXHIBITED

New York, The Museum of Primitive Art, 1969, no. 137, illustrated.
Leningrad, 1976, no. 150, illustrated.

PUBLISHED

Emmerich, 1979, page 96, plate II.

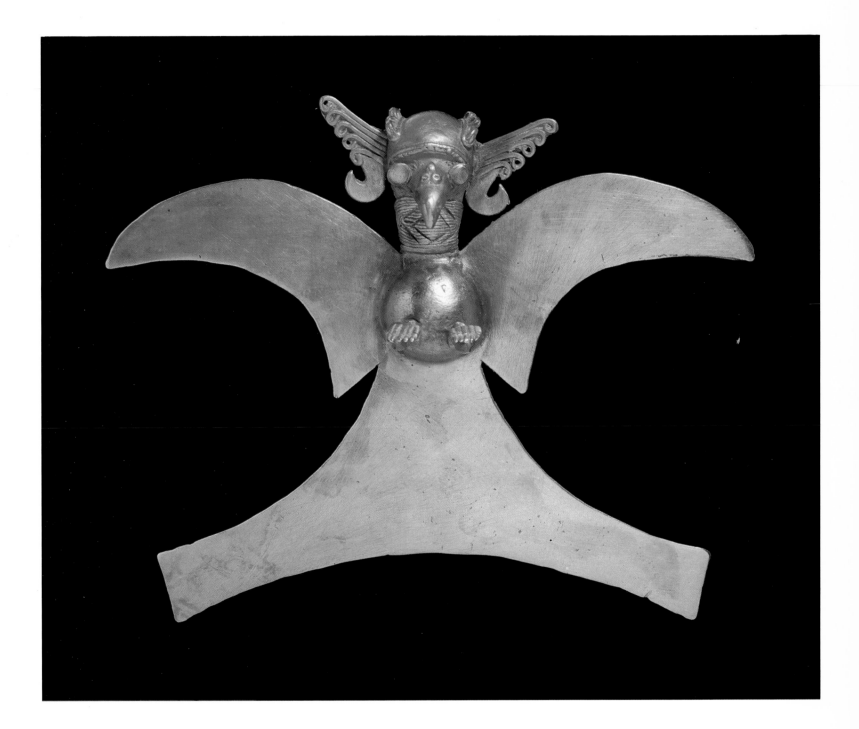

16

Double-figure pendant

CHIRIQUÍ (?)

11TH–MID-16TH CENTURY

H. 3½ in. | 8·9 cm.   W. 5¾ in. | 14·6 cm.

Pairs of human figures appear frequently among the gold ornaments. Male figures of similar, if not identical, detail were customarily joined, and the ideas clustering around the dual images were many. Figures with masks, often with bat features and/or 'warrior' attributes, were most commonly rendered. Here human faces with no animal features have been given 'tusk'-shaped bodies. The tusk shape is known and may take its significance from the objects of ivory and bone discovered at the burial site of Sitio Conte in central Panama.

At Sitio Conte many works of whale-tooth ivory and manatee-rib bone were unearthed, and crocodilian features were frequently incorporated into them. Many pendants combine gold parts with tusk-shaped ivory and bone bodies. Heads, in these instances, are often made of gold. The tusk shape appears to have assumed a separate meaning, however, for it continues to be found in pendants with bat and, later, jaguar, attributes. In this case, the pendant has no animal features.   JJ

DESCRIPTION

Two figures with round, tapered bodies are joined at the head to a long, horizontal plaque. The plaque has a slightly concave topline and incurvate lateral ends. In their outer hands, the figures hold short hook-end poles that are attached on top to the plaque. The figures have identical human faces with coffee-bean eyes, straight noses with flaring nostrils, and linear mouths. On their heads is a raised headband with five evenly spaced double scrolls surmounting it. There are nine wedge-shaped open sections in the plaque behind them. They wear spiral ear ornaments and a four-strand decorative band around their upper bodies. They have no inner arms. In back, two suspension loops appear at the outside edge of each neck.

Prominent on this pendant are the three danglers that hang from bars attached to the shoulders of the figure. Each bar ends in two large loops which support the danglers. The entire ornament was made by the lost-wax technique; the danglers were added after casting.

HK

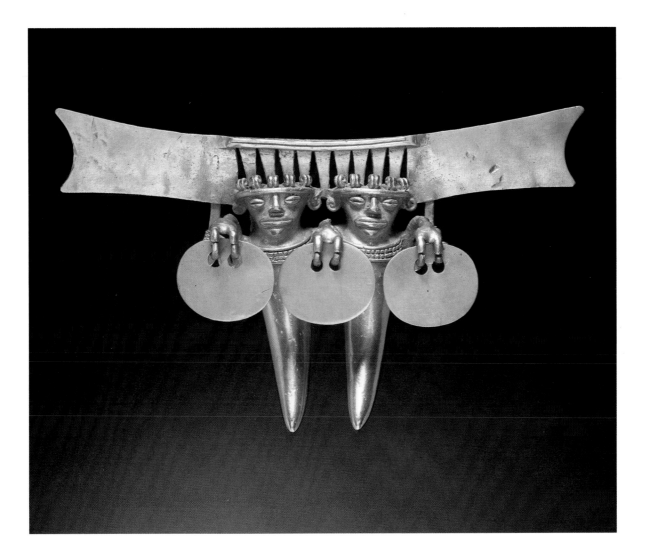

17

Double-figure pendant

PARITA, REPORTEDLY FROM THE AZUERO PENINSULA
12TH–14TH CENTURY
H. 2⅞ in. | 7·4 cm.   W. 4⅜ in. | 11·2 cm.

An interesting group of double-figure pendants are those called 'warriors.' The warrior designation comes from the paddle-shaped clubs that are held in the figures' outside hands (Cooke and Bray, this volume). Most of the warrior figures are masked as bats, the principal identifying feature of which is the big loop nose. Pop eyes, achieved by mounting the eyes on stalklike projections, are frequently present as well. Snarling, toothed mouths are part of the bat symbolism also, but such mouths are used as attributes of other creatures and are therefore not a clear diagnostic detail. The rows of danglers hanging to the side of each of the bat-head figures are noteworthy. Danglers are not found as often on Parita warrior pendants as they are on the bat-head figures of Diquís. The association between bats and warriors may be based on the qualities identified with vampire bats, which are common in Panama.

Many of the warrior pendants are said to come from Panama's Azuero Peninsula, where they were unearthed in the early 1960s (Biese 1967). The important ancient site of El Hatillo, believed to have been the main source of these pendants, is located close to the banks of the Parita River and was at one time known as Parita, hence the name of the style. Parita is the latest development of the Conte gold style.

JJ

DESCRIPTION

Two anthropomorphic figures stand side by side and hold paddle clubs in their outer hands. The male bodies are rendered with remarkable realism, displaying an almost fleshy quality in the representation of chest and belly. The heads of the figures are particularly ornate with the large upturned noses flanked by tightly wound spirals, ringed eyes on stems, and a broad open mouth, outlined by a raised edge. Four fangs are displayed. Each headdress consists of a cap with a pair of elevated, flattish crests running from back to front and resting on inverted triangles at the sides. The edges of the crests are outlined by raised double moldings that terminate in spirals in front. Side hooks, flat and upturned, project from the back of the crests. The figures wear trapezoidal loincloths tied with a two-strand belt and double ligatures around their lower legs. Cuplike elements appear to the sides of each waist from which reptilian streamers descend. The arms of the figures are thin, and, in their inner hands, each holds a pole to which three danglers are attached. Two more poles with danglers are in front of the clubs, connected to the figures' arms by cross-pieces. The two figures were cast separately by the lost-wax method and joined in the back by three rods inserted through rows of loops behind the heads, hips, and feet. There are two suspension rings in the back of each figure at shoulder level. The danglers were added after casting; some are replaced.   HK

EXHIBITED
New York, The Museum of Primitive Art, 1969, no. 146.

PUBLISHED
Emmerich, 1965, facing page 104, plate II; page 99, fig. 123.

18

Two pectoral discs (patenas)

MACARACAS

8TH–12TH CENTURY

Diam. 5⅜ *in.* | 13·6 *cm.*   6¾ *in.* | 17·1 *cm.*

Circular plaques of hammered sheet metal are ubiquitous among the Isthmian gold objects. Their average diameter is five to six inches, and there are two holes through them, by which they were attached, presumably to a garment or a neckband of some kind. The plaques are also called discs, medallions, breastplates, and *patenas*. At their simplest, the patenas are ornamented at the periphery with rows of raised dots. On others, the dots are supplemented with a tasteful framing rim accented by small bosses. Larger centrally positioned bosses were also used. On yet other discs, designs become more complex and figural elements appear. The discs embellished only with bosses appear to come from all of the gold-using areas of the Isthmus.

While on his fourth voyage to the New World, in 1502, Christopher Columbus sailed along the coast of Central America from present-day Hondurás south to Darién, in Panama. During this part of the voyage, he and his men saw and traded with the Indians for 'mirrors' of gold. The Indians wore the 'mirrors' around their necks (Colón 1959). Unfortunately, no description of the 'mirrors' was recorded, but it is possible that these gold discs are of the type later called 'mirrors' by Columbus.

JJ

DESCRIPTION

These circular plaques have a concave center and a narrow rim, which is slightly bent backward. They are embellished with embossed decoration encircling the rim. An embossed row of dots at the edge, and another near the juncture of the rim and the concave center, adorn the larger disc, and rows of short dashes the smaller. Two holes are punched through the center of each disc near the rim. On the smaller disc, between the embossed lines, are two rows of tiny stamped motifs, one in the center of the rim, the other near the inner embossed line.   HK

19

Diadem

COSTA RICA OR PANAMA
11TH–MID-16TH CENTURY (?)
H. 3⅛ *in.*|8 *cm.*   Cir. 20½ *in.*| 52 *cm.*

Diadems, or ornamental headbands, are among the many types of gold ornaments made in ancient America. Fabricated of flexible sheet metal that bends easily, they vary in height, and thereby in presence—the higher they are, the grander they appear. The illustrated example is of impressive size. Decoration, when present, is simple and consists of a row of raised bosses or circles close to each rim edge. The ends of the diadems overlap and would have been laced or sewn together by means of a cord or other material passing through the paired holes. So simple are these diadems that it is difficult to place them, in light of current published evidence: the present example could come from Colombia as well as Costa Rica or Panama.

Headdresses of gold, either as diadems or caps, or as the ornaments worn in 'hats' of organic materials, were an important part of the group of decorative forms used in Precolumbian times for precious metals. Crownlike diadems, in basic construction little different from this one, are among the earliest worked gold objects from South America.

JJ

DESCRIPTION

This sheet gold diadem is embellished at the top and bottom edges by a row of evenly spaced embossed circles. At the ends there are two holes on either side, through which a narrow, twisted band of gold is pulled.   HK

EX. COLL.
Sale, Köln, Lempertz, December 14, 1966, lot 1815.

20

Pair of cuffs

COSTA RICA OR PANAMA
11TH–16TH CENTURY (?)
H. 2¾ in.| 7 cm.   Cir. 9 in.|22·9 cm.

Paired cuffs of gold have been found in Isthmian graves. Arms cuffs, or bracelets, are more frequently encountered but ankle cuffs are known. The bracelets come in many lengths—some almost reach the elbow—and many different patterns enhance them, including elaborate figurative ones. The patterns, elaborate or simple, are worked the length of the cuff on both sides of the opening. Arm ornaments were made also in Colombia, but, as a rule, they were not decorated in this manner.

Arm ornaments are not among the more commonly used of ancient American gold forms. Gold decoration was primarily for the head—neck, ears, nose, and the top of the head—and each had its own ornament or ornaments. Even the mouth had a lip plug. This predilection for head embellishment is present in objects of other media as well. Everything precious, from jade to feathers, was used for the purpose. Less attention was directed at decorating other parts of the body. Characteristically, hands were not bedecked; nor were wrists or fingers, nor ankles or feet. Waists and knees were given rather more attention, but nothing compared to that lavished upon the head.

JJ

DESCRIPTION

Adorning these cuffs are vertical decorative bands at either side of the arm opening. The embossed bands consist of two parallel lines that frame a row of six raised circles. One hole is provided on either side of the opening so that the cuffs could be closed. These holes have been enlarged, apparently with use. On one of the cuffs an additional hole on one side and a pair of holes on the other have been placed close to the main attachment hole. The surface is not highly polished; some discoloration is present on the inside of the cuffs.   HK

EX. COLL.

Sale, Köln, Lempertz, December 14, 1966, lot 1817.

21

Pectoral plaque with masked figure

MACARACAS, REPORTEDLY FROM THE AZUERO PENINSULA
8TH–12TH CENTURY
H. 5 *in.*|12·7 *cm.*   W. 4⅝ *in.*|11·7 *cm.*

Many of the gold plaques of central Panama are embellished with reptilian imagery in zoomorphic and anthropomorphic form. Crocodilians, the group of reptiles that includes crocodiles, alligators, and caimans, are among the most ancient inhabitants of the earth and live in both the Old and New Worlds. The New World varieties are creatures of the American tropics. How they were considered in Precolumbian times is not well understood today. Crocodilian images on Panamanian plaques are usually depicted with large, double, serrated crests, which have led to their being called 'crested crocodiles' or 'crested dragons.' The crests appear on the anthropomorphic versions as well, other salient features of which are a wide mouth and many pointed teeth, and long claws on hands and feet, all aspects present on the plaque illustrated here. The anthropomorphic images have long been called 'crocodile gods,' but, in recent years, the term has fallen into disfavor.

Archaeological excavation undertaken during the past fifteen years or so has established a more detailed chronology for ancient Panama (Cooke 1984a), and earlier work has been integrated into these findings. The important site of Sitio Conte, in the Coclé province of central Panama, was excavated in the 1930s, and gold objects found at the time were grouped loosely into a style named Coclé, after the province. The Coclé style has since been found to have many distinct parts (Bray, n.d.); among them are Conte, previously called early Coclé, and Macaracas, previously late Coclé. The new names come from the polychrome ceramics with which the gold objects were associated in the Sitio Conte burials.

JJ

DESCRIPTION

The anthropomorphic crocodile is shown in a rectangular format with a distinct raised band framing the design. The figure has a square face with big, staring eyes; flaring nostrils; and ferocious-looking mouth, studded with pointed teeth. From the top of his head emerge crests with triangular elements, which have been interpreted as plumes or scales. His body is human, while his hands and feet are clawed. He wears a belt around his waist with streamers to either side terminating in hooks. These streamers are an abbreviated version of the reptilian belt found on more elaborately executed examples. The design is worked in the repoussé technique, and there are four pairs of attachment holes, two close to the sides near the top and two beside the feet.

HK

EX. COLL.
André Emmerich, New York. Sale, Basel, March 1964, lot 19.

EXHIBITED
New York, The Metropolitan Museum of Art, 1970, no. 237, illustrated.
Leningrad, 1976, no. 143, illustrated.

PUBLISHED
Emmerich, 1965, page 93, fig. 112.
Emmerich, 1979, page 96, plate IV.

22

Double-crocodile pendant

MACARACAS

8TH–12TH CENTURY

H. 3¾ in. | 9·6 cm.   W. 3 in. | 7·5 cm.

The double-crocodile pendants to which 'tails' of other media have been added are particularly pleasing in the juxtaposition of their different materials. The cast gold of the crocodilian heads and torsos is generously elaborate in detail, and it contrasts well with the smooth textures of the stone, ivory, or shell inlays. The 'crested crocodiles' here have tails of shell, and the slightly grainy texture of the gold bodies is underscored by the drier substance and chalky color of their tails.

Few Precolumbian peoples incorporated additional materials into gold objects. Perhaps the most successful of those that did were the people of central Panama in the second half of the first millennium AD. Among them was the goldsmith who made this pendant. Ornate, carefully crafted, subtly colored works, the Coclé objects are among some of the most extraordinary of the extant New World gold pieces.

Certain facial details on the crocodiles appear to be those associated with bats—for instance, the eyes, nose, and ears. The implication of the overlap of reptilian and bat features, if indeed specific symbols were discrete to either reptiles or bats at this time, is not presently clear. Although the reptiles central to this Isthmian iconography have long been thought to be crocodilian, recent study suggests that the role may belong to lizards, especially iguanas (Helms 1977). Ethnographic evidence that associates lizards with rulership, the iguana's crest, and the ability of the animal to walk on its hind feet are among reasons given in this new interpretation.   JJ

DESCRIPTION

Two side-by-side animals support their bodies on bent legs. Their heads are raised and jut out in opposite directions. A central crest made of a row of upward-projecting hooks and side streamers runs down their heads. In front the hooks of the crest become a flat band that rises to a triangular peak at the top of the head. The side streamers are flat bands with triangles (crocodilian scales?); at the bottom, they end in other hook motifs. The ears, to either side of the crest, are large and triangular, ending in another hook.

The mouths of these fantastic creatures are open; the ridge is marked by a raised border. The upper and lower teeth are displayed, as well as four fangs. Two elegantly curved streamers emerge from the sides of the mouths and end in scrolls. The end of the snout is a wide upturned 'nose,' which is flanked by tightly wound spirals, perhaps representing nostrils. The bulging eyes are surrounded by three rings. The bodies end at a braided element, where the tails, which are made of shell, begin. The shell tails are inserted into a hollow in the lost-wax casting and are squared off on the sides with tapering, upcurved ends. Suspension loops are under each of the four front feet.

HK

EXHIBITED

New York, The Museum, of Primitive Art, 1969, no. 143, illustrated.
New York, The Metropolitan Museum of Art, 1970, no. 230, illustrated.
Leningrad, 1976, no.128, illustrated.

23

Double-end animal pendant

CONTE (?)

6TH–8TH CENTURY

H. 2 *in.*|5·1 *cm.*   W. 3 *in.*|7·6 *cm.*

Pendants made up of four animals joined body-to-body were made in distinct types. The most significant are the big-tailed ones known as curly-tailed animals and those in which the creatures become double-ended, with an identical head at both top and bottom. One of the curly-tailed variety was excavated at Sitio Conte in the 1930s, when the multiple-animal pendants were considered Coclé in style. The double-end animals may have originated somewhat earlier than the curly-tailed examples, although in overall shape and size, if not in all details of manufacture, they are very similar. Both types appear to have been made over a length of time sufficient for changes to occur, and it is possible that different periods of manufacture are indicated by details such as the suspension loops, which in some examples are formed by holes through the front feet of the animals and in others by rings on separate rods which run through the feet.

Sitio Conte, the ancient site noted for its rich burials, is located on the banks of the Río Grande in the Coclé province of central Panama. It first came to public notice when a large group of gold and stone objects reached the antiquities market in Panama, after having been washed out of graves along the river bank during floods in 1927. The site was named for the Conte family, its owners during the 1930s when controlled excavation took place.   JJ

DESCRIPTION

Four identical animals stand side by side, their legs apart, joined top and bottom by a rod going through the feet. Each animal has identical heads at its front and tail ends. The identity of the animals has not been determined, but they have flat, long snouts and open mouths with a single row of teeth. The mouths are encircled by an outlining element. The slightly domed heads have two small crests made up of three ridges, running front to back. The eyes are truncated cones and jut out to the sides of the head. The ornament was cast all together in one lost-wax process and is open on the underside. The animals' heads still have remains of core material in them. Three suspension loops are on the top tie rod, one at each end and one in the middle.

HK

24

Curly-tailed animal pendant

'INTERNATIONAL' STYLE
5TH–10TH CENTURY
H. 1⅜ *in.*|3·4 *cm.*   W. 1⅛ *in.*|2·8 *cm.*

Pendants in the shape of animals with large curled-over tails were made in Panama, both in cast gold and in semiprecious stone. They are among the very few Isthmian pendant forms that exist in both materials. A good number were excavated at Sitio Conte in the 1930s, when the source of their distinctive tail shape was considered to be the cebus monkey (Lothrop 1937). The stone curly-tailed animals, often carved of agate, were perforated to be worn with the animal hanging downward, while those of metal were made to be suspended with the animal facing upward. Except for the tail, the outlines of which remain constant, the curly-tailed animals vary substantially, and they have been identified as everything from dogs to ducks. Many appear to have bird features as well. The present example, with its 'beak' and the rows of 'tufts' on its head, may be a bird.

The discovery of the curly-tailed animals at Sitio Conte led to their assignation to the Coclé style. More recent work, both excavation and review of existing collections, has put them into the International group (Bray, n.d.). They come from a much wider area of Costa Rica and Panama than had been supposed.

JJ

DESCRIPTION

An animal with birdlike head and a quadruped body has a broad, curved tail arching over its body. Three rows of parallel notched projections run from front to back on the head, and the beaklike mouth is marked by a line. Round, protruding eyes are located on either side of the head. The front paws were worked as suspension loops, but the loops are worn through. Each front leg is also perforated. The object was cast by the lost-wax process; core material remains in all four legs.   HK

EXHIBITED
Leningrad, 1976, no. 131, illustrated.

PUBLISHED
Von Winning, 1968, page 384, fig. 589.

25

Curly-tailed animal pendant

'INTERNATIONAL' STYLE
5TH–10TH CENTURY
H. 2¼ *in.*|5·8 *cm.* W. 1⅛ *in.*|2·7 *cm.*

Curly-tailed animals are similar to one another in body-tail configuration, but they differ in the details of the head; individual animals are not always distinguishable among them, and some have human faces. Styles, too, differ, as a comparison of this pendant with the preceding example will show. The rather perky animal here has body volumes that have been squared off and their bulk diminished. The surfaces of the ornament are highly polished and glistening. In contrast, the preceding curly-tailed animal is muscular and a bit squat; it is not as sleek in outline nor as shiny of surface. Such differences, and the large region from which the pendants have been reported to come, suggest that they reflect a degree of 'internationalism' in the metalwork of the Isthmus (Bray, n.d.). This period of internationalism is thought to date from the mid to late centuries of the first millennium AD.

A number of 'International'-style objects come from early Sitio Conte burials. Samuel Lothrop (1937) thought them to be sufficiently different from other Sitio Conte works to indicate influence, if not importation, from the Sinú area of Colombia. As one result of this opinion, the style of the objects has been called both Coclé, from the documentation of their Sitio Conte provenance, and Sinú, following Lothrop's published statement.

JJ

DESCRIPTION

This curly-tailed animal has a quadruped body and a broad, elongated, flat-end tail, which curves over the back almost touching the head. The head is laterally flattened, rounded in back, and has a narrow, raised band outlining the edges. Two small dotlike eyes are raised on the sides of the head, and a long mouth is topped by a snout with two nostrils. The front paws are suspension loops. The pendant was cast by the lost-wax process. Remains of the core are still in place inside the head and tail.

HK

EXHIBITED
New York, The Metropolitan Museum of Art, 1970, no. 224, illustrated.
Leningrad, 1976, no. 132, illustrated.

PUBLISHED
Von Winning, 1968, page 384, fig. 590.

26

Figure pendant

'INTERNATIONAL' STYLE
5TH–10TH CENTURY
H. 2⅛ *in.*|5·5 *cm.*   W. 1⅜ *in.*|3·5 *cm.*

The stylized figure pendants of the 'International' group are especially intriguing. Their bodies are rudimentary, and their arm and leglike appendages appear to be conventionalized fish-fins. The faces of the figures are usually human. Their headdresses are quite specific in detail, consisting of large, sweeping side elements and a central cone. Headdresses of this type appear also on gold figure pendants from Colombia (Falchetti 1976), as do the finlike appendages. A somewhat simpler pendant of this kind was found in one of the gold-rich Sitio Conte burials, that numbered Burial B, Grave 32 (Lothrop 1937). Also in Grave 32 were three gold discs with raised seahorse designs. In the designs of the seahorse discs there is a secondary element in the distinctive shape of the notched feet-tail configuration seen here. The feet-tail shape, then, may be an oblique reference to seahorses. Pendants in the form of seahorses are found in the 'International group'.

'International' style objects are noteworthy for a number of significant qualities which distinguish them from later Panamanian works. Differences exist in form and in imagery; the combinations of human and animal characteristics are not those of later compositions. Conceptually, the ornaments are both elegant and simple, with few, if any, of the many additive parts so plentiful on other Isthmian examples. Surfaces are so smooth that they appear silken; they glisten in a well-bred manner that is never overwhelming. The 'International' style objects have links to the Quimbaya area of Colombia, a region famous for its gold objects.   JJ

DESCRIPTION

This effigy pendant shows a figure with a highly stylized body and a relatively naturalistic human face. The face has two round eyes set into sockets under protruding eyebrows. The chin juts forward, and the mouth is indicated by a short horizontal line. The figure wears ear ornaments and a prominent headdress. The latter consists of a cap surmounted by a tapering element in the center with two big hook shapes on either side. Each hook has five notches at the top. Body and limbs are abstract, almost geometric forms; the body is a slightly raised rectangle with stylized 'arms,' pointing down, on either side. At the bottom is a crescent-shaped element with a wide groove in the center. The front of the ornament is well burnished, while the back, which is flat, is uneven and less well finished. It was cast by the lost-wax process in the round. The central core still remains and is visible through a hole in back caused by the loss of a casting plug. A suspension loop is at the back of the head.   HK

27

Nose ornament

QUIMBAYA

5TH–10TH CENTURY

H. 1⅛ *in.*|3 *cm.*   W. 2⅛ *in.*|5·4 *cm.*

Ornaments made to be worn in the nose were widely used in Precolumbian America. Nose ornaments, or nose rings, as they are also called, were usually made to be hung from the septum, and those of gold were particularly favored in South America. Ancient examples are known from Panama, but there are many fewer there than remain from adjacent Colombia. Colombian nose ornaments are amazing in their invention and variety, far surpassing those of other Precolumbian areas in their degree of elaboration. The nose ornament here is of great simplicity. It is decorous and refined, and it has been polished to a lustrous sheen. Contrary to first impressions, it was not made by casting; rather, it was shaped by hammering, and the rounded sides were joined at the outer edge. So well done is the join and so well polished the surface that the seam can best be distinguished from the inside.

Such hammered and soldered works are among those of the Quimbaya style, the style associated with the main body of works from a well-known 'Treasure' discovered in Colombia in 1891 (Restrepo Tirado 1929). The 'Treasure of the Quimbayas,' which actually represents the contents of two tombs, was found at La Soledad, in the municipality of Filandia, now in the department of Quindio. The 'Treasure' is perhaps the single most famous group of Precolumbian gold objects extant today.

JJ

DESCRIPTION

The hollow, bean-shaped ornament has an opening like a keyhole on its top—and straight—side. The only decoration consists of three parallel ridges on both sides of the opening; the edges of the circle below are bent inward. The ornament was made of two pieces of sheet gold that were soldered together. The surface is polished to a high gloss.

HK

EXHIBITED

New York, The Museum of Primitive Art, 1969, no. 166.
Leningrad, 1976, no. 63, illustrated.

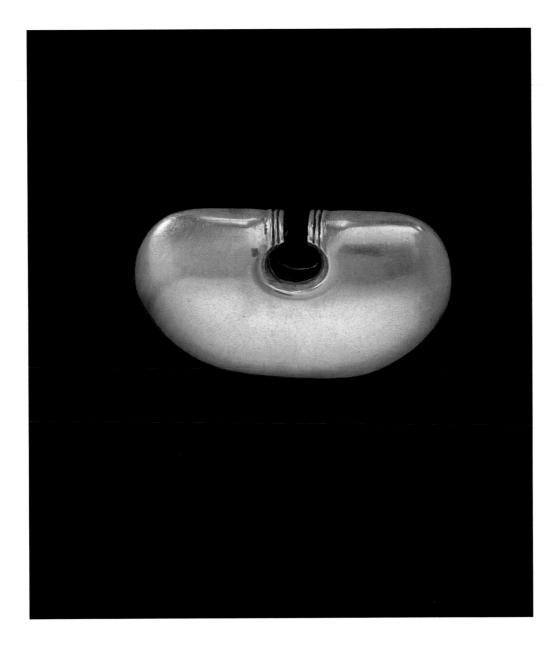

28

Lime container (poporo)

QUIMBAYA
5TH–10TH CENTURY
H. 9 in. | 23 cm.   W. 5¼ in. | 13·3 cm.

In Andean South America, there is an indigenous tradition for the ritual use of coca leaves. In Precolumbian times, coca was used chiefly by placing a quid of leaves into the mouth and adding a small amount of powdered lime, usually made from calcined sea shells. The coca paraphernalia, a small bag for the leaves and a container and a spatula for the lime, have—in the past five thousand years—been made in an infinity of materials. At certain times and places, great attention was lavished on them, and bag, bottle, and spatula could become very elaborate. Such an episode occurred in the Quimbaya region of Colombia, along the middle reaches of the Cauca River valley, in the second half of the first millennium AD. During that time, particularly impressive lime bottles were made of gold.

The lime containers, known as *poporos* in Colombia, were cast in the form of nude human figures or as flasks incorporating raised images of them. They exhibit great elegance of conception, manufacture, and finish. The shouldered bottle here, adorned on either side with a female figure, still contains powdered lime.

In the 'Treasure of the Quimbayas' there were six anthropomorphic poporos (Plazas 1978) and eleven in other shapes. While the 'Treasure' is said to represent the mortuary offerings of two tombs, it is believed that each tomb held multiple burials.

JJ

DESCRIPTION

The laterally flattened bottle is a narrow rectangle with rounded corners. The incurvate sides have mushroomlike protruberances at the shoulders and a pronounced ledge at the base. The neck is constricted but then swells and tapers upward. Set into the recesses on the two broad faces of the container are nude female figures in high relief. The hands are held to the stomachs of the plump, fleshy bodies, which are well-proportioned.

The faces are broad, and the line of the wide noses continues into the eyebrows; the nostrils flare, and the mouths are closed. Five circular ear ornaments rim the earlobes. Double-strand ligatures appear across the forehead and around the neck, wrists, knees, and ankles. Fingers and toes are indicated by short grooves, and the feet protrude. There are four plugged core support holes, two at the top and two at the bottom of the bottle's lateral projections. The object was cast by the lost-wax technique. The black deposits on the surface are copper corrosion products.   HK

EX. COLL.
Collection Hoffmann, Geneva.

EXHIBITED
New York, The Museum of Primitive Art, 1969, no. 152, illustrated.
New York, The Metropolitan Museum of Art, 1972.
New York, The Museum of Primitive Art, 1974, no. 36, illustrated.
Leningrad, 1976, no. 60, illustrated.

PUBLISHED
Lapiner, 1976, page 382, fig. 816.
Knauth et al., 1974, page 149.
Emmerich, 1979, page 95, fig. 2.

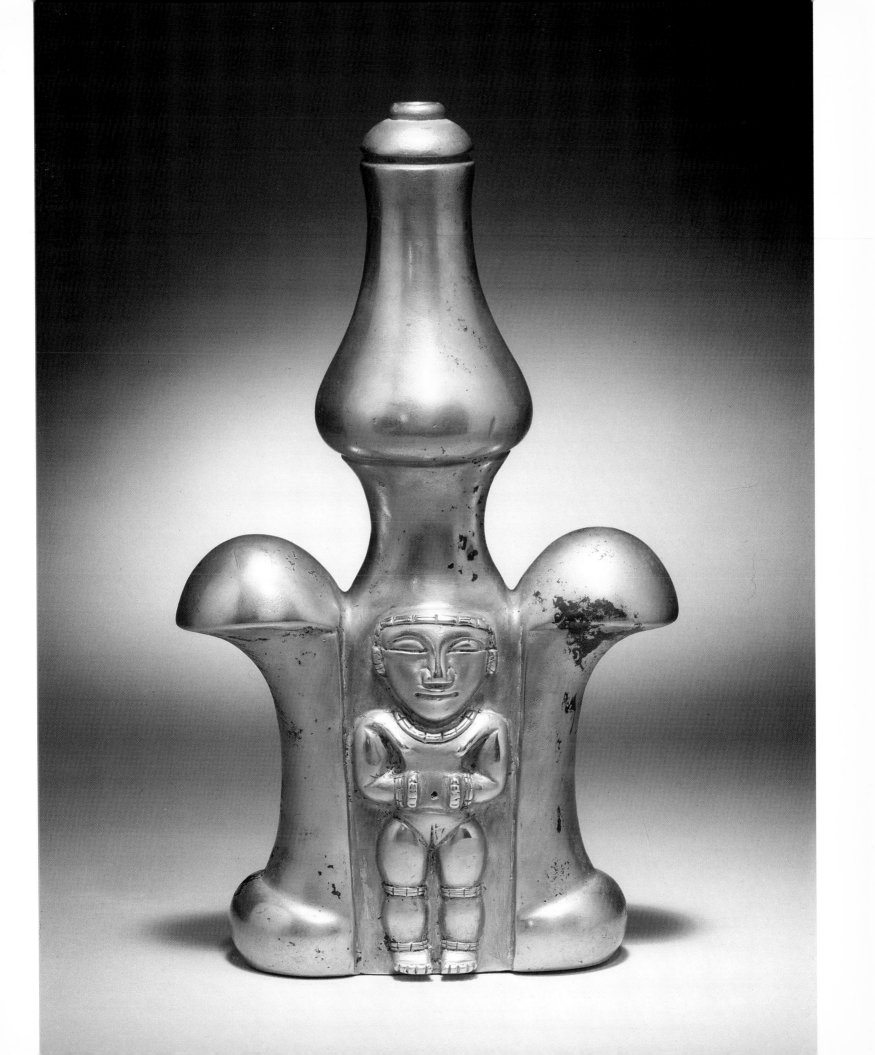

29

Lime spatula or pin

QUIMBAYA (?)

5TH–10TH CENTURY

H. *top* 2⅛ *in.*|5·4 *cm.*   H. *total* 22¼ *in.*|56·5 *cm.*

The lime spatulas, or dippers, that were part of the coca ritual equipment in South America were nowhere more grandly produced than in southwestern Colombia, where some were of such size and impressiveness that they were considered, when discovered, to be scepters. Such a spatula is shown here; it is almost two feet tall. Lime spatulas were used to dip powdered lime from container to mouth. In Precolumbian times, they were made in many different materials, including cast gold. Because of their length and general appearance, they are also frequently called pins or *alfilers*.

On the finial of the spatula there is a very engaging, puffed-up bird standing on an equally engaging 'monster.' The grinning monster, which is all head, legs, and arms, is most enigmatic, for it is also a dual-aspect creature; it can be read as two back-to-back profile figures. Overall, this complex double image is far from being understood. The image, however, is a specific one, which occurs on other spatulas, often very large ones. At least one of the eight gold spatulas in the 'Treasure of the Quimbayas' (Plazas 1978) was of this type. The 'Treasure' is now in the Museo de América in Madrid, where it came to rest after being exhibited with other ancient Colombian gold objects in 1892, in the Exposición Histórico-Americano, a large exhibition assembled on the occasion of the four-hundredth anniversary of the discovery of America.

JJ

DESCRIPTION

This spatula is topped by a three-dimensionally cast bird, which has a broad head with a curved beak and raised coffee-bean eyes. It stands on a two-dimensional composite creature combining human and animal features. On its head, the bird has sideways curving crests; the larger, outer elements have a groove in the center and notches on top. In back, a trapezoidal tail hangs down, and the sides of the wings meet in an elongated upward curve. Beneath the bird, the composite carrier figure also has tufts or crests on its head, as well as raised-dot eyes and a large mouth displaying two rows of teeth. Profile mouths are on the 'cheeks.' The figure, details of which are the same front and back, does not have a body; its large, almond-shaped head sits immediately on two straight legs, from which arms project to the sides. Fingers are indicated. The object was cast by the lost-wax process, and the shaft was extended by working.

HK

EXHIBITED

New York, The Museum of Primitive Art, 1969, no. 151.

30

Two lime spatulas or pins

QUIMBAYA OR CALIMA
5TH–10TH CENTURY (?)
H. 10⅜ *in.* | 26·3 *cm.*   16⅜ *in.* | 41·7 *cm.*

The figurative tops of the so-called lime spatulas appear to fall into certain groups distinguished by image. The squat, crested bird, seen here on the right, is one that is observable in a number of guises, of which this is the simplest. The bird can be bigger and more stylized—particularly in details of crest and eyes—and it sometimes appears perched on other elements or figures. Of the nonfigurative finials, the golf-tee shape was most frequently employed.

The tall, cast spatulas or pins have long been thought to have been made in the Calima region of Colombia, to the southwest of the Quimbaya area. The discovery of the spatulas in regions other than the Calima area, however—for example, those from the 'Treasure of the Quimbayas'—indicates that the type of object was either traded widely from Calima or that certain examples were manufactured outside the region. Although there is little doubt that the gold objects were traded among various groups of Precolumbian peoples, it is sometimes difficult to know, with the present state of information, what specific directions the trade in certain types of objects took.

JJ

DESCRIPTION

Left   A lime dipper with a well-burnished shaft tapers slightly towards the bottom. At the top, a conical shape rises from a double molding; on the flat top, a broad rim encircles the central cavity.

Right   A little bird stands on the flat, conical top of this lime dipper. The bird's beak is narrow and pointed; the eyes protrude slightly from the sides of the head. A two-part crest, made up of four scrolls for each part, runs from the front to the back of the head. A trapezoidal tail hangs down in the back, and the wings end, pointing upward, above the tail. There are three claws on each foot.

Both spatulas were cast by the lost-wax process, and the shafts have been extended by working.   HK

EX. COLL.
Sale, right only, Köln, Lempertz, December 14, 1966, lot 1810.

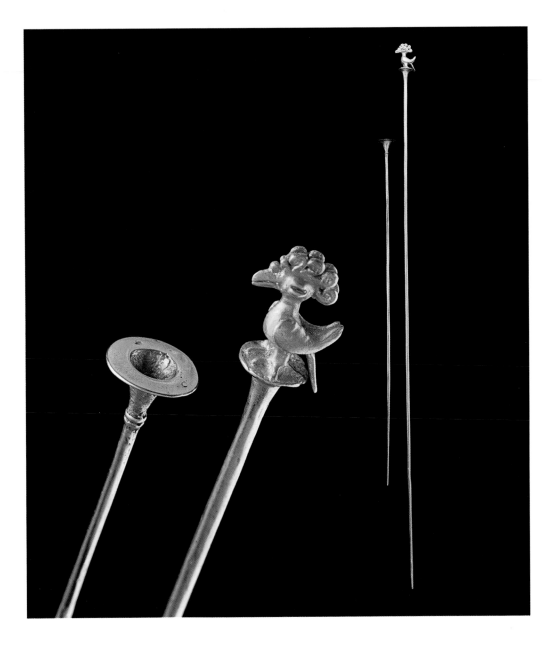

31

Three 'flying-fish' pendants

QUIMBAYA (?)

5TH–10TH CENTURY

H. 2¼ in.|5·8 cm.   1⅞ in.|4·8 cm.   1¾ in.|4·5 cm.

W. 1⅞ in.|4·9 cm.   1¾ in.|4·3 cm.   1⅝ in.|4·1 cm.

Ornaments that have been identified variously as flying fish, winged crocodiles, or, more simply, as fishlike shapes, are elaborate in detail and puzzling in form. The standard representations have domed heads with long snouts that show many teeth, broad wings spread like those of a bird, and a pair of small 'fins' placed at the juncture of the tail, which is upright and large, and the body, which is round and smooth. Surfaces, except for the loaflike bodies, are highly patterned. Here a tiny, linear grid follows the contours of wings and tail. The wings of other examples are less abstract in their patterning when more featherlike indications appear. Curlicues can also embellish the toplines of wings and tail, as on the present trio.

There is little consensus on the derivation of these images, as the uncertainty in a name identifying them implies. Certain South American flying fish, however, their pectoral fins functioning as wings, skim rapidly over the surface of the water. When on the surface, the speed at which they travel and the glistening tonalities of their wet bodies give them a brief, twitching dazzle. Perhaps it was this quality that was meant to be caught by the particular elaboration of these pendants.   JJ

DESCRIPTION

The ornaments have heads with bulging brows and long snouts in which specifically indicated upper and lower teeth are displayed. Atop the snouts are raised arrow-shaped elements marking the nostrils and the nose ridges. The round eyes protrude somewhat. There is a constriction between head and body, and, on both sides of the body, 'wings' spread out and curve elegantly. They are stepped toward the head and carry bands of decoration. Between wings and tail are lanceolate-shaped lateral projections, also marked with geometric patterns. The tail is an upright triangle with the same decorative bands as the 'wings.' On the upper side of wings and tail, there are coiled scrolls. The objects, cast by the lost-wax technique, are solid, except for the heads, which are open in back. Suspension loops are on the underside, just below the heads. The largest ornament has a double loop.

HK

EXHIBITED

New York, The Museum of Primitive Art, 1969, no. 161.
Leningrad, 1976, no. 95, 96, 97, illustrated.

PUBLISHED

Emmerich, 1979, page 98, fig. 4.

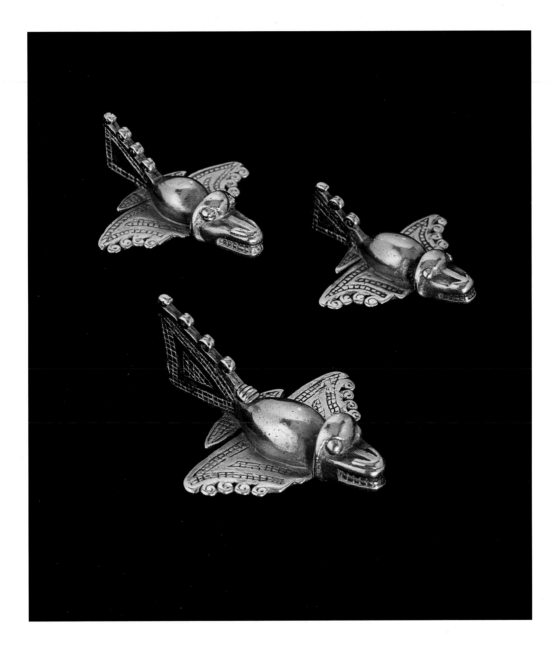

32

Double-insect pendant

STYLE UNDETERMINED
5TH–10TH CENTURY (?)
H. 2¼ in.|5·7 cm.   W. 1⅞ in.|4·8 cm.

Pendants that have danglers suspended before them were made in Colombia, as they were in the Isthmian areas. Many of these ornaments used danglers in much the same manner, that is, they were hung in front of the object in such a way as to partially obscure it. In extreme cases, the numbers and the placement of the danglers completely hide the depiction beneath. The placement of the danglers in the ornament here is most judicious, for it allows the identification of the heads of the insects—their eyes are just visible—and it also balances visually the upper and lower pendant pairs. The slightly-more-than-half-moon shape of the danglers echoes, but does not duplicate, the outline of the insect bodies, and, in another subtle contrast, the vibrating, hammered sheet of the danglers sets off the smooth, solid surfaces of the cast, segmented bodies.

Insect representations such as these are thought to come principally from the Quimbaya region of the middle Cauca Valley. They do not, however, all belong to the Quimbaya style, i.e., the style defined by the salient features of the 'Treasure of the Quimbayas.' The insect ornaments vary from realistic to abstract in a range of stylistic diversity. The components of that diversity, whether the result of time, distance, or the personal inspiration of the maker, remain to be detailed.   JJ

DESCRIPTION

The almond-shaped bodies of these ornamental insects are divided roughly in half, with differing grooved patterns top and bottom. The striated rear sections terminate in small knobs that may be the remains of the casting sprues. The front ends are grooved with what may be a closed-wing pattern, and the heads have two small, ball eyes and a central raised ridge. This element runs from the top to the underside of the heads, which are hollow. The suspension loops are also on the underside. Two pairs of semilunate danglers are attached to the insects by rods joined just behind the head and near the tail. The danglers are hammered and were added after casting. The insects were cast by the lost-wax process, and it is possible that the rods and the insects were joined after they were cast.

HK

EXHIBITED

New York, The Museum of Primitive Art, 1969, no. 171.

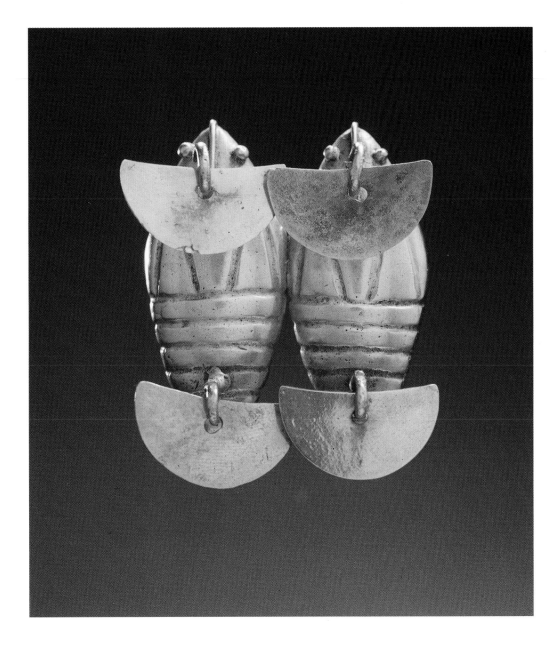

33

Fish pendant

STYLE UNDETERMINED

5TH–10TH CENTURY

H. 2⅝ *in.*|6·5 *cm.*   W. 1¼ *in.*|3·2 *cm.*

Cast ornaments in series, made to be strung together in necklaces, were a characteristic Colombian form. Serial necklace ornaments also come from Peru, where they were fabricated of sheet gold, and from Mexico, where they were cast, as were many of the Colombian examples. Multipiece necklaces of cast-gold elements were among the objects so much admired in Mexico when first seen by the Spaniards in the 1520s (Muller, this volume). It is not known what significant distinction there may have been between necklace ornaments and individual pendants; the latter were apparently worn one at a time about the neck.

The fish ornament here, a good-sized one for a necklace ornament, was threaded through the 'tube' at the front of the nose. It is possible that the 'tube' is meant to be a representation of whiskers; if so, it would indicate more specifically the type of fish depicted.

JJ

DESCRIPTION

A fish pendant with rounded, tapering body and broad head is hollow underneath. The ridge running down its back ends in the tail fin; a dorsal and two lateral fins are present. The fins are grooved. The eyes and nostrils are worked as circles of raised gold. A wide, coiled tube in the mouth of the fish would have functioned as the means of suspension. The ornament was cast by the lost-wax process.

HK

EXHIBITED

New York, The Museum of Primitive Art, 1969, no. 172.

34

Figure pendant

TOLIMA (?)

5TH–10TH CENTURY (?)

H. 3⅞ in. | 10 cm.   W. 2⅜ in. | 6·1 cm.

Pendants in the form of human figures were produced in some quantity in ancient Colombia. Many are straightforward human images without further distinguishing features, such as animal masks or musical instruments. One group of them was once said to belong to an 'invasionist' style. The pendants of this group were usually male, often with nose ornaments and elaborate headdresses; the hands were either raised to the front or placed on the hips. While the pendants did not form a stylistic unit, their imagery was very similar. One of the raised-arm variety is illustrated here.

The 'invasionist' style was thought to represent changes wrought by an influx of peoples of the Amazon, to the east of the Colombian Andes (Pérez de Barradas 1966). Entering from the southeast and following along the Magdalena and Cauca River valleys, the 'inva-sionist' style was seen as representing a significant change in goldwork, which became simpler in both form and decoration as a result (Plazas and Falchetti, this volume).

JJ

DESCRIPTION

The nude male figure stands with flexed knees and arms bent upward and forward. Except for the arms that are rounded, the body and head are flat, almost geometric shapes; the legs are long rectangles, and the upper body is a square. A four-strand belt encircles the body just above the genitals. Multistring bracelets are worn on the upraised arms, and the five-fingered hands are open. The toes are turned under and grooved.

The flat face is outlined by a raised double element, the outer of which ends in the two spirals that form the ear ornaments. The face has coffee-bean-type eyes and a prominent hooked nose. No mouth is indicated. There appear to be two nose ornaments, one a large, open ring, which is free-hanging, and another that projects upward, nail-like, above it. The headdress consists of fourteen squared-off 'rays' arranged in a half-circle. The ornament, which was cast by the lost-wax technique, has a suspension loop at the back of the neck. The nose ring was shaped by hammering and added after casting.

HK

EXHIBITED

New York, The Museum of Primitive Art, 1969, no. 160, illustrated.
Leningrad, 1976, no. 89, illustrated.

35

Figure pendant

TOLIMA (?)

5TH–10TH CENTURY (?)

H. 3⅞ in. | 9·7 cm.   W. 2 in. | 5·2 cm.

Without indication of body bulk of any kind, this figure pendant is formed of a layer of metal of substantial, almost-even thickness. The basic figure—head, torso, and limbs—is discreetly elaborated by a few added details, raised levels for knees and feet, and a simple rounding for the arms. In all, it is a sophisticated, yet elemental, stylization of the human body. The extreme flatness of figures such as this is exceeded, in Colombian gold, only by Muisca figures. These are thin sheets of metal, completely flat, on which all surface detail is supplementary, in the manner of cake decoration.

Tolima works exhibit an interest in the design possibilities of two-dimensional form. Their two-dimensionality was exploited more for the drama of outline than for use as a vehicle for added surface detail.   JJ

DESCRIPTION

The nude male figure stands with flexed knees and arms bent upward and forward. Except for the arms, which are rounded, the body and head are flat, almost-geometric shapes; the legs are long rectangles, and the upper body is a square. A two-strand belt encircles the body just above the genitals. The four raised fingers are stubby, and no toes are indicated. The face, outlined by a raised double element, has bug eyes and an aquiline nose, but no mouth is defined. There is a large, free-hanging ring in the nose. The headdress, shaped like a bishop's miter, is connected to the head by five crossbars decorated with grooves. Cast by the lost-wax technique, the ornament has a suspension loop at the back of the neck. The nose ring was shaped by hammering and added after casting.

HK

EXHIBITED

New York, The Museum of Primitive Art, 1969, no. 160, illustrated.
Leningrad, 1976, no. 90, illustrated.

36

Two figure pendants

STYLE UNDETERMINED
5TH–10TH CENTURY (?)
H. 1¾ in. | 4·3 cm.   2⅜ in. | 5·9 cm.
W. 1⅜ in. | 3·5 cm.   1½ in. | 3·9 cm.

The large, hatchet noses of these two small pendants are remarkable for the degree of character—verging on caricature—that they impart to the stylized faces they adorn. The noses are made yet more impressive by the ornaments that appear as small, round projections to either side of the nostrils. Nose ornaments were made in countless shapes in ancient Colombia; those seen on the figures here are among their simplest versions. Precolumbian ceramic and stone images, as well as those of gold, depict the wearing of nose ornaments. They were extensively used in Precolumbian South America, and were particularly inventively shaped in Colombia.

A certain amount of Colombian goldwork is difficult to isolate by style. In the collection of Bogotá's Museo del Oro, figure pendants similar to those illustrated here are without provenance (Pérez de Barradas 1965: nos. 275, 276). The Museo del Oro was established in 1939, under the auspices of the Colombia's Banco de la República, to acknowledge the importance and value of the country's Precolumbian heritage of gold, and to create a means by which it could be collected and studied.   JJ

DESCRIPTION
The figures here are essentially flat with flexed knees. Their hands rest on their stomachs, and their chests are slightly raised. The fingers and toes are indicated by simple grooves. They wear two-strand belts, necklaces, and false-filigree headdresses. They have coffee-bean eyes, added mouths, and large triangular noses from which rods project. Their headdresses are a series of lateral scrolls, with the addition of a top structure on the figure to the right. This structure is an upside-down triangle on a wide shaft with three scrolls on the top. Suspension loops are at the back of the head; the ornaments were cast by the lost-wax process.   HK

EX. COLL.
Sale, Köln, Lempertz, December 14, 1966, lots 1821, 1822.

EXHIBITED
New York, The Museum of Primitive Art, 1969, no. 159.

37

Figure pendant

STYLE UNDETERMINED

5TH–10TH CENTURY (?)

H. $2\frac{3}{4}$ in. | 7 cm.   W. $1\frac{7}{8}$ in. | 4·9 cm.

Colombian figure pendants, without masks, are among the simplest depictions of human beings produced in Precolumbian goldwork. While these figures are known in sufficient variety to indicate stylistic, if not temporal, differences, they seem to be composed of a certain basic set of features. The pendants represent nude, standing males, wearing large headdresses, sometimes elaborate ones. 'Belts' are customary, but not mandatory, and nose or ear ornaments, necklaces, and armbands can be worn. Phalli are frequently depicted, at times erect, in what may be ceremonial representations (Cooke and Bray, this volume).

The pendant here is a good example of this figure type. The necklace and nose ornament are optional. The nose ornament is a short, broad rod. In some Colombian images, two short rods are worn in the nose at the same time. The figure, which is fabricated flat, has been given vestiges of body bulk by a gentle rounding through the center of the torso and legs.   JJ

DESCRIPTION

The figure is essentially flat with flexed knees, but the sides of the figure are bent backwards, giving it a slight profile. The grooved hands rest on the chest, and the genitals are depicted. The figure wears a two-strand belt around the lower torso, and a three-string necklace. The flat face is outlined by an angular double molding. The eyes are of the coffee-bean type, and the mouth is made by incision. The slightly hooked nose is enormous; there is a round-end rod through the tip. The false-filigree headdress consists of two rows of adjoining scrolls projecting laterally from the head and across the top of it. After casting by the lost-wax process, excess gold was not removed from the spaces between the legs, and between the body and arms, nor at the neck. A suspension loop is at the back of the neck.   HK

EX. COLL.

Sale, London, Sotheby and Co., March 29, 1965, lot 51.

EXHIBITED

New York, The Museum of Primitive Art, 1969, no. 159.

38

Figure pendant

TOLIMA

5TH–10TH CENTURY (?)

H. 5⅞ in.|14·8 cm.   W. 3½ in.|8·9 cm.

The stylized figures of Tolima are the most geometrized of the pendants that include zoomorphic and/or anthropomorphic references. There are two basic configurations: one in which the pendant has a 'winged' body, the other in which the body is all splayed arms and legs, like this one. The bodies of the winged figures have, below the wings, elaborated middles, perhaps to be read as feathers, and they can be given a tail of differing shapes. The customary tail is an 'anchor' with extended, rounded-off ends. Both pendant forms are flat, with only the details of the face raised; mouths, particularly, can be emphasized. Rabbitlike ears atop the head are customary, although series of short, straight projections also appear. On occasion, both elements are used.

The pendant figures with the splayed arms and legs are interesting for the equality of parts. Arms and legs always have the same length, width, and angles of bend, and no anatomical details ever appear on them. The long, anchor-shaped tail is a curious but consistent feature of most of the pendants with this image, although there are a few with no tail at all. The pendants appear to have been made over a considerable period of time and with considerable continuity of meaning. The prehistory of the Tolima region, in southwestern Colombia, is poorly known, however. It has received little professional archaeological attention.   JJ

DESCRIPTION

This pectoral depicts a flat, abstract anthropomorphic figure with raised bent arms and splayed bent legs arranged as mirror images along a vertical and horizontal axis; it terminates in an anchor-shaped element. A triangular face with an arched forehead, outlined by a single raised molding, sits on the narrow neck. The eyes and mouth are small ovals, while the nose is a short, vertical bar, slightly constricted at the bridge and connected to the figure's forehead. The headdress has ten raylike projections, which might imitate plumes. The object was made by lost-wax casting, and the extremities were stretched by hammering. A suspension loop is at the back of the neck. Except for the recessed areas of the face and neck, the piece is totally smooth and has a high polish.

HK

EXHIBITED

New York, The Museum of Primitive Art, 1969, no. 154.

39

Face pendant

TOLIMA (?)

5TH–10TH CENTURY (?)

H. 2½ *in.*|6·2 *cm.*   W. 2 *in.*|5·2 *cm.*

One of the intriguing aspects of certain Colombian pendants is the depiction of human figures that themselves wear pendants. An incidence of this can be seen here on a pendant in the form of a human head. The face is adorned with a neck ornament and a fancy headdress with sweeping side elements and a central core made of carefully wrought swirls. A tiny neck ornament, although only half-an-inch high, is clearly visible and recognizable as a type of stylized Tolima figure pendant. The full-sized Tolima pendants are flat and totally schematized, qualities that are rendered in the tiny image here. Furthermore, eyes and mouth are indicated in the simple round head of the image, and the geometrized body is 'striped'; these are, again, features that have counterparts in full-sized Tolima pendants. Below the tiny ornament, the pendant ends in a shape akin to that of tweezer tongs.

Colombia's department of Tolima has given its name to the distinctive schematized figures. So distinctive is the schematization, in fact, that its presence has been the only certain diagnostic feature for Tolima objects. Tolima images are much more surely identified than is a Tolima style.   JJ

DESCRIPTION

The ornament features a human face with an elaborate headdress and a crescent element at the bottom. The face, worked in relief, has coffee-bean-type eyes set into sockets formed by the nose and forehead ridges. Across the top of the head is a tripartite band, of which the central element is twisted. The front element ends in scrolls on the sides of the head at eye level. Above it, the false-filigree headdress rises, a series of adjoining wires terminating in scrolls, the inner ones coiling downward, the outer ones upward. Under the chin, the image of a Tolima figure is worked in low relief. The crescent shape at the bottom is slightly convex. The edges are rounded and bend backward. The piece was made by lost-wax casting, and the head is hollow. Two holes through the back of the head provided the means by which the piece was suspended. The front of the ornament is well polished and smooth. The back shows casting roughness.

HK

EXHIBITED

New York, The Museum of Primitive Art, 1969, no. 158, illustrated.
Leningrad, 1976, no. 87, illustrated.

40

Two nose ornaments

SINÚ

5TH–10TH CENTURY (?)

H. 1¼ *in.* | 3·2 *cm.*   1¾ *in.* | 4·4 *cm.*

W. 1⅜ *in.* | 3·6 *cm.*   1⅞ *in.* | 4·8 *cm.*

Of the very many varieties of ancient Colombian nose ornament, the paradigmatic type is the U-shaped one illustrated here. Elementally simple, the U-shaped ornaments are severely designed, the caps at the ends adding the only contrasting notes. The U, of course, can be modified. There are ornaments with straight sides, some are round-sided, and then there are those with sides that belly out, as these do. These ornaments are particularly substantial, for they are solid gold, and thus as weighty in fact as they are in aspect.

Significant Precolumbian development in the low-lying Sinú region was focused along the rivers, the Sinú, San Jorge, and Cauca. The last two waterways connect to the Magdalena, Colombia's most important river and north-to-south route through the country. Of the three Sinú 'provinces,' each associated with a river, it was Zenúfana that supplied the gold. Zenúfana was located along the lower Cauca and its tributary the Nechí, where gold sources were known (Plazas and Falchetti, this volume).

JJ

DESCRIPTION

These inverted U-shaped nose ornaments were made solid by hammering sheet metal into the appropriate shapes. The caps, in the form of 'nail heads,' were added separately. The surfaces are smooth and well polished.   HK

EXHIBITED

New York, The Museum of Primitive Art, 1969, no.165.

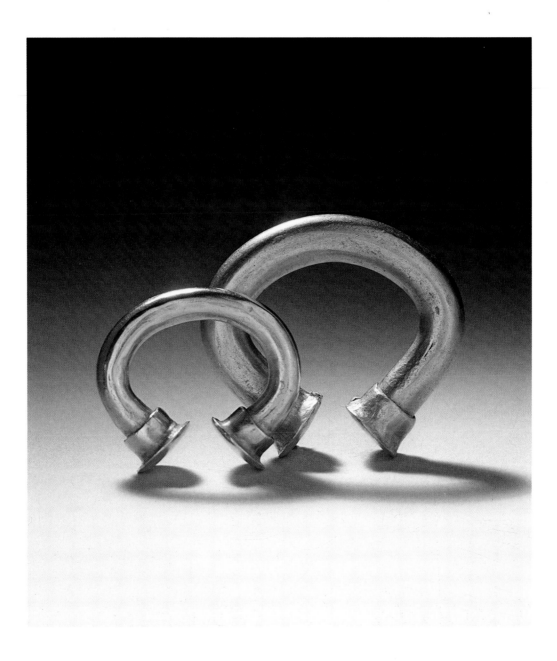

41

Two pairs of ear pendants

SINÚ

10TH–MID-16TH CENTURY (?)

W. 4⅜ in. | 11·1 cm.   2 in. | 5 cm.

Ear ornaments are ubiquitous in the personal jewelry of ancient America. South American peoples were especially fond of their use, and, for millennia, they made the ornaments in an enormous variety of pattern, size, and material. Many of the shapes and sizes of these ornaments are so extraordinary that to people of twentieth-century sensibility they seem unwearable. That is not the case with the pairs of ear pendants here, for they conform to a familiar, present-day pattern. They could be worn, more or less comfortably, hanging from the ear lobes. The delicate wire work of which they are composed gives the ornaments a light and graceful aspect of great appeal. Indeed, they were apparently much admired in ancient times too, for this type of ornament was made in some quantity (Plazas et al. 1979).

During the sixteenth century, the Sinú region of Caribbean Colombia, where ornaments of this type have been identified, was very rich in gold, a fact much commented upon by the Spanish conquerors. The desire for gold soon led them to search not only the living but the dead, and the looting of ancient graves began. Gold objects had been important mortuary offerings in the Sinú for centuries.

JJ

DESCRIPTION

The two pairs of fan-shaped ear ornaments are made of false filigree, which gives them a lacelike quality. Rows of openwork alternate with narrow, tripartite bands to form the body of the 'fan.' On top, the suspension rings are quite thick and enlarged at the opening. At the outermost top edges of the smaller pair, there is a decorative element that may be a stylized animal. The ornaments were cast by the lost-wax method.

HK

EXHIBITED

Smaller pair only: New York, The Museum of Primitive Art, 1969, no. 163.

42

Cache figure (tunjo)

MUISCA

10TH–MID-16TH CENTURY

H. 5⅞ *in.* | 15 *cm.*   W. 1⅝ *in.* | 4·2 *cm.*

Human images are the most common type of Muisca *tunjo*, the class of metal objects found in the high Andes around Bogotá, the present capital of Colombia, established by the Spaniards in 1539. The figures were used as votive objects; they were always differentiated by sex, and a great amount of specific detail was worked into them. Mothers and children, warriors, and coca chewers are common tunjo representations (Plazas and Falchetti, this volume). Published information on the specific groupings of the objects as they were cached—the chief manner of offering—is scant. The Museo del Oro in Bogotá has documented a good-sized group said to be the contents of a cache that was found shallowly buried in an open field in Funza, Cundinamarca (Duque Gomez 1979a).

Muisca tunjos were not worked after casting. Flaws were not corrected, excess metal was not removed, surfaces were not polished; they were left as they came out of the mold. Even molding sprues could remain. In the tunjo illustrated, the sprues can be seen beneath the figure's feet. The spontaneity of manufacture plus the artistic means—i.e., the flat surfaces on which all distinguishing detail is supplementary—and the manner in which they were used, set the Muisca tunjos apart from other Precolumbian gold objects.

JJ

DESCRIPTION

A flat plaque in the shape of a stylized male figure has details of face, arms, hands, genitals, legs, and feet made of round or flat wirelike elements. Ear ornaments, a prominent necklace, a single-strand belt, and a rectangular 'hat' are worn. The hat has outlined edges and, on either side, paired triangular perforations. The arms bend at the elbows, and an object is held in each hand. In the left is a coiled, rattle-shaped object and, in the right, two short 'staffs,' broken off at the top. The object was cast by the lost-wax technique; the rattle, like the staffs, appears to be broken at the top, all possibly a result of difficulty in casting. The unworked surface is plainly visible.   HK

EXHIBITED

Leningrad, 1976, no. 116, illustrated.

43

Three cache objects (tunjos)

MUISCA

10TH–MID-16TH CENTURY

L. 4½ *in.*|11·6 *cm.*   4⅜ *in.*|11·3 *cm.*   3 *in.*|7·5 *cm.*

The *tunjos* of the Muisca peoples were principally votive objects, and they were made in the forms of a variety of subjects, both animate and inanimate. Human figures with different accoutrements were the primary subject depicted, but tunjos in the shape of small staffs, spearthrowers, lime containers, snuffing tablets, hammocks, seashells, animals, and snakes were among the many that were produced. It is an intriguing array of apparently specific subjects. The snakes are often represented with whiskered or 'hairy' heads, as can be seen here.

As votive objects, the tunjos could be offered to sacred lakes. The Muisca ceremony that gave rise to the legend of El Dorado, the Gilded Man, is one in which offerings were made to Lake Guatavita. The oblation was performed at dawn when the Muisca ruler, covered with gold dust, was taken to the middle of the lake to make the offerings. As the light of the rising sun illuminated his 'golden' body, the legend of 'El Dorado' was born.

The Muiscas had lived in, and dominated, the high Andean plains of the present-day Cundinamarca and Boyáca departments for centuries when the Spaniards reached them in the 1530s. During many of those centuries, they had made gold objects—beginning as early as the seventh century—but just when they began to make the tunjos is not known.   JJ

DESCRIPTION

Left   The tunjo is a flat, wavy strip, on top of which a double, twisted thread follows the body undulations; the knob at its end is possibly the casting button. The body and head of the snake are outlined by a thin wirelike element and a central thread continues across the head and projects from the mouth like a tongue. Eyes, large 'coiled' ears, and whiskers are present.

Center   The flat, undulating body of the serpent has a cordlike element running along its center line, ending in what may be a casting button. Two small legs with tiny toes are just behind the head, which has eyes, small ears, and whiskers. In addition, a lower jaw is worked as a semicircle of adjoining threads under the head. The mouth is half open; inside, there may be a tongue.

Right   The serpent's body is decorated with a linear pattern, and the narrow head has a long snout and a pair of large projecting ears. The small eyes are of the dot-and-circle type; one dot is particularly tiny. Whiskers are present on one side of the mouth only; the others are missing.

All three serpents were cast by the lost-wax technique.

HK

EX. COLL.

Sale, right only, Köln, Lempertz, December 14, 1966, lot 1886.

EXHIBITED

Center only, Leningrad, 1976, no. 112, illustrated.

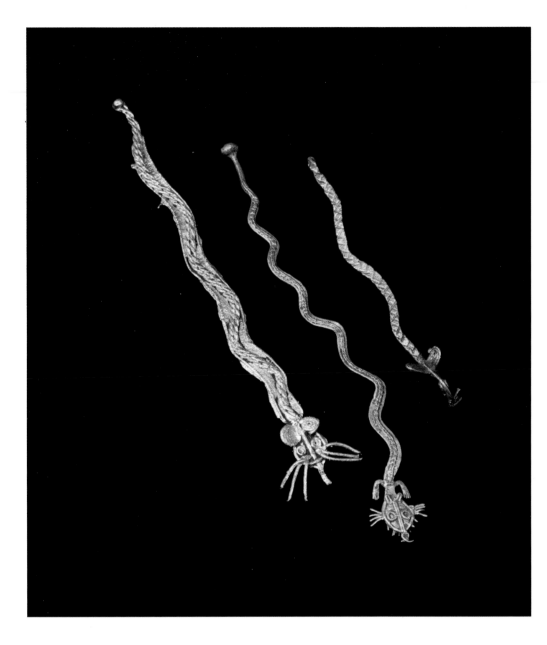

44

Masked-figure pendant

TAIRONA

10TH–MID-16TH CENTURY

H. 5¼ in. | 13.3 cm.   W. 5¾ in. | 14·6 cm.

Few Precolumbian gold pendants are as purposefully theatrical as the so-called Tairona *caciques*. Cacique, the word most frequently used by the Spaniards to mean 'chieftain' during the years of the Conquest, has maintained much the same meaning to this day. In Colombia, it has been applied to the Tairona pendants of the type illustrated, as a mark of respect for the flamboyant ornaments. Enormous headdresses, made up of big-beaked birds, spirals, stylized heads, and other elements, are worn by figures with a bold presence that belies their apparent ornamental function. Beneath the great headdress here, the figure wears a large bat mask (Legast 1982) with a prominent muzzle that is topped by a diamond-shaped nose. The big muzzle has often been identified as that of a crocodile or alligator (Lothrop et al. 1957). Other customary aspects of the cacique pendants are the hands-upon-hips stance and the double-spiral objects held in the hands. Tairona gold objects are markedly uniform in style. That style is quite individual, with complex elaborative detail wedded to smooth, polished surfaces. A distinct interest in three-dimensional form also characterizes Tairona works.   JJ

DESCRIPTION

This impressive pendant has a stylized male body shown standing with arms and legs bent. His hands, which rest on his hips, are indicated by five thin, gold wirelike elements; each holds an object made up of opposing scrolls. The figure's face is dominated by the squared-off snout displaying big teeth. The round eyes are set under two arched ridges that run from the corner of the chin to the front of the snout. Circular ear ornaments flank the head, and a ring for a dangler, now missing, is under the chin. Bands circle the shoulders, elbows, wrists, and waist. They do not continue on the back of the figure. A short central band decorates the leaf snout, and five raised balls of different sizes further articulate it. The toes are represented, and there are thin twisted bands at the ankles. The genitals are present.

The headdress is composed of a cap on which a pair of big-beaked birds are rendered three-dimensionally. Their hooked beaks end in a dangler. A circle with a raised ball decorates the center of the cap band. Behind the birds appear paired stylized animal heads in profile and paired groups of spirals. Danglers are in place at the outermost edges of the spirals, but are missing from the 'snouts' of the stylized animals. The object was cast by the lost-wax technique, and much core material remains inside. The danglers and some of the balls were added after casting. A pair of suspension loops is set at the back of the top of the head. Modern repair is visible in back.

HK

EX. COLL.

Collection Hoffmann, Geneva.

EXHIBITED

New York, The Museum of Primitive Art, 1969, no. 174, illustrated.
Leningrad, 1976, no. 119, illustrated.

PUBLISHED

Lapiner, 1976, page 389, fig. 830. Emmerich, 1979, page 95, fig. 3.

45

Bird spatula

POPOYÁN

11TH–MID-16TH CENTURY

H. 5⅜ *in.* | 13.8 *cm.*   W. 1⅞ *in.* | 4·7 *cm.*

Bird imagery is pervasive in objects from all the goldworking regions of Precolumbian America. The Isthmian eagle pendants, with their particular frontal display stance, are the best known, but ornaments of other bird-shapes were made. The present example depicts a 'diving' bird with displayed wings and tail visualized from the back. The linear patterns on them are a rendition of feathers, and their openness adds to the material, as well as the visual, weightlessness of the bird. The bird head is done with great economy; the curved lines of neck, beak, and crest tightly define its form and, at the same time, give it a strongly expressive character. The bird adorns the top of a lime spatula, the shaft of which is quite short. Spatulas were used to transfer the powdered lime from a container to the mouth when it was added to coca leaves for chewing. Coca-chewing paraphernalia was made in elaborate materials in Precolumbian times.

Objects in Popoyán style are few. They get their name from the city of Popoyán, in southwest Colombia, where a significant find, made in the 1920s (Braunholtz 1939), led to the definition of the style in goldwork. The style has also been called Cauca, after the department in which Popoyán is located.   JJ

DESCRIPTION

A bird, with long arched neck, is set at the top of the spatula, with a horizontal spread of tail and elegantly curved wings as its continuation. The bird's head is laterally flattened and has a crest of truncated triangles. Eyes, formed by coils, are on the sides of its head. The openwork design on the tail and wings is outlined by a precisely executed pattern. The narrow, squared-off shaft of the spatula was worked after casting, while the bird is in an as-cast state.   HK

EXHIBITED

Leningrad, 1976, no. 78, illustrated.

46

Nose ornament

CALDÁS (?)

13TH–MID-16TH CENTURY

H. 1⅝ *in.*|4·2 *cm.*   W. 2⅜ *in.*|5·9 *cm.*

Ornaments made from sheet gold worked by hammering are as common in Colombia as are objects of cast metal. Some Precolumbian peoples had a clear preference for using one method of working precious metals over the other, but there were those who used both methods with equally felicitous results. Such was the case in much of ancient Colombia. The nose ornament here, which is of a classic Colombian shape, was cast and then hammered. It has a pair of wingless birds facing each other across the nose opening. A good number of Colombian nose ornaments have pairs of similar birds, similarly placed, as their main decorative element.

At present it is difficult to assign these ornaments surely to a particular time, but it is possible that they are part of the Caldás complex, which dates to the last centuries before the Conquest. The Caldás complex is found in the middle Cauca River Valley, in much the same region that produced objects of Quimbaya style several centuries earlier.

JJ

DESCRIPTION

Two stylized birds embellish this semicircular nose ornament. The birds are in profile and are located to either side of a thickened ring that encircles the nose opening. The raised ring ends on, and reinforces, the support prongs of the ornament. The birds have open beaks, slender necks, and pointed tails; there are no wings. Their long legs are bent, and each has three toes. The outside edge is finely stippled. The object was worked and embossed after casting.   HK

EXHIBITED

New York, The Museum of Primitive Art, 1969, no. 166.

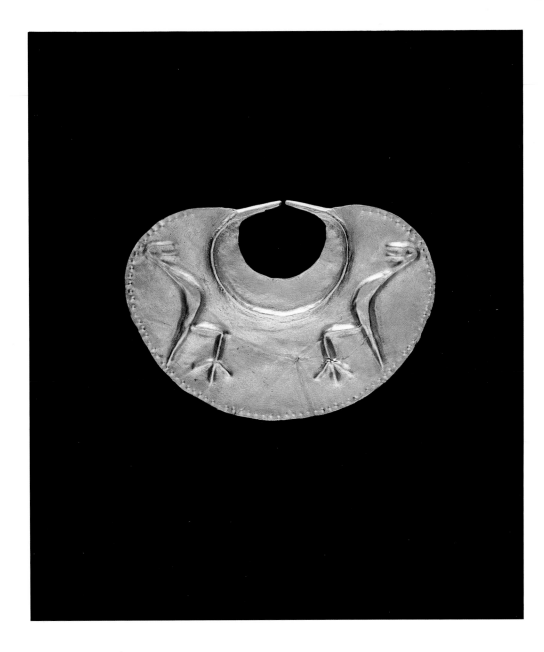

47

Pectoral disc with figure

CALDÁS (?)

13TH–MID-16TH CENTURY

Diam. 4⅞ in.|12·5 cm.

Among Colombian pectoral discs, there is a group in which a stylized, splayed figure appears; it is seen in the disc here. The figure is distinguished by the geometrized arms and legs, which are always shown in this schematized manner. The body and head can vary in detail. One of the curious aspects of the figure, however, is that it can be given a tail, which is usually long and bipartite, ending in spirals. On this disc, the spiraled tail is present; furthermore, similar tail elements have been used on either side of the figure, where they form a strong horizontal, effectively balancing the design. The representational meaning of these 'side-tails' is unclear, but it is possible that they functioned more as an artistic device than as a meaningful detail.

Some of the discs with this type of figure include images of birds similar to those on the preceding nose ornament. The discs may also belong to the Caldás complex of the Cauca River Valley. Hammered-gold objects are characteristic of southwestern Colombia in the late centuries of the Precolumbian era (Plazas and Falchetti, this volume).

JJ

DESCRIPTION

A stylized, composite figure is worked in repoussé on this pectoral disc. Two continuous lines and a row of small bosses encircle the rim, framing the symmetrically arranged composition. The figure is linear, with spread-out, raised arms and splayed, bent legs. The representation of the fingers and toes recalls organic forms. Eyes, nose, and nose ring are present on the face. To the sides of the body and between the legs are two straight projections ending in opposing scrolls. The latter may be a tail. A hole for suspension is provided above the head of the figure.   HK

EXHIBITED

New York, The Museum of Primitive Art, 1969, no. 179.

48

Two nose ornaments

CALDÁS OR SONSO (?)

13TH–MID-16TH CENTURY (?)

H. 3½ *in.* | 8·9 *cm.*   3⅞ *in.* | 9·8 *cm.*

W. 8⅜ *in.* | 21·3 *cm.*   10 *in.* | 25·5 *cm.*

Some of the very many ancient American nose ornaments have strong resemblances to natural forms, in marked contrast to those of artful or inorganic design. The two nose ornaments illustrated here, their long projections bristling and balancing sedately outwards, bring to the mind of the modern viewer exaggerated mustaches or whiskers. Because indigenous American peoples have little facial hair, it is unlikely that the ornaments were thought of as mustachelike to their makers, but it is possible that they had animal associations. For instance, the nose ornaments may have represented feline whiskers, and were possibly seen as an abbreviated version of an animal mask. An unusual feature of these particular ornaments is the extraordinarily long central section, which would have obscured the mouth of the wearer.   JJ

DESCRIPTION

The side projections of these two nose ornaments extend upwards, like cat whiskers, giving the whole a slightly concave topline. At the center of this line, there is a semicircular opening, the bottom of which is folded over the top, reinforcing the crosspiece of the opening. To the sides of the nose openings are holes, one at either side on the smaller ornaments, and two at either side on the larger. Several gold strips are pulled through the paired holes on the larger ornament. There are three pairs of 'whiskers' on the small ornament and four on the large. One of the whiskers on the smaller ornament was broken and repaired in ancient times; it was reattached by stapling. Beneath the nose openings, the ornaments end in a half-oval shape that would have covered the mouth.

HK

EX. COLL.
Sale, Köln, Lempertz, December 14, 1966, lots 1807, 1808.

EXHIBITED
New York, The Museum of Primitive Art, 1969, no. 181.

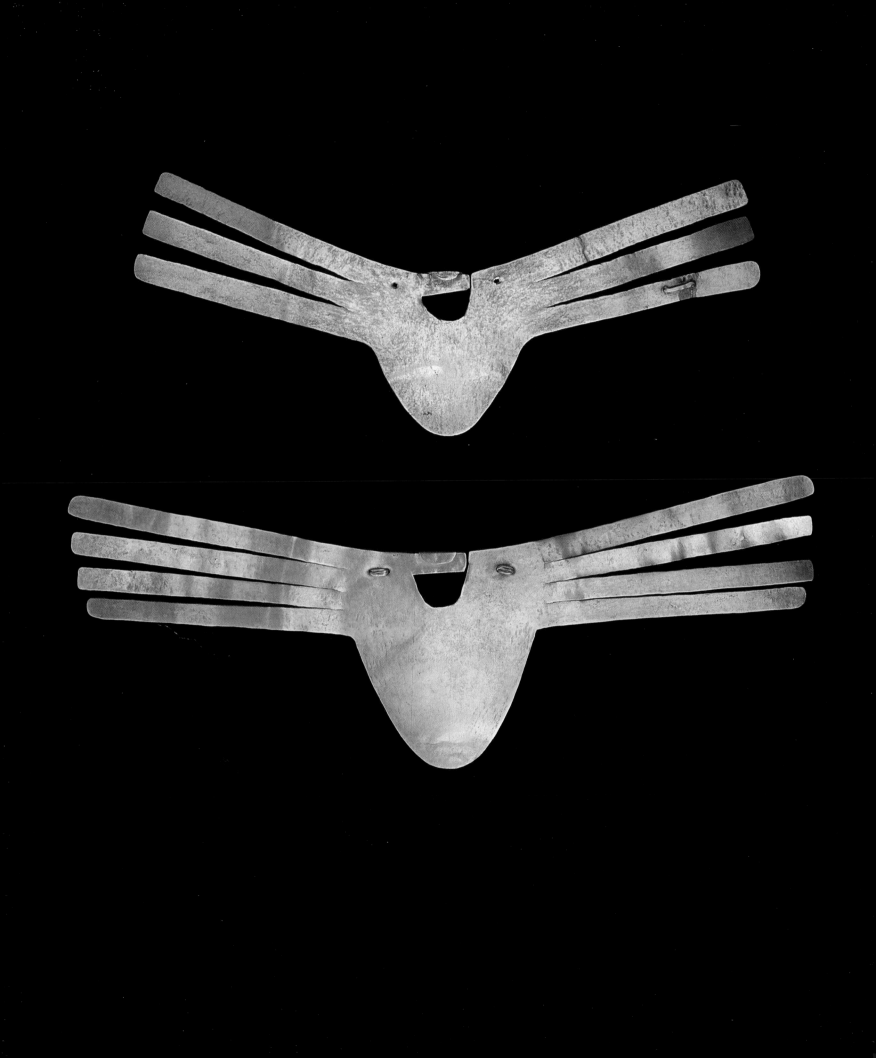

49

Pectoral ornament

CALDÁS OR SONSO (?)
13TH–MID-16TH CENTURY (?)
H. 14⅜ in. | 36·4 cm.   W. 10¼ in. | 26 cm.

Pectorals of very large size, which would have fully covered the chest, are among the ornamental gold forms used in ancient Colombia. Many of these ornaments are without decoration, relying completely on carefully outlined shape for their presence and character. Such is the case here with the tall, slender pectoral, which is almost calligraphic in the elegance and simplicity of its conception. Pure in its plainness, it is almost line itself.

The majority of the large, hammered, pectoral ornaments come from the Calima area and are earlier in time than the present example, and much more decorated. The Calima goldworking region, on the Pacific side of southwestern Colombia, was named for the Calima River, near the headwaters of which burials with major gold objects were found during the early part of this century. At that time, new towns were being established, and ancient remains were discovered as the land was cleared.

JJ

DESCRIPTION

This chest ornament, in the shape of the letter T, has raised arms and a concave topline. There is a hole near the middle of the topline, and several strips of flat gold sheet are wound through the hole and over the edge. It is possible that this is meant as a decorative element. One surface of this hammered ornament is somewhat more carefully finished than the other.   HK

EX. COLL.
Sale, Köln, Lempertz, December 14, 1966, lot 1806.

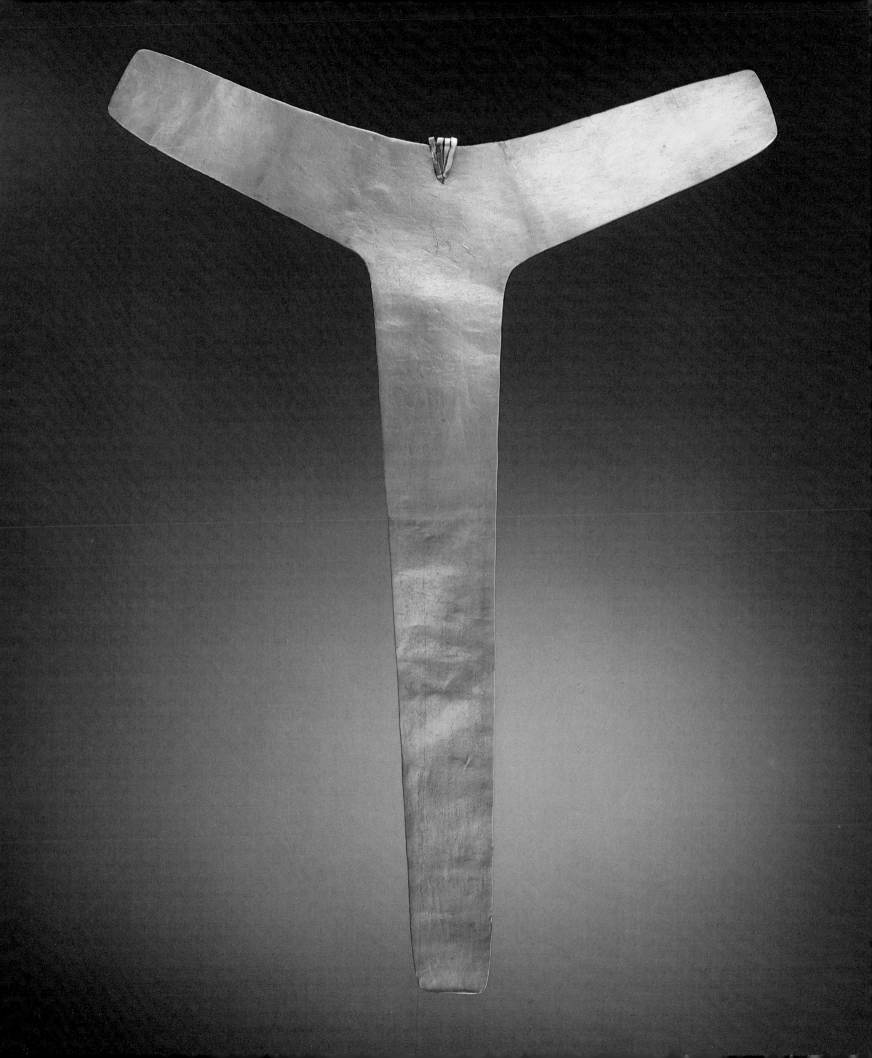

50

Pectoral ornament with face

CALDÁS OR SONSO (?)

13TH–MID-16TH CENTURY (?)

H. 13¼ in. | 33·6 cm.　W. 12¼ in. | 31.3 cm.

Facial details on objects of inorganic shape, particularly when no head is defined, are intriguing in their dimension of meaning. They can be interpreted either as anthropomorphized 'shapes' or as shorthand notations for fuller human images, without direct relationship to the flat surfaces they embellish. A sizable number of early pectorals with faces, such as those in Calima style, have clearly delimited heads that are rendered in high relief (Cat. no. 55, this volume). The pectoral illustrated here, on the other hand, has eyes, nose, mouth, and beard indicated near the top, but there is no definition of the head.

Large, flat pectorals, when provenance information is available, come from southwestern Colombia. A pectoral very close in many of its details to the present example is in the Museo del Oro in Bogotá. It is without provenance (Pérez de Barradas, 1965, no. 234).

JJ

DESCRIPTION

A chest ornament of sheet metal in the shape of a T, with slightly raised arms and a concave topline, has a row of small bosses along its entire outside edge. A face is worked in repoussé in the center of the topline. Oval eyes, a broad nose, and two narrow lips, with a series of vertical parallel ridges beneath them to form a beard, make up the face. Two large cracks on either side of the shaft were mended in ancient times with gold strips. Another crack on the top of the right arm has been more recently mended. A hole for suspension is above the nose.　　　　　　HK

EXHIBITED

New York, The Museum of Primitive Art, 1969, no. 180.

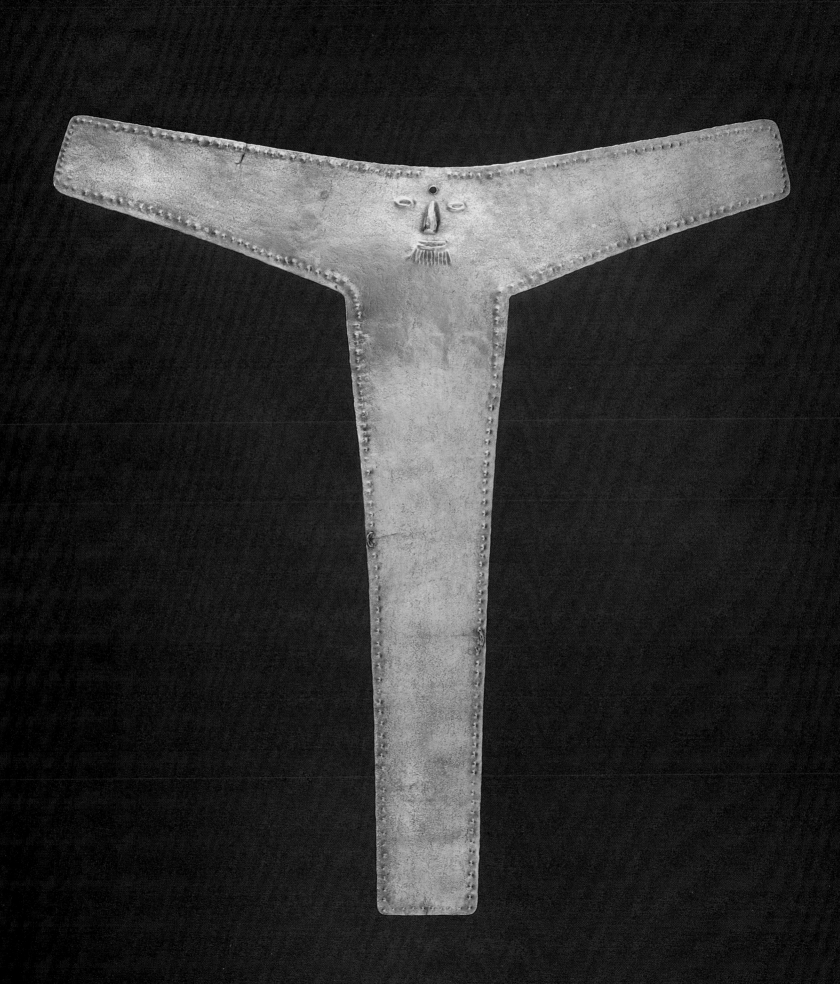

51

Pair of ear pendants

CALDÁS OR SONSO (?)

13TH–MID-16TH CENTURY (?)

H. 9⅝ in.|24·5 cm.   Diam. discs 3¾ in.|9·5 cm.

Precolumbian ear ornaments composed with large, circular, pendant attachments infrequently survive intact. They are known today primarily from the pendant discs, which remain more routinely than the assemblies that supported them. The assemblies seem to have been attached in an impermanent manner, possibly for greater flexibility of the whole, or perhaps to allow for an interchanging of parts. Many of the assemblies were mere hoops of gold wire, which could be easily lost. Pairs of discs exist in openwork examples as well as in a variety of closed shapes akin to those illustrated here. The illustrated pair is still intact, with its major supports in place, showing how grand the ornaments can be.

Pendant discs for ear ornaments appear to come principally from the Calima and Nariño regions of Colombia.   JJ

DESCRIPTION

These ear ornaments are made up of a long supporting element, about an inch wide, which is attached to a pendant disc at the bottom. At both ends of the support, the sheet gold is shaped into thin, round wire. The wire is bent at the top for insertion into the ear lobes; at the bottom, the wire goes through a hole in the disc and is wound around the rim. The discs have a raised center, outlined by the two embossed ridges on the adjacent rims. In almost evenly spaced quadrants, three embossed rays project to the edge of the rim.

HK

52

Pair of ear ornaments

SONSO

13TH–MID-16TH CENTURY

L. 5 *in.*|12·7 *cm.*   4¾ *in.*|12·2 *cm.*

A mid-sixteenth century Spanish description of the Calima region mentioned gold in use in the following manner:

Both men and women have their noses pierced, and wear a sort of twisted nails in them of gold, about the thickness of a finger, called caricuris. *They also wear necklaces of fine gold, rarely worked, and ear rings of twisted gold. Their former dress consisted of a small cloth in front, and another over the shoulders, the women covering themselves from the waist downwards with a cotton mantle. When their chiefs die, they make large and deep tombs inside their houses, into which they put a good supply of food, arms, and gold, with the bodies.*
(Cieza de Leon 1864: 102)

Archaeology has defined a phase in Calima that covers the last few centuries before the Conquest. The phase, named Sonso, was first identified by excavation in the Cauca Valley (Bray and Moseley 1969–70), along one of the main north-south waterways in Colombia. The phase name is now applied to the gold objects assigned to that time period, and the twisted wire ear ornaments are among them. The pair illustrated here is larger than the average Sonso 'ear rings.'   JJ

DESCRIPTION

Gold wire, made of hammered sheet, has been bent into the shape of ear ornaments. Ten and eleven loops, respectively, are twisted into the side of each ornament, which ends in a large spiral. The other, straight, side terminates in a simple blunt end.

HK

EXHIBITED

Leningrad, 1976, no. 76, illustrated.

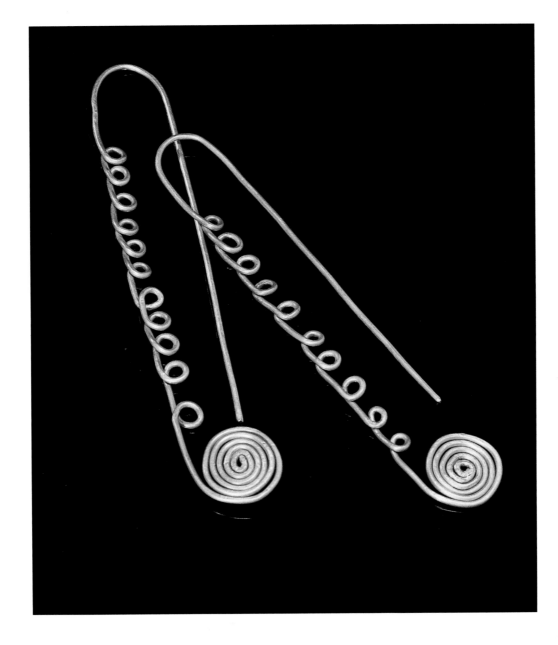

53

Funerary mask

CALIMA

3RD–10TH CENTURY (?)

H. 7¾ in. | 19·7 cm.   W. 9½ in. | 24·2 cm.

The face-sized masks of Calima are among the most impressive of extant Precolumbian gold objects. Substantial in scale, they are always human in aspect. The masks were produced in a considerable range of depth, from flat ones to those in high relief. The flat masks are large and almost round; only the nose and the outlines of eyes and mouth are raised from their surfaces. These masks have small, pupil-like holes pierced through the center of the eyes. Another flat group has, additionally, elevated cheeks. Next are the masks of schematized volumes, where a semblance of natural bulk and weight has been worked into the face, as is seen here. These have pierced pupils also, but the rectangular mouth is fully open. Finally, there are masks made with the depth of a human face, without the convention of the schematized background shape or particularized volumes like the 'apple' cheeks. This last group has a complete opening for the eyes as well as for the mouth. It is interesting to note the consistency with which certain features—eyes, nose, mouth, and cheeks—are emphasized throughout the entire assemblage.

The manner of mortuary use of the masks is conjectural. It is usually assumed that, in the tomb, they were placed in some relationship to the head of the deceased, either over the face or as a 'false' head on a mummy bundle or coffin. In late periods in Calima, wood coffins were used (Schuler-Schömig 1981), and it is possible that they were employed in early times as well. There is evidence from nearby Tierradentro that an early mask was permanently attached to a wood support (Bray 1981b: 84).

JJ

DESCRIPTION

A broad, oval, sheet-gold mask has nose, mouth, and cheeks worked in strong relief. The top of the mask is flat, forming a narrow forehead, while the lower part has a more naturalistic roundness to the chin and jaws. The almond-shaped eyes, spectacle-like in outline, are set under a brow ridge of similar shape. The eyes have cut out, perfectly circular pupils; there are 'bags' beneath the eyes. The broad, fleshy nose has flaring nostrils, and between it and the bulging round cheeks are deep depressions. There is a marked degree of naturalism in the treatment of the nose and the area under the eyes. The cheeks are pronounced round shapes. The rectangular mouth is cut out, and the edges of the opening are bent in such a manner as to make the lips quite thick. The surface is well polished; chased details are present. There are three small holes on either side of the cheeks for attachment.

HK

EXHIBITED

New York, The Museum of Primitive Art, 1969, no. 148, illustrated.
New York, The Metropolitan Museum of Art, 1972.
Leningrad, 1976, no. 52, illustrated.

PUBLISHED

Lapiner, 1976, page 383, fig. 820.
Emmerich, 1979, page 94, fig. 1.

54

Headdress ornament

CALIMA

3RD–10TH CENTURY (?)

H. 10 *in.* | 25·4 *cm.*   W. 9⅜ *in.* | 23·6 *cm.*

Calima headdress ornaments are flamboyant, ostentatious objects, with many appurtenances—featherlike projections, multiple danglers, added parts—that would have swayed and fluttered when moved, catching and reflecting light. Imposing and stately, the ornaments may have been attached to turbanlike headdresses, necessarily of sufficient material to support both the weight and the presence of the gold ornament. The example illustrated here is a traditional Calima type. A central arrow-shaped element at the bottom would have hung down over the forehead and nose; worked on it, in repoussé, is a human face. In the center of the ornament is the main elaborative detail, a human head rendered in high relief. This head, which has two big dish-shaped pendants in its ears, wears a nose ornament so large that it virtually obscures the face. Upside-down profile heads, possibly of birds, appear at the sides of the main head. The repoussé surfaces merge into the plainer ones of the paired 'plumes' at the top. One of the intriguing aspects of these ornaments is the compounding of faces. In addition to the central, important one, there are two other faces on the ornament here. All of this would have appeared above the face of the wearer.

An archaeologically important part of the Calima region is the area near the headwaters of the Calima river and along the adjacent section of the Cauca River Valley of the Cordillera Occidental. Major gold finds were made there in the early twentieth century, when many Calima-style gold objects entered private collections in Colombia.

JJ

DESCRIPTION

At the center of this diadem, a human head was worked in high relief. The face has closed eyes and a big nose with well-defined nostrils. It wears a caplike headdress, which is three-tiered and semicircular. No mouth is indicated. Much of the face is concealed by an H-shaped nose ornament and large saucer-shaped ear discs, all of which are attached by means of heavy gold wire. In the middle of the nose ornament is an embossed face, and, at each of its four ends, there are birds' heads in profile. An extension beneath the central head is decorated with an embossed face and rows of circles along the lower edge. Beside it are lateral projections, possibly birds' heads, with a circular eye, rectangular mouth band, and upward-pointing beaks.

Along the lower edge of each lateral projection are ten holes on either side, to which long, half-round danglers are strapped. Further repoussé decoration includes rows of bosses and mouth bands. Between the lateral projections and the plumes, there are triangular pro-truberances with three-pointed 'stars,' and, beneath them, there are embossed animals, the tails of which extend up the smaller plumes. The large central plumes are well burnished; the smaller ones carry five half-round danglers. The central face seems to have been raised from the front over a mold.   HK

EXHIBITED

New York, The Museum of Primitive Art, 1969, no. 149.

55

Pectoral ornament with face

CALIMA

3RD–10TH CENTURY (?)

H. 6⅝ in. | 16·8 cm.   W. 7⅝ in. | 19·4 cm.

The raised heads on Calima pectorals have the same puffy-eyed, prominent-nosed human faces that appear on the Calima headdress pieces; they wear the same close-fitting caps and enormous ear and nose pendants. Whether on chest or head ornaments, there is remarkably little variation in these faces. One or two types of caps and certain embossed details on the nose pendant represent the widest margins of variability. The most frequently depicted cap is that with the small rectangular crest seen here. The nose pendant, with minor exceptions, is a large H with an embossed face at its center. The specifics of the embossed face and the elements along the edge of the H are not standard; apparently, these features did not need to conform so rigidly to prescribed patterns. The closed eyes, which are such a conspicuous part of the heads, are associated with death in many Precolumbian contexts. They may have that meaning here, but no other detail points to this interpretation.

The pectorals that these standardized heads embellish are known in a given number of shapes. The kidney shape, shown in the illustrated example, was perhaps that most customarily employed.   JJ

DESCRIPTION

This chest ornament, of notched elliptical shape, has a central, high-relief mask. Made by being pressed into a mold, the mask shows the wrinkles characteristic of metal worked in this manner; there are wrinkles under the nose and around the chin and ear ornaments. The face itself has closed eyes and a mouth that is not visible. It wears a cap with a stepped structure on top and hanging ornaments in the nose and ears. The septum and ear lobes are perforated, and gold wire attaches the ornaments through these holes. The H-shaped nose ornament is decorated with a central face and three circles on each side. The ear ornaments are concave discs with simple repoussé line decoration.

Around the border of the pectoral a repeat pattern of diagonally arranged hook motifs is worked in repoussé. The hook motifs alternate with bands of horizontal lines worked from the front. The pectoral was suspended by means of the two holes at the top.

HK

56

Pair of ear spools

CALIMA

1ST–3RD CENTURY (?)

Diam. 2¼ in.|5·7 cm.   L. 2½ in.|6·3 cm.

Biconical, or spool-shaped, ear ornaments are known from the Calima region of Colombia. Details of manufacture point to an early date for them. The spools, made of relatively light-weight gold, are fabricated by crimping or pinning the parts together. The round, decorated ends of the examples here were crimped to the cone-shaped sides, and the sides were pinned together along a clearly visible, many-holed seam. The spools probably had wood cores, making them a good deal less fragile and more wearable than they are now. There is some evidence that the spools were worn lengthwise as pendants, hanging from the ear instead of being placed through the lobe.

Objects fabricated in this manner have recently been published from a Calima-region tomb (Plazas 1983). The gold objects of this tomb are ambitious, often of hollow, three-dimensional form; they may be early in date. Lime containers in the shape of human and animal figures are the most complex works. Ear spools from nearby Tierradentro, also thought to be early in date (Bray 1978: no. 459), are similar in many respects to the Calima ear spools. They are about the same size and are round and double-ended, but they are very different in detail. Tierradentro examples are straight-sided and visibly hollow through the center, and the patterned decoration is on the central shaft.

JJ

DESCRIPTION

These biconical ear ornaments are made of thin sheet gold. They are hollow; no core is present. The central cones of each ornament are made of a single piece of metal, which is joined at a seam with holes along the edge. The original, tiny attachment pins or nails that went through these holes are lost. On the flat ends of the cones, separate, circular discs of decorated sheet are attached by crimp fastening. The geometric decoration on the discs was achieved by working from the front, perhaps against a form. A four-pointed 'star' and regularly repeated scrolls, dots, and dashes fill the surfaces. There is a central hole in each. These ornaments have suffered considerable damage and have been mended; modern repair can be seen in many places. HK

57

Ornamented tweezer

CALIMA

3RD–10TH CENTURY (?)

H. $3\frac{7}{8}$ *in.* | 9·9 *cm.*   W. $1\frac{3}{4}$ *in.* | 4·5 *cm.*

This embellished pair of tweezers, decorated both front and back with 'grinning' faces, is a good indication that the ancient use of these small implements was more than functional. Indeed, such is the elaboration here that it is hard to conceive of the object as being employed for a mundane matter like the plucking of facial hair. The transformation of functional forms into elaborated pieces, made of precious materials and indicative of special status, is a known phenomenon in Precolumbian America. Particularly true of celt and/or knifelike shapes, it is possible that such a transformation occurred in the Calima-area gold tweezers. On the tweezers illustrated here, two superimposed faces, with fine sets of teeth, might be interpreted as skeletal, were it not for the rather fleshy-looking noses.

The Calima collections of Bogotá's Museo del Oro are particularly strong, for important finds were made near the municipality of Restrepo in the years immediately following the founding of the museum in 1939. Many of the gold objects unearthed at that time entered the new museum and were published in the early 1950s (Pérez de Barradas 1954), when the institution began its considerable efforts to inform its public.

JJ

DESCRIPTION

The object was made of sheet gold; when fully formed, the tapered shaft was bent double. Each side is decorated with two fantastic faces, one above the other, in the center of the tweezer. The eyes and mouths, displaying two rows of teeth, are worked on the front surface by many small inscribed lines, while the noses were raised from the back. The edges of the rectangular jaws alternate curvilinear and angular forms, and scroll patterns continue onto them, worked out from the faces.

HK

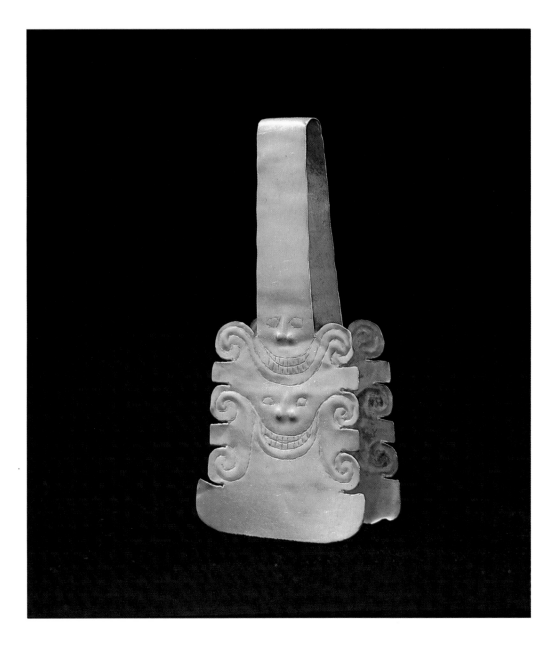

58

Three pairs of tweezers

CALIMA

1ST–10TH CENTURY (?)

H. 2⅛ in.|5·5 cm.   3⅝ in.|9·2 cm.   1⅞ in.|4·7 cm.

Of the utilitarian forms in gold—chisels, needles, fish hooks, and the like—tweezers are by far the largest and most impressive. While they may, indeed, have been used for the elimination of sparse facial hair, as is often said, even undecorated tweezers were made in sizes, and with a presence, that exceed utility. The plain ones have carefully balanced, pleasing shapes. This lack of ornamentation would make them difficult, if not impossible, to place if they had not been discovered with sufficient regularity in the Calima region to assign them to it. They have also, however, been found throughout much of southwestern Colombia.

A recent report of a tomb find made along the Río Chiquito, in the Tierradentro region (Duque Gomez 1979b), has a pair of tweezers among its contents. Other items of gold in this find were bracelets, a long pin, and a pair of ornaments, apparently ear pendants.

JJ

DESCRIPTION

Three pairs of anchor-shaped tweezers have jaws with curved blades and slightly convex surfaces. They were made by hammering and have been worked to a well-polished finish.

HK

EX. COLL.

Sale, right only, Köln, Lempertz, December 14, 1966, lot 1837.

EXHIBITED

Center and right only:
New York, The Museum of Primitive Art, 1969, no. 167.

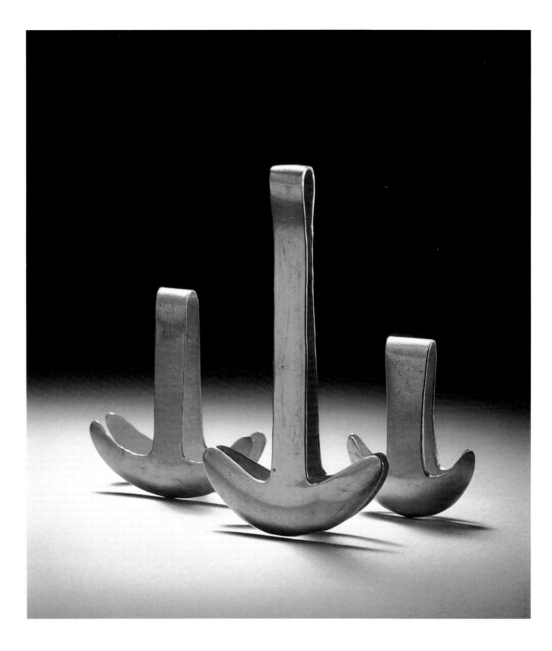

59

Nose ornament

PIARTAL
7TH–12TH CENTURY (?)
H. 2⅛ *in.*|5·4 *cm.*   W. 5¾ *in.*|14·6 *cm.*

The high Andean plateau of the department of Nariño in Colombia continues into adjacent Ecuador, and, in ancient times, it was a continuous culture area. The styles of goldwork on either side of the border are the same. These styles, however, are a peculiar, perhaps unique, combination of elements. While northern, or Colombian, and southern, or Ecuadorian, features can be pointed out in them, the Nariño works are not quite like either one (Plazas 1977–78).

One group, called Piartal or Piartal–Tuza, includes a great number of nose ornaments. These ornaments are composed almost exclusively of geometric shapes with no human or animal references. Such an ornament is that illustrated here, which is as carefully and abstractly designed as any contemporary goldsmith could wish. The manipulation of shape itself appears to be the underlying concern of the makers of these ornaments. Few Piartal nose ornaments are exactly alike, as if there had been, at that time, a premium on inventiveness. This is one of the reasons why the Piartal group is so striking, for much Precolumbian goldwork appears to be more concerned with the able execution of traditional forms.

JJ

DESCRIPTION

This sheet metal nose ornament is made up of a central section with horizontal projections. The center is a semicircle with a keyhole-shaped opening in the middle of the upper, straight side, and a crescent with a triangular 'tail' beneath it. The L-shaped projections at the sides support bow-tie-like shapes. The surface of the object is totally smooth and well polished.

HK

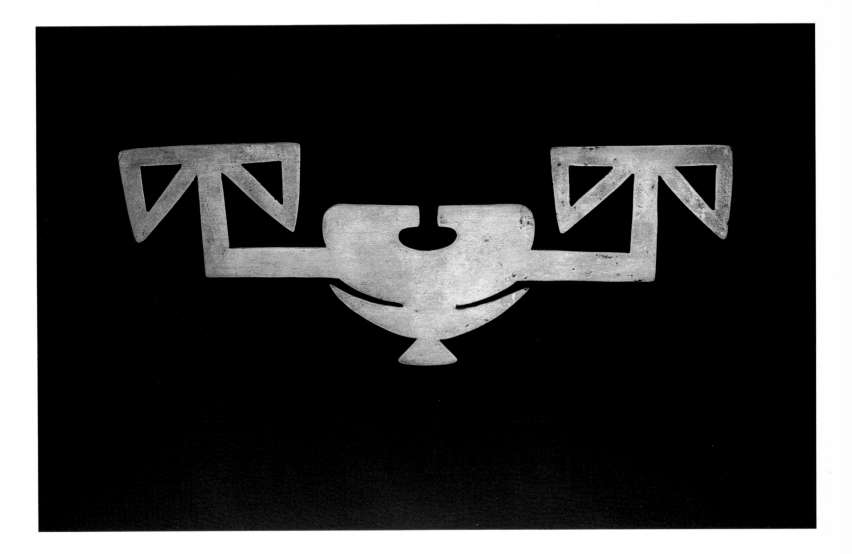

60

Pectoral disc

CAPULÍ (?)

7TH–12TH CENTURY (?)

Diam. 8 in. | 20·2 cm.

Many plain gold discs of different sizes come from the Nariño area of highland Colombia and Ecuador. These are named Capulí for the archaeological phase to which they belong. Capulí works, when other than severely elegant, like the disc seen here, exhibit much the same type of individuality noted for other Nariño objects. Many of the plain Capulí discs exist in pairs and were worn as ear ornaments, the large pendant circles hanging at the bottom of a hooplike gold wire. The present example is clearly too large for such use; it would have been a pectoral.

The four suspension holes raise the intriguing question of how the disc was strung to be worn. With the exception of a few of those found on the desert-dry Pacific coast of Peru, ancient American 'stringings' seldom remain even partially intact. Reconstructions of Precolumbian neck-ornament assemblies are thus routinely hypothetical. While more than one hole was necessary for stability when stringing a disc of this size, four is more than sufficient. The additional holes, however, would have allowed for a more-ornamented stringing, with cords or thongs of different colors, and/or the inclusion of elements like tassels, knots, or even smaller gold discs as danglers.

JJ

DESCRIPTION

This hammered circular disc is slightly convex. Some of the working texture remains on the surface. A row of four suspension holes is centrally placed near the top.

HK

61

Helmet

STYLE UNDETERMINED

3RD–10TH CENTURY (?)

H. 3½ in.|9 cm.   Cir. 21¾ in.|55 cm.

Gold helmets in the shape of close-fitting, round caps were made in both Colombia and the Isthmus in Precolumbian times. Such a basinlike cap was placed on the head of the famous Panamanian leader Parita, when he was made ready for burial in 1519 (Cook and Bray, this volume). Many of these helmets were embossed with elaborate decoration, while others were plain. The plain ones appear to have been embellished with added materials, perhaps feathers or gold danglers.

In Colombia, the plain helmets can have a double row of holes running from one side to the other over the crest of the cap, as in the example illustrated here. The holes are thought to have held the added decoration, and various attempts at reconstructing this adornment have been made at the Museo del Oro in Bogotá (Bogotá 1982: 19). Some of the helmets are thought to have been tied onto the head by means of 'chinstraps' attached to the side holes near the bottom edge.   JJ

DESCRIPTION

This plain hemispherical helmet has two rows of sixteen holes running across the top of the cap. One pair of holes appears at the center (of the back?) near the rim. The holes were punched through from the underside. The sheet-gold helmet was formed by raising.

HK

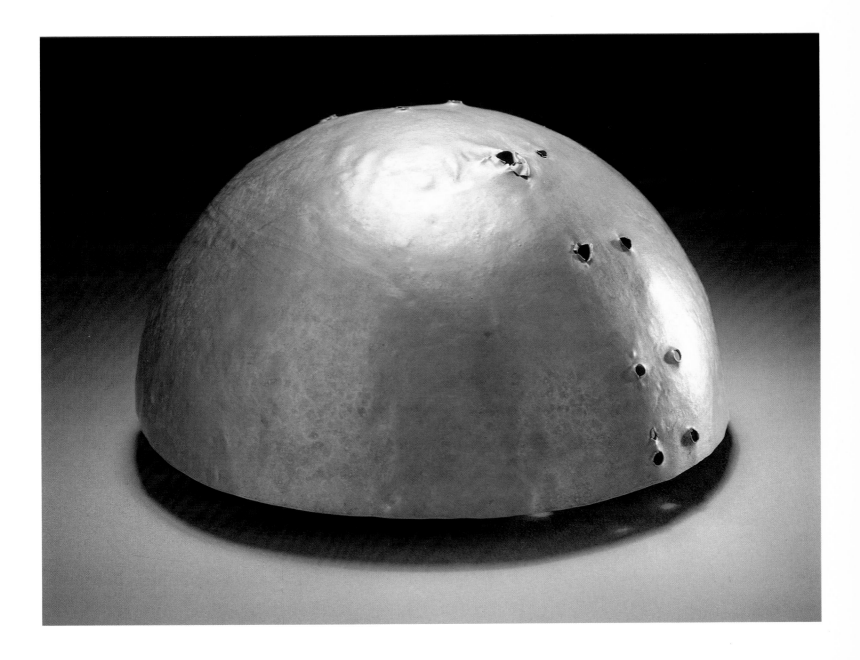

62

Nose ornament with snakes

STYLE UNDETERMINED
2ND CENTURY BC–2ND CENTURY AD (?)
H. 2¼ in. | 5·6 cm.   W. 3¼ in. | 8·4 cm.

The part of Andean South America that is today Peru is the region in which gold was initially worked in the Western Hemisphere. The earliest gold yet known from Peru consists of nine tiny bits of thin foil that accompanied the burial of a young man who died sometime near the middle of the second millennium BC (Grossman 1972). The bits of hammered gold foil had been placed, together with a few lapis lazuli beads, in his mouth and hands. Not far away, and not part of the burial itself, was a metalworker's tool kit—a small stone anvil and three stone hammers. From this modest beginning, the use of gold grew through the following millennia to the proportions that awed the conquering sixteenth-century Spaniards (Jones 1974).

The earliest Peruvian works of art in gold date to about a thousand years after the aforementioned burial. They are splendid and fully realized objects of personal adornment; diadem-crowns, ear and nose ornaments, and pectorals are among these works (Lothrop 1941, 1951). The present nose ring, which probably comes from northern Peru, was made when the tradition for such ornaments was well established. Vigorous yet restrained, its simplicity of organization is exemplary.   JJ

DESCRIPTION

This semicircular nose ornament has a large oval opening in the interior of its upper portion. The support ends, which are thus formed, taper and thicken towards the nose opening, and the topline is incurvate as a result. On either side of the oval ornament, a stylized snake is traced, heading downward. The zigzag snake bodies are 'spotted,' and their heads have round eyes and open mouths. Made of hammered sheet, the object is very smooth and well polished.   HK

EXHIBITED

Leningrad, 1976, no. 11, illustrated.

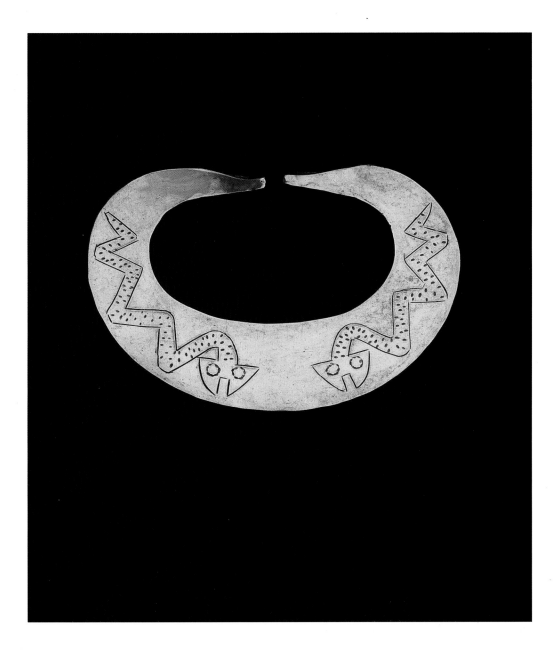

63

Nose ornament with face

VICÚS

1ST–3RD CENTURY (?)

H. 2⅝ in. | 6·7 cm.   W. 3⅝ in. | 9·3 cm.

Vicús-style nose ornaments apparently come from shaft tombs in the vicinity of Cerro Vicús, in the far north of coastal Peru (Disselhoff 1971). The tombs at Vicús are deeply buried—the deepest are said to be almost fifty feet down—and have yielded material in two distinct styles. Nose ornaments of the kind illustrated here are characteristic of one style, that termed Vicús, and the images of the face and the two cats are typical of it. There are even nose ornaments on which both motifs are used together.

Nose ornaments, which are among the earliest of American jewelry forms, begin to fall from favor in Peru in about the mid–first millennium AD. They are seldom used in the late-preconquest centuries.   JJ

DESCRIPTION

The main motif on this semicircular nose ornament is a fantastic face with a grinning mouth, broad nose, and round eyes under a strongly marked brow ridge. Two big S-shapes extend like a large mustache up the side of the face. Under the mouth, a series of six stepped, vertical lines ending in hooks, probably indicates a beard. The ornament is bordered by a double row of small dots, followed by a row of bosses with a raised central dot. The sheet metal ornament has a small circular hole with a narrow opening for the nose.

HK

64

Nose ornament with cats

VICÚS

1ST–3RD CENTURY (?)

H. 3⅜ in. | 8·7 cm.   W. 4⅜ in. | 11·2 cm.

DESCRIPTION

Two mirror-image felines are worked in repoussé on this semicircular nose ornament. The felines have heart-shaped faces with open eyes, snub noses, and whiskered mouths; pointed ears top their heads. Plump bodies, long upturned tails, and straight legs, with semicircular bosses for toes, complete the animals. Above their heads, beneath their feet, and between them, are bosses with a central raised dot. The ornament is bordered by a triple row of small dots, and there is a small circular hole with a narrow opening for the nose. The piece is made from sheet metal, and small cracks are present on the rim, probably the result of the hammering process.   HK

65

Figure whistle

MOCHE

3RD–7TH CENTURY

H. 2 *in.* | 5·2 *cm.*   L. 2¾ *in.* | 6·9 *cm.*

The ancient Peruvians had a notable preference for the hammering of gold; they seldom cast either gold or silver. Specific qualities of sheet metal, when shaped by hammering, must have had significance for them, since the tradition lasted from the earliest recorded working of gold in the second millennium BC until indigenous practices were disrupted by the Spanish conquest in the sixteenth century. Within this hammering tradition, three-dimensional objects form a particularly interesting group because of inherent construction problems. There are some Peruvian works of such complexity of construction that nineteen pieces of shaped sheet metal were used to make gold heads that are only about three-quarters of an inch high (Lechtman 1984a).

The construction methods of the Moche people, the makers of the figure illustrated here, are not quite as complex, although they are far from simple. This figure, which is actually a small whistle, is joined front and back along the sides, the most common point of joining sheet-metal objects of this sort. Other parts have been added separately: the right arm is individually worked and joined to the body, the 'headlight' ornaments are attached by staplelike straps, and the three-part whistle assembly is attached to the back. Originally, the figure held in its extended hand, an object that was pinned to it by means of a tiny 'nail,' which goes through the hand; now only the 'nail' remains.

JJ

DESCRIPTION

This whistle features a standing human figure dressed in a tunic and mantle. The mantle hangs over the figure's shoulders and down its sides. The details of the face—the big, almond-shaped eyes under the arching brows; the long nose; and the thin, wide mouth with worry lines—are delicately worked in low relief. The figure wears round ear ornaments and a caplike headdress, to which two big discs are attached by straps. The discs have wide rims and central cavities which might originally have been inlaid. The figure's extremities are rather rudimentarily worked, and the lower right arm is a separate piece, attached at the elbow. The right hand projects forward and originally held a now-missing object. At the back of the figure's neck, there is a tube, 1⅝ in. (4·2 cm) long and ⅜ in. (0·8 cm.) wide, and beneath it are two spherical sounding chambers. The object was made of several separate pieces of sheet gold, worked by repoussé and presumably joined by soldering. Some of the seams have been resoldered in modern times.

HK

EXHIBITED

New York, The Museum of Primitive Art, 1969, no. 185.
Leningrad, 1976, no. 14, illustrated.

PUBLISHED

Jones, 1979, page 69, fig. 15.

66

Head-form ornaments

MOCHE

3RD–7TH CENTURY

H. 1¼ *in.* | 3·1 *cm.*   W. 1 *in.* | 2·5 *cm.*

During much of the first millennium of our era, the northern Pacific coast of Peru was ruled by the Mochica peoples. The Mochica, or the Moche, as they are also known, built their capital in the dry, coastal valley of Moche, where the main construction was the Huaca del Sol, the so-called Pyramid of the Sun, the largest adobe structure built in Pre-columbian South America. The great pyramid, made of over 143 million adobe bricks, was clearly visible and easily accessible during Colonial times, and it received extraordinary attentions from early treasure hunters (Bray, this volume). As a result of such attentions, little of the wealth in precious metals that the Moche peoples are believed to have possessed remains in its ancient form today. Those works that do remain are all the more important because of their rarity.

Among the surviving works are a number of small, hollow heads that appear to have been made as necklace ornaments to be used in a series. Six such ornaments are pictured here, and they are quintessentially Moche in the delineation of the human face. Moche art has often been noted for its realism, a quality present in these small heads. The expression on the faces, remote, detached, and curiously deadpan, is another characteristic of Moche depictions in metal. The meaning of this expression is not presently clear.

JJ

DESCRIPTION

The well-defined facial features of these hollow heads were worked in repoussé. The faces have big, lozenge-shaped eyes (originally inlaid?), prominent aquiline noses, and closed mouths, the corners of which turn down slightly. The eyebrows are thin, arched lines of fine stippling; the large ears wear circular ornaments. The hair, represented by striation, is worn in tonsure fashion. The heads were made in two halves and joined by soldering along a clearly visible seam; they are closed at the bottom. Paired holes, arranged vertically, are found on either side of the back of the head.

HK

67

Ceremonial knife (tumi)

SICÁN

MID-9TH–MID-11TH CENTURY

H. 13½ *in.*|34·5 *cm.*   W. 5¼ *in.*|13·3 *cm.*

With the waning of the Mochica authority on the Peruvian north coast, new centers of power began to coalesce, and one of these, by the ninth century, had taken on the character and individuality that would distinguish it historically. Three hundred kilometers to the north of the Moche Valley, the important religious enclave of Batán Grande, in the Lambayeque Valley complex, grew rich and powerful. A necropolis of great antiquity, Batán Grande was ruled by a dynasty of 'Lords,' who, for two centuries, apparently ruled this ancient and important religious-funerary center as something akin to a Vatican state.

During those times—which are called Middle Sicán, from the archaeological phase name—the ruling lords amassed great wealth, much of which was taken to the grave with them. The Major Batán Grande graves had more lavish gold and silver mortuary offerings than those of any other documented Precolumbian-era tomb (Carcedo and Shimada, this volume). Large, decorated *tumis* or ceremonial knives, such as that illustrated here, were significant offerings in these tombs. The blade shape is known also in copper, where it is a simple, utilitarian, but valued, form. Tumis of gold and silver are bigger than the copper ones and are often elaborated with the depiction of a figure, perhaps mythical, that is the central image of Batán Grande art during this period. Here, the figure is represented seated and holding a tumi in its proper left hand.   JJ

DESCRIPTION

A repoussé human figure sits cross-legged, left leg over right, on a rectangular base atop a plain gold blade. The face of the figure has eyes in the shape of inverted commas, a broad nose, and a narrow mouth framed by two lines running from nose to chin. Turquoise ear plugs are set in beaded gold rims on either side of the head, and a cap with a semicircular filigree crest is worn. The crest, composed of strip-metal zigzags and scrolls in alternate rows, is topped by a line of small spheres. The figure wears a collar and holds a ceremonial knife in the left hand, while the other hand grasps an unidentified circular object. The arms and legs are worked in high relief, and above the elbows is a separately attached pair of 'wings.'

On the back of the head, there is a rosette of concentric circles with a decorated trapezoidal element at the bottom. Below that, over the back of the figure, are three rows of four embossed circles and a 'fringe' of truncated triangles, which appears to represent the headdress and/or garment. Cinnabar remains in recessed areas of the back. Below the shaft, the knife ends in a hemispherical blade.

The object was made of numerous pieces of sheet gold joined by either crimping or soldering. The beads, made from molten metal, were soldered in place.

HK

68

Ceremonial knife (tumi)

SICÁN

MID-9TH–MID-11TH CENTURY

H. 13 *in.*|33 *cm.*   W. 5⅛ *in.*|13 *cm.*

An account written down in the sixteenth century tells of dynastic rulers of Lambayeque who controlled the Valley from the time a lord named Naymlap arrived there by sea (Donnan 1978). The Naymlap dynasty prospered and ruled for a conjectured three hundred years, until the last of the line was drowned by angry subjects. Because the written account did not fix the legendary dynasty in time, it has been difficult to relate it to a specific archaeological manifestation. Recent excavation in Lambayeque, particularly at Batán Grande, in beginning to unravel the area's prehistory (Shimada 1981), has led to the suggestions that Naymlap was the first Lord of the dynasty that ruled Batán Grande at the turn of the first millennium AD and that perhaps it is his image that prevails on so many of the gold objects.

The facial features are depicted on both sides of this tumi, surmounted by the traditional, and imposing, fanned-out headdress. The back of the tumi is differentiated from the front by a row of long danglers, corresponding to the danglers that decorate the long 'back-flaps' of the big headdresses on the full-figure tumis. This tumi was reported to have been found with Cat. nos. 73, right, and 74 (Los Angeles 1964: 70–72).

JJ

DESCRIPTION

The top of this ceremonial knife is decorated front and back with the same human face, worked by repoussé; it has eyes in the shape of inverted commas, a broad nose, and a narrow mouth framed by two lines running from nose to chin. Turquoise ear plugs set in beaded gold rims are seen at the bottom of the conventionalized ears, and the figure also wears a cap with a semicircular crest. The crest is composed of zigzags and scrolls, made of strip-metal, in alternate rows; it is topped by a line of small spheres. There is a recessed semicircular area with turquoise inlay in the center of the cap. Beneath the chin of the face on the back of the tumi, there are six free-hanging danglers. At the top of the shaft, two vertical rows of turquoise discs are set in beaded rims. These discs are supported on the back by horizontal straps. All the pieces of turquoise inlay on the tumi are pierced by holes. Two repoussé birds appear at either side of the shaft; originally, there were four on each side. Below the shaft, the knife ends in a hemispherical blade.

The object was made of numerous pieces of sheet gold joined by either crimping or soldering. The beads were made from molten metal and soldered in place. Modern repair is visible.

HK

EX. COLL.

Paul A. Clifford and Paul R. Cheesman, Miami

EXHIBITED

Los Angeles County Museum, 1964, no. 211, illustrated.
New York, The Museum of Primitive Art, 1969, no. 192, illustrated.
Leningrad, 1976, no. 37, illustrated.

PUBLISHED

Lapiner, 1976, page 284, no. 647.

69

Beaker

SICÁN

MID-9TH–MID-11TH CENTURY

H. 10¼ in. | 26 cm.   Diam. 7⅞ in. | 20 cm.

In the late 1950s, a major tomb was discovered at Batán Grande that was said to have held some two hundred precious metal objects (Carcedo and Shimada, this volume). One hundred and seventy-six of the gold and silver objects were beakers in various sizes and shapes. The beakers were grouped in stacks—often as many as ten to a stack—and/or separately placed. Those in stacks were apparently similar in image and size, while the individually placed beakers were correspondingly more individual in their depictions. Among the stacked variety are those of largest size. There are reports of the finding of a stack of four or five beakers approximately three feet high in a Bátan Grande burial.

Among the larger beakers, those with faces that are upright when the beaker itself is upside-down are common in the Batán Grande tomb finds. The beakers with upside-down images usually have faces with many teeth (interpreted by some as fangs) as well as the distinctive inverted-comma-shaped eyes that are characteristic of Sicán Lord representations.   JJ

DESCRIPTION

This tall effigy beaker has a repoussé face worked upside-down on its circumference. Open, comma-shaped eyes, a straight nose with flaring nostrils, and a mouth with prominent teeth are depicted in relatively high relief on one side. Between nose and squared-off chin, two lines frame the mouth. The mouth has many teeth (fangs?) and what may be a protruding tongue indicated over the lower lip. The ears are worked as raised ovals that constrict near the bottom, where round ear ornaments are indicated.

Above the short, straight-browed forehead, a bulging element represents the brow band of a cap. The cap continues around the beaker, and from it, in back, hangs the hair, apparently dressed in neat rows (braids?) and decorated at the bottom by a row of discs. A wide decorative band with a chevron pattern and a central medallion also hangs from the cap. Beneath the face, a raised molding is worked, collarlike, around the beaker. The lip of the beaker is wide and flaring.

The cup was raised over a mold. The nose caused problems in the making and was patched.   HK

EX. COLL.

Paul A. Clifford and Paul R. Cheesman, Miami.
Sale, Köln, Lempertz, December 14, 1966, lot 1800.

EXHIBITED

Los Angeles County Museum, 1964, no. 191, illustrated.

70

Beaker

SICÁN

MID-9TH–MID-11TH CENTURY

H. 5¼ *in.* | 13·3 *cm.*   Diam. 4⅝ *in.* | 11·9 *cm.*

The large Sicán beakers on which depictions of faces or heads appear upside-down are intriguing, for there is little precedent in ancient Peruvian art for upside-down renditions. Among the beakers of Batán Grande, however, the convention appears frequently. The face customarily used on these beakers is that with 'displayed teeth.' The beaker here is unusual in being Janus-faced; each side bears the same 'smiling/snarling' likeness. Routinely, beakers with this image have details consistent with head representations, i.e., a whole head is depicted. The use of the same face on opposing sides of the beaker recalls the ceremonial knives on which the Sicán Lord face appears both front and back.

Sicán, a word from Muchik, the language of the northern Peruvian coast before the Inca conquest, was the ancient name of Batán Grande. It is now used by archaeologists to designate the cultural manifestations exemplified by the great gold-bearing tombs of that ancient religious center.   JJ

DESCRIPTION

Two repoussé faces are worked upside-down on the circumference of this effigy beaker. Open, comma-shaped eyes, a straight nose with flaring nostrils, and a mouth with prominent teeth are depicted in relatively high relief on both sides. Between each nose and squared-off chin, two lines frame the mouth. The mouths have many teeth (fangs?); what may be a tongue overlaps the lower lips. The conjoined ears protrude, and ear plugs go through the joint lobe. Above the straight brow line, a cap is articulated with a rounded band, and, beneath the faces, a raised molding is worked, collarlike, around the beaker. The lip of the beaker is wide and flaring.

The beaker was raised over a mold. On one side, the nose and upper lip were patched in the making, and on the other side there is a long crack in the 'collar'.

HK

EX. COLL.
Paul A. Clifford, Miami

EXHIBITED
Los Angeles County Museum, 1964, no. 192.

71

Two beakers

SICÁN

MID-9TH–MID 11TH CENTURY

H. 7⅞ in. | 20 cm.   Diam. 7⅛ in. | 18 cm.

In Sicán-period Batán Grande, gold beakers were among the chief mortuary offerings in major tombs. Reports exist of many dozens being found together (Carcedo and Shimada, this volume, fig. 2), and, in these incidences, some of the beakers were of such similar size and weight as to suggest a common prototype or mold. The two beakers illustrated here, one pictured from the front and the other from the back, are a case in point, for they carry the same image and are of the same size. They differ in only one respect—the central medallion hanging from the back of the cap is not identical in the two examples.

The details of cap and hair on these beakers are particularly Peruvian in character, because head coverings of a wide variety of form and material were much valued there from early Precolumbian times. The hair indicated on the back of the Sicán beakers, for instance, possibly represents hair that is grouped into thick strands and finished and decorated at the bottom. The finishing may have been done by tying the ends with colorful threads, 'weaving' or 'knotting' them, and adding danglers or tassels. Examples of hair worked in this fashion are known on extant caps.   JJ

DESCRIPTION

These effigy beakers have a repoussé face worked upside-down on their circumference. Open, comma-shaped eyes, a straight nose with flaring nostrils, and a mouth with prominent teeth are depicted in relatively high relief on one side. Between nose and squared-off chin, two lines frame the mouth. The mouths have many teeth (fangs?), and what may be a protruding tongue is indicated over the lower lips. The ears are worked as raised ovals that constrict near the bottom, where round ear ornaments are shown.

Above the short, straight-browed foreheads, a bulging element represents the brow band of a cap. The caps continue around the beakers, and from them, in back, hangs the hair, apparently dressed in neat rows (braids?) and decorated at the bottom by a row of discs. Wide bands with chevron patterns and central medallions also hang from the caps. In the middle of the medallion on the beaker at the left, two concentric circles are worked. Beneath the faces, a raised molding encircles each beaker like a collar. The lips of the beakers are wide and flaring. The vessels were raised over molds.

HK

EX. COLL.

Sale, Köln, Lempertz, December 14, 1966, lots 1798, 1799.

72

Beaker

SICÁN

MID-9TH–MID-11TH CENTURY

H. 10⅜ in. | 26·3 cm.   Diam. 8 in. | 20·3 cm.

Frontal human faces depicted upright on the Sicán vessels are usually given an abbreviated torso; the hands are often shown with a shell, possibly a *Spondylus*, held between them. The *Spondylus* is a mollusk that has a very colorful, spiny shell; it was widely used in ancient Peru for a variety of purposes. Some fourteen hundred years or so before the Sicán Lords were powerful in Batán Grande, a deity image was carved in central Peru that showed the figure holding a *Spondylus* shell in one hand (Rowe 1967, fig. 21). For centuries, the pink-orange color of the prickly shell had great appeal for ornamental use. The *Spondylus* appears also as a solitary, but repeated, motif on smaller Sicán beakers. It is said that, when Naymlap, the legendary founder of the Lambayeque dynasty, arrived in the Valley, he had among his retinue a Preparer of the Way, a man whose special duty it was to scatter the dust of sea shells before his lord when he walked.

The upright-image beakers have much the same kind of hair depictions on the back as do the upside-down cups. Slightly more elaborate in detail, and certainly longer, the hair arrangements are done in a similar manner. It is interesting to note, however, that the distinctive inverted-comma-shaped eyes do not appear on the beakers with figures holding shells; thus, these perhaps do not represent a Sicán Lord.

JJ

DESCRIPTION

A broad human face worked in high relief by the repoussé technique decorates the front of this large beaker. The face has open, almond-shaped eyes, a straight nose with flaring nostrils, and a narrow mouth. Between the nose and the squared-off chin, two lines frame the mouth. The large, detailed ears are adorned with circular plugs that go through the lobe. Above the straight brow line, a cap with a raised brow band appears; it ends in the flaring rim of the beaker. Beneath the face, the arms and hands are raised across the chest, with the outstretched fingers touching a shell patterned with vertical and horizontal grooves.

The hair hangs from the back of the cap in two layers; the longer layer is embellished at the bottom with a row of discs. A wide decorative band with a chevron pattern and central medallion also hangs from the cap. The medallion has two central concentric circles surrounded by seven small ones.

The beaker was raised over a mold. There is a rectangular repair patch on the cap in back.   HK

EXHIBITED

New York, The Museum of Primitive Art, 1969, no. 189.
Leningrad, 1976, no. 32, illustrated.

PUBLISHED

Emmerich, 1965, page 37, fig. 48.
Emmerich, 1979, page 97, plate VI.

73

Two beakers

SICÁN

MID-9TH–MID-11TH CENTURY

H. 6½ in.|16·4 cm.   5⅛ in.|13 cm.

Diam. 4⅝ in.|11·7 cm.   4⅜ in.|11·2 cm.

On a number of smaller beakers, the face of the Sicán Lord appears as a repeated motif. In these faces, the comma-shaped eyes, the conventionalized ears, and the semicircular headdress are all present. The patterns in the central area of the headdress are probably meant as representations of turquoise inlay. The heads customarily appear with frogs, usually four of each to a beaker, as seen here. The meaning of the conjoined motifs is not presently clear. The beaker on the right was reported to have been found with Cat. nos. 68 and 74 (Los Angeles 1964: 70–72).

Burials at Batán Grande were placed in shaft tombs; among the mortuary offerings, together with objects of precious materials, were fine ceramic vessels and objects of carved wood. Human and animal sacrifices were also present in important burials.

JJ

DESCRIPTION

Two beakers of different size are similar in shape and decoration. The repoussé ornamentation consists of four evenly spaced frogs, around the lower half, and four human heads above. The faces have eyes of inverted-comma shape, a broad, flat nose, and a small mouth with lines framing it. Ear plugs and a semicircular headdress are worn. The caplike interior part of the headdress has a pattern of bosses. The frogs are shown from above, with their front and back legs extended to the sides of their bodies. Two parallel rows of circles appear on their backs. The heads look upward; their round eyes, under arched brows, are separated by nose ridges; the mouths are grooves. The beakers were raised over molds.

HK

EX. COLL.
Right only, Paul A. Clifford and Paul R. Cheesman, Miami.
Left only, Sale, Köln, Lempertz, December 14, 1966, lot 1797.

EXHIBITED
Right only, Los Angeles, 1964, no. 202, illustrated.

74

Beaker

SICÁN

MID-9TH–MID-11TH CENTURY

H. 5¼ in.|15 cm.   Diam. 4¼ in.|10·9 cm.

Full-figure images of the Sicán Lord, in frontal or profile versions, appear in low relief on the gold beakers; both versions hold tall staffs. The staffs, extended to either side of the frontal figures, belong to the long Peruvian tradition of important, role-declaring staffs. Deity and/or warrior figures often carry staffs or maces, and images of anthropomorphic staffs are known. Here, the staffs have paired profile faces at the top, and a frontal face can be read between the two. The main figure wears a headdress of unusual shape. Topped by 'feathers,' the 'hat' portion of the headdress is not semicircular, but, rather, is a large tau. Beneath the figure, a row of stylized birds is depicted, beak upward. The bird is another motif often seen on Sicán gold objects.

The great quantities of beakers found in individual Sicán tombs have led to the suggestion that they were not made just for burial. The resources and manpower needed to make quickly such a quantity of metal objects would have strained the capacities of the Sicán community. The beakers may have been made, and were possibly used, during the lifetime of the owner. Accumulating gradually, the many beakers would then have been available for interment when the occasion demanded (Carcedo and Shimada, this volume).

JJ

DESCRIPTION

Two frontal figures are worked in repoussé on either side of this beaker. They wear prominent plumed headdresses with a graduated middle section; paired bosses embellish the three extensions on each. The faces have eyes of inverted-comma shape, a broad, flat nose, and a small mouth with lines at the sides framing it; they wear circular ear ornaments. The arms of the figures are outstretched, and, in each hand, a tall staff is held. On the staffs, just above the hands, there are shields and, above them, faces with peaked hats. The figures themselves are rather squat, and their feet are splayed sideways. They appear to be wearing shirts or tunics decorated at the bottom with triangular motifs, and there are triangular 'wings' at the elbows. The figures, contained by a 'framing line,' stand on a 'ground line' that separates them from the bird pattern beneath them. A band of nine birds encircles the beaker. The birds are joined wing to wing and have large round eyes and beaks that point upward. The beaker was made by raising over a mold.

HK

EX. COLL.
Paul A. Clifford and Paul R. Cheesman, Miami.

EXHIBITED
Los Angeles County Museum, 1964, fig. 204, illustrated.

75

Rattle beaker

SICÁN

MID-9TH–MID-11TH CENTURY

H. 6¼ in. | 16 cm.   Diam. 4¼ in. | 10·5 cm.

A small group of the Sicán beakers has false bottoms, and, in the resulting space between false and real bottoms, there are pellets that rattle when the beaker is moved. Many of the rattle beakers are distinguished further by turquoise inlays, which add to their specialness. Available information suggests that the special beakers were found in tombs that numbered ceremonial tumis among their other mortuary contents. The rattle beakers may have had a particular function, possibly one associated with the funerary ceremonies.

Excavations began in the Batán Grande Archaeological Complex in 1978, and it is from this work that the details of the religious-funerary nature of the complex have come to be known (Shimada et al. 1981). Batán Grande, named for the modern hacienda on which it is located, was first used by the ancient Peruvians as a cemetery in the second millennium BC and was still so used in Sicán times. Why the area took on its particular religious significance and why it was used so extensively as a necropolis is not known. It is believed, however, to have been the largest cemetery in Precolumbian America.

JJ

DESCRIPTION

This elegant beaker with flaring sides has a hollow bottom that contains two pellets (of stone?). Four cross-shaped openings pierce the walls of the hollow bottom. An encircling repoussé band of stepped chevrons, a row of rectangular turquoise inlays, and a repoussé band of animals decorate the cup. The animals have large round eyes, beaklike mouths, and humped backs with short, upright tails. There are seven turquoise inlays, all of which have been pierced by holes; some of the inlays may have been replaced in modern times. One authority (Moseley 1978) has suggested that turquoise inlay was reused, thereby explaining the ever-present holes.

The beaker was raised over a mold, and the false bottom was crimped into place. There is a pair of holes on the underside of the beaker.

HK

EX. COLL.
Sale, Köln, Lempertz, December 14, 1966, lot 1796.

EXHIBITED
New York, The Museum of Primitive Art, 1969, no. 191.
Leningrad, 1976, no. 28, illustrated.

76

Necklace

SICÁN OR CHIMÚ

9TH–15TH CENTURY

Diam. 1⅛ to 1¼ in. | 2·8 to 3·2 cm.

Hollow gold beads made during the late Precolumbian era in northern Peru range in size from those that are the circumference of a shirt button to those that are almost the size of tennis balls. The method of manufacture was always the same, whatever their size. They are made in two halves and joined at the middle. As is true of other necklace elements from ancient America, it is often difficult to reconstruct the original stringing of these hollow gold ornaments, for the cords do not usually survive burial. When restrung today, the plain beads are often assembled by graduated size, as they are strung here.

In very late Preconquest times, the north coast of Peru was dominated by the Chimú kingdom, which ruled from its capital city of Chan Chan, in the Moche Valley. At Chan Chan, the dynasty of Chimú kings built large, individual, royal compounds that were high-walled and imposing structures of adobe. Within those high, and presumably closely guarded, walls, the many-chambered royal mausolea were filled with various, valued contents, drawn from throughout the wealthy Chimú realm. Only slight remnants of those contents exist today. Like the equally visible and impressive earlier adobe structures, the royal compounds of Chan Chan, with their well-stocked tombs, have been the targets of treasure-hunters from early Colonial times until the present day (Moseley and Day 1982).

JJ

DESCRIPTION

These round, hollow beads were made from sheet metal raised into hemispheres, which were then soldered by the granulation technique. The central seams are clearly visible. There is one hole at either end of each bead, by means of which they can be strung together. The present stringing is modern.   HK

77

Pair of ear plugs

CHIMÚ

12TH–15TH CENTURY

Diam. of frontal 2⅜ in. | 6 cm.

Total length 3½ in. | 8·9 cm.

From Moche times onward on the Peruvian north coast, ear ornaments were customarily made with a wide, flat, decorated frontal, the weight of which was counterbalanced by a long shaft in back. It is this configuration, with the long shaft, that has led the ornaments to be called ear plugs. Other Moche conventions for ear ornaments were continued into later times, too—for example, the multipiece central motifs of the frontals and the gold balls that rim the frame.

During the Chimú era, which occurred several hundred years after that of the Moche, the detailing of the ornaments became very fine and small in scale, qualities present in this pair. The patterning on the headdresses and clothes of the central figures is regular, almost meticulous, echoing the rhythm of the small spheres on the periphery of the ornaments. Richly dressed Chimú Lords, for this is what the figures are thought to be, hold pairs of beakers in their outstretched hands; they appear to have profile animal- (or snake-) head ornaments on their collars. Both beakers and the profile animal heads are characteristic of earlier Sicán works.   JJ

DESCRIPTION

A pair of ear plugs has, recessed into the front of each one, a half-figure wearing an elaborate headdress. The repoussé figures are made of several separate pieces of worked sheet metal. Their facial features include lozenge-shaped eyes, a broad nose and a wide, but closed, mouth. The headdress rising above their foreheads is made of two layers of metal that are embossed with decorative bands of geometric elements. A flat dangler is attached by a strap near either end of the fanned-out crest. Beneath the face of each figure, there is a wide collar, from which profile animal heads protrude on either side. The animal heads have a long upsweeping tongue and a large ear. The tunics that are worn have decorative bands top and bottom, and six drop-shaped danglers are strapped to the lower edge. The figures have no legs or feet. Their arms are raised sideways, and a beaker is held in each hand.

A raised enclosing rim on the face of the ear plug frontals forms a shallow space for the worked figures. After embossing, the various elements were cut out from the front, and joined by stapling or soldering. The beads on the rim were made from molten metal and soldered in place. Centrally, on the back of the ear plug frontals, tubular shafts of sheet, 3⅛ inches (8 cm.) long and ⅜ inches (0·9 cm.) in diameter, are soldered. The tubes are closed at the shaft end by an additional round of metal, which is pierced.

HK

EXHIBITED

New York, The Museum of Primitive Art, 1969, no. 190.

78

Pair of ear plugs

CHIMÚ

12TH–15TH CENTURY

Diam. of frontal 5¼ in. | 13·5 cm.

Total length 5¼ in. | 13·4 cm.

Amazingly complex scenes appear on large Chimú ear plugs, as the ornaments here amply illustrate. Multipiece and ambitious in its component parts, the present scene shows a Chimú Lord standing on a litter. The litter is supported by two men, of sufficiently high rank to wear large headdresses, and there is one other attendant figure. The standing Chimú Lord holds a beaker in one hand and a fan in the other. It is interesting to note that, on one ear plug, the beaker is in the figure's right hand and, on the other, it is in the left. This right-to-left reversal is true of the rest of the scene as well. The litter-bearers are moving in opposite directions on each ear plug frontal. Reversed direction, in anything other than a centrally organized design, is another convention that began with the Moche and was followed by the Chimú centuries later. It is another indication of the very traditional nature of ancient Peruvian metalwork.   JJ

DESCRIPTION

These impressive ear plugs are decorated with four figures set into concave discs with beaded borders. The repoussé figures are made up of several pieces of worked sheet metal. The principal figures stand full-face on a litter with animal head ends. A dangler is attached at either extremity. The facial features of the figures include lozenge-shaped eyes, a prominent nose, and a closed mouth. A tunic, ear ornaments, and a huge headdress, consisting of a stepped front section and a fanned-out crest, are worn. Two danglers attached by straps are placed near the extremities of either side of the crest. The arms and feet of each figure project forward. A beaker is held in one hand, a fan in the other. Three tiny danglers hang from the fan.

The litter-bearers have frontal faces and profile bodies. Their legs are rendered as if they were moving forward. Simple ear ornaments, semicircular headdresses, and loincloths are worn. Their outer arms are three-dimensional, and a keyhole-shaped dangler is strapped to each. A small profile figure stands between the bearers, wearing a loincloth and cap and carrying a double-spout vessel; a keyhole-shaped dangler is attached to the outer hand. On the backs of the three figures are representations of what may be gourd lime containers.

The ornaments are made of many pieces of sheet metal joined by stapling or soldering. After embossing, various elements were cut out from the front. The beads on the rim are hollow—made in two halves—and they are strung on a wire and soldered in place. Tubular shafts are soldered, centrally, on the back of the ear plug frontals. The shafts, 4¼ inches (10·7 cm.) long and 1¼ inches (3·1 cm.) in diameter, are decorated with a traced repeat of crested birds in a diamond pattern. The ear plugs have been repaired in modern times.   HK

79

Ceremonial knife (tumi)

SICÁN (?)

9TH–12TH CENTURY (?)

H. 9½ in. | 24·3 cm.　　W. 4¼ in. | 11 cm.

Gold ceremonial knives that are decorated on the shaft with finely traced, overall patterns were made in northern Peru, possibly at the same time as the tumis with decorated tops (see Cat. nos. 67, 68). The tradition for the embellishment of tool shapes was an old one in Peru, and, in precious metals, the tradition either derived from, or overlapped with, that of copper. There are copper knives with shapes similar to that of the gold tumis. Notably similar are the Mochica copper knives that are depicted held in one hand by a frontal figure, while a trophy head is held in the other hand (Jones 1979, fig. 37). The depicted knife differs somewhat in shape, yet it may be the symbolic ancestor of the later, richly made, north-coast tumis. The Mochica image of the figure with displayed knife and trophy head is one that implicitly states triumph or power over others. It is, thus, tempting to speculate that the knife with a long shaft and curved blade, of later times, may carry the whole meaning of the Mochica scene, and that, with time, the knife itself became a symbol of power over others or of the right to rule.

JJ

DESCRIPTION

The shaft of this ceremonial knife carries the same traced decoration on both sides. It consists of two diamond shapes, each containing a crested figure (?) with a tail. A wide band with a compartmentalized step-fret pattern outlines the diamonds. Set-off rectangles, top and bottom, enclose animal forms, and stippled dots are used for filler in various places. The hemispherical blade is plain. Hammered from sheet metal, the surface of the knife is smoothed and well polished.　　　　HK

EXHIBITED

Leningrad, 1976, no. 34, illustrated.

80

Pectoral plaque

CONDORHUASI
4TH–7TH CENTURY
H. $4\frac{1}{2}$ in.|11·5 cm. W. $3\frac{7}{8}$ in.|9·8 cm.

The goldwork of northwestern Argentina is not well known today. Metallurgically, it belongs to the region of the southern Andes, an area that includes the highlands of southern Peru and Bolivia and adjacent parts of Argentina and Chile (Lechtman 1980). The metalworking tradition of this area differs from that of central and northern Peru, the region from which the Peruvian objects in the preceding pages of this Catalog have come. The origins of the southern Andean tradition are particularly obscure, although there is some evidence for the working of copper as early as 1200 BC. The tradition is believed to be well established, however, by the early first millennium AD and the rise of the great city of Tiahuanaco on the Bolivian altiplano. An Argentinian gold plaque, attributed to Condorhuasi, as is the illustrated example, was discovered with Tiahuanaco ceramic vessels and other items of gold—including a beaker with repoussé decoration—in a burial on the small island of Pariti in Lake Titicaca (Posnansky 1957).

Condorhuasi objects, which are only known in ornamental forms, are made in gold, silver, and copper. Plaques, bracelets, and ear ornaments are definitely among them, and there are other objects that may be nose ornaments or necklace elements. The major pieces are the gold plaques with their distinctive outline and central perforation. It is unusual that no utilitarian forms in metal appear in Condorhuasi graves, and ceramic offerings are often not included either (Gonzalez 1979).   JJ

DESCRIPTION

This plaque is in the form of an elongated hexagon with rounded corners. In the middle of it, there is a cut-out in the shape of centrally overlapped triangles. Two holes near the top edge are for suspension. The plaque is made of hammered sheet metal, cut to shape and smoothed; the surface is more thoroughly finished on one side than on the other, implying that the plaque had a right and a wrong side.

HK

Bibliography

Accola, Richard M.
1980   Sitio Nacascolo. *In* Memoria del Congreso sobre el Mundo Centroamericano de su Tiempo: IV Centenario de Gonzalo Fernández de Oviedo: 167–174. Editorial Texto, San José.

Acosta, Joaquín
1848   Compendio Histórico del Descubrimiento y Colonización de la Nueva Granada en el Siglo Décimo Sexto. Paris.

Adrián de Ufeldre or de Santo Tomas, Fray
1965   Conquista de la Provincia del Guaymí por el venerable padre maestro Fr. Adrian de Ufeldre . . . *Hombre y Cultura* 1(4): 72–121. Panama.

Aguilar, Carlos H.
1972a   Colección de objetos indígenas de oro del Banco Central de Costa Rica. *Publicaciones de la Universidad de Costa Rica, Serie Historia y Geografía* 13. San José.
1972b   Guayabo de Turrialba. Editorial Costa Rica, San José.
1980   Presencia temprano del cobre en el intermontano central de Costa Rica. *In* La Antropología Americanista en la Actualidad: Homenaje a Raphael Girard 1: 363–368. Editores Mexicanos Unidos, Mexico.

Alva Alva, Walter
1984   Neuere deutsch-peruanische Forschungen im Norden Perus. *In* Peru durch die Jahrtausende (exhibition catalogue): 216–218. Verlag Aurel Bongers, Dortmund.

Andagoya, Pascual de
1913   Relación de los sucesos de Pedrarias Dávila en las Provincias de Tierra Firme . . . *In* J. T. Medina, ed., El Descubrimiento del Océano Pacífico . . . 2: 191–207. Imprenta Universitaria, Santiago de Chile.

Anghiera, Petro Martire d'
1912   De Orbe Novo: The Eight Decades of Peter Martyr d'Anghera. 2 vols. (Trans. and ed. by F. A. MacNutt.) G. P. Putnam's Sons, New York.

Balboa, Vasco Núñez de
1913   Carta dirigida al Rey por Vasco Núñez de Balboa . . . 1513. *In* J. T. Medina, ed., El Descubrimiento del Océano Pacífico . . . 2: 129–138. Imprenta Universitaria, Santiago de Chile.

Balser, Carlos
1966   Los objectos de oro de los estilos estranjeros de Costa Rica. *In* Actas y Memorias, 36 Congreso Internacional de Americanistas 1: 391–398. Seville.

Basel, Münzen und Medaillen A.G.
1964   Gold- und Silberschmuck aus dem präcolumbischen Amerika, Sammlung André Emmerich, New York (sales catalogue), March. Basel.

Benzoni, Girolamo
1857   History of the New World. The Hakluyt Society, London. (1970, Burt Franklin, New York.)

Bergsøe, Paul
1937   The Metallurgy and Technology of Gold and Platinum among the Pre-Columbian Indians. *Ingeniørvidenskabelige Skrifter* A44. Copenhagen.
1938   The Gilding Process and the Metallurgy of Copper and Lead among the Pre-Columbian Indians. *Ingeniørvidenskabelige Skrifter* A46. Copenhagen.

Bernal, Ignacio
1980   A History of Mexican Archaeology. Thames and Hudson, London.

Biese, Leo
1967   The Gold of Parita. *Archaeology* 20(3): 202–208. New York.

Bischof, Henning
1969   Contribuciones a la cronología de la Cultura Tairona. *And* La Cultura Tairona en el área Intermedio. *In* Verhandlungen des 38 Internationalen Amerikanistenkongresses 1: 259–269 and 271–280. Munich.

Bogotá, Museo del Oro
1982   Noticias Breves, El Museo del Oro en el exterior. *Boletín Museo del Oro* 5 (enero-abril): 19. Bogotá

Bollaert, William
1860   Antiquarian, Ethnological and Other Researches in New Granada, Equador, Peru, and Chile . . . Trübner & Co., London.

Boomert, Aad
1975   A Contribution to the Classification of Spectro-Analyses of Prehistoric Metal Objects. *Helinium* 15: 134–161. Wetteren, Belgium.

Bouchard, Jean-François
1979   Hilos de oro martillado hallados en la costa pacífica del sur de Colombia. *Boletín Museo del Oro* 2 (mayo-agosto): 21–24. Bogotá.

Bozzoli [de Wille], María Eugenia
1975   Birth and Death in the Belief System of the Bribri Indians of Costa Rica. Unpub. Ph.D. diss., Department of Anthropology, University of Georgia, Athens.
1977   Narraciones Bribris. *Vínculos* 2(2): 165–199; 3 (1–2): 67–104. San José.
1979   El nacimiento y la muerte entre los Bribris. Editorial Universidad de Costa Rica, San José.

Braunholtz, H. J.
1939   A Gold Pendant from Ancient Colombia. *The British Museum Quarterly* 13(1): 19–21. London.

Bray, Warwick
1972   Ancient American Metal-Smiths. *Proceedings of the Royal Anthropological Institute of Great Britain and Ireland for 1971*: 25–43. London.
1977   Maya Metalwork and its External Connections. *In* N. Hammond, ed., Social Process in Maya Prehistory: 365–403. Academic Press, New York.
1978   The Gold of El Dorado (exhibition catalogue). The Royal Academy of Arts and Times Books, London.
1981a   Gold Work. *In* Between Continents/Between Seas: Precolumbian Art of Costa Rica (exhibition catalogue): 153–166. Harry N. Abrams, New York, and The Detroit Institute of Arts.
1981b   Plate Captions. *In* Sweat of the Sun, Tears of the Moon (exhibition catalogue): 48–96. Natural History Museum of Los Angeles County, Los Angeles.
1984   Across the Darien Gap. *In* F. W. Lange and D. Z. Stone, eds., The Archaeology of Lower Central America: 305–338. Albuquerque.
n.d.   The Prehispanic Metalwork of Central Panama. Manuscript submitted for publication to Editorial Universitaria, Panama.

Bray, Warwick, and M. Edward Moseley
1969–70   An Archaeological Sequence from the Vicinity of Buga, Colombia. *Ñawpa Pacha* 7–8: 85–104. Berkeley.

Bray, Warwick, Leonor Herrera, and Marianne Cardale de Schrimpff
1981   [Report on the 1980 Field Season in Calima.] *Pro Calima* 2: 1–22. Solothurn.
1983   Report on the 1981 Field Season in Calima. *Pro Calima* 3: 2–31. Basel.

Bruhns, Karen
1969–70   Stylistic Affinities between the Quimbaya Gold Style and a little known Ceramic Style in the Middle Cauca Valley, Colombia. *Ñawpa Pacha* 7–8: 65–84. Berkeley.
1976   Ancient Pottery of Middle Cauca Valley, Colombia. *Cespedesia* 5(17–18): 101–196. Cali.

Brüning, Heinrich
1922–23   Estudios monográficos del Departamento de Lambayeque. D. Mendoza, Chiclayo.

Bull, Thelma
n.d.a   Additional Report on Archaeological Investigations in the Province of Los Santos, District of Guararé, Republic of Panama. Unpub. manuscript.

n.d.b   A Preliminary Report on Archaeological Investigations in the Province of Los
             Santos, District of Guararé, Republic of Panama. Unpub. manuscript.
Butler, J. J., and J. D. van der Waals
1964   Metal Analysis, SAM I, and European Prehistory. *Helinium* 4: 3–39. Wetteren,
             Belgium.
Caciques e Indios
n.d.   Caciques e Indios, 16. F.574.v. Archivo Nacional, Bogotá.
Cadavid, Gilberto, and Luisa Fernanda de Turbay
1977   Arqueología de la Sierra Nevada de Santa Marta: investigaciones culturales en
             el área Tairona. Unpub. manuscript. Bogotá.
Caley, Earle R., and Dudley T. Easby, Jr.
1959   The Smelting of Sulfide Ores of Copper in Preconquest Peru. *American Antiquity*
             25(1): 59–65. Washington.
Caley, Earle R., and Lowell W. Shank
1971   Composition of Ancient Peruvian Copper. *Ohio Journal of Science* 71(3):
             181–187. Columbus.
Carcedo Muro, Paloma
n.d.   Análisis de una litera "Chimú." *Revista Española de Antropología Americana.*
             Madrid. In press.
Cardale de Schrimpff, Marianne
1976   Investigaciones arqueológicas en la zona de Pubenza, Tocaima. *Revista
             Colombiana de Antropología* 20: 335–496. Bogotá.
Carrión Cachot, Rebeca
1940   La luna y su personficación ornitomorfa en el arte Chimú. *In* Actas y Trabajos
             Cientificos del 27 Congreso Internacional de Americanistas 1: 571–587. Lima.
C[asimir] de Brizuela, Gladys
1971   Informe preliminar de las excavaciones en el sitio arqueológico Las Huacas,
             Distrito de Soná, Veraguas. *In* Actas del 2 Simposium Nacional de
             Antropología, Arqueología y Etnohistoria de Panamá: 249–256. Panama.
1972   Investigaciones arqueológicas en la Provincia de Veraguas. *Hombre y Cultura*
             2(3): 119–137. Panama.
1973   Síntesis de Arqueología de Panamá. Editorial Universitaria, Panama.
Caso, Alfonso
1969   El Tesoro de Monte Albán. *Memorias del Instituto Nacional de Antropología e
             Historia* 3. Mexico.
Castillero Calvo, Alfredo
1967   Estructuras sociales y economicas de Veraguas desde sus origenes históricos,
             siglos XVI y XVII. Editora Panamá, Panama.
Cavallaro, Raffael
1982   Social and Religious Considerations of Adobe Manufacture and Marking in
             Monumental Architecture at Batán Grande, Peru. Unpub. B. A. thesis,
             Department of Anthropology, Princeton University.
Cavallaro, Raffael, and Izumi Shimada
n.d.   Sicán Marked Adobes and Labor Organization: Evaluating Hypotheses. Unpub.
             manuscript.
Charles, J. A.
1972   Physical Science and Archaeology. *Antiquity* 46(182): 134–139. Cambridge,
             England.
Chaves, Alvaro, and Mauricio Puerta
1973–79   Excavaciones arqueológicas en Tierradentro. Unpub. reports. Fundación de
             Investigaciones Arqueológicas Nacionales, Bogotá.
1980   Entierros primarios de Tierradentro. *Publicación de la Fundación de Investigaciones
             Arqueológicas Nacionales* 4. Bogotá.
Cieza de León, Pedro de
1864   The . . . First Part of his Chronicle of Peru. (Trans. and ed. by C. R. Markham).
             The Hakluyt Society, London.
1883   The Second Part of the Chronicle of Peru . . . (Trans. and ed. by C. R. Markham).
             The Hakluyt Society, London.
Colón, Fernando
1959   The Life of the Admiral Christopher Columbus by His Son Ferdinand.
             (Trans. by B. Keen.) Rutgers University Press, New Brunswick.
Cooke, Richard G.
1972   The Archaeology of the Western Coclé Province of Panama. Unpub. Ph.D. diss.,
             Institute of Archaeology, University of London.
1976a   Informe sobre excavaciones en el sitio CHO-3, Miraflores, río Bayano, febrero
             1973. *In* Actas del 4 Simposium Nacional de Antropología, Arqueologiá y

Etnohistoria de Panamá: 367–426. Panama.
1976b   Panamá: Región Central. *Vínculos* 2(1): 122–140. San José.
1976c   Rescate arqueológico en El Caño (NA-20), Panamá. *In* Actas del 4 Simposium
             Nacional de Antropología, Arqueología y Etnohistoria de Panamá: 445–482.
             Panamá.
1976d   Una nueva mirada a la evolucion de la ceramica en las Provincias Centrales de
             Panamá. *In* Actas del 4 Simposium Nacional de Antropología, Arqueología y
             Etnohistoria de Panama: 307–365. Panamá.
1979   Los impactos de las comunidades agrícolas precolombinas sobre los ambientes
             del Tropico estacional. *In* Actas del 4 Simposium Internacional de Ecologia
             Tropical 3: 917–973. Panama.
1981   Los hábitos alimentarios de los indígenas precolombinas de Panamá. *Revista
             Médica de Panamá* 6: 65–89. Panama.
1984a   Archaeological Research in Central and Eastern Panama. *In* F. W. Lange and
             D. Z. Stone, eds., The Archaeology of Lower Central America: 263–301.
             Albuquerque.
1984b   Birds and Men in Prehistoric central Panama. *In* Recent Developments in
             Isthmian Archaeology. Proceedings, 44 International Congress of Americanists:
             243–281. Oxford.
n.d.   La arqueología de Panamá y su importancia para los pueblos de habla chibcha.
             In 1 Congreso Cientifico sobre los Indigenas de Costa Rica. San José. In press.
Creamer, Winifred
1983   Production and Exchange on Two Islands in the Gulf of Nicoya, Costa Rica,
             AD 1200–1550. Unpub. Ph.D. diss., Department of Anthropology, Tulane
             University, New Orleans.
Cubillos, Julio César
1954   Arqueología de Rioblanco (Chaparral, Tolima). *Boletín de Arqueología* 1: 519–
             591. Bogotá.
Dade, Philip
1960   Rancho Sancho de la Isla. *Panama Archaeologist* 3: 66–87. Canal Zone.
1972   Bottles from Parita. *Archaeology* 25(1): 35–43. New York.
Daniel, Glyn E.
1950   *A Hundred Years of Archaeology.* Duckworth, London.
de la Rocha, Fray Antonio
1964   Del Padre Fray Antonio de la Rocha y de la Conversión de los Indios . . . en
             el Reino de Panamá . . . *Hombre y Cultura* 1(3): 87–132. Panama.
de Zeltner, M. A.
1866   Note sur les Sépultures Indiennes de Departement de Chiriqui (État de Panamá).
             Imprimerie de T. M. Cash, Panama.
Detroit, The Detroit Institute of Arts
1981   Between Continents/Between Seas: Precolumbian Art of Costa Rica (exhibition
             catalogue). Harry N. Abrams, New York, and The Detroit Institute of Arts.
Díaz del Castillo, Bernal
1905–16   A True History of the Conquest of New Spain. (Ed. by A. P. Maudslay). 5 vols.
             The Hakluyt Society, London.
Disselhoff, Hans D.
1971   Vicús. *Monumenta Americana* 7. Berlin.
Donnan, Christopher B.
1973   A Precolumbian Smelter from Northern Peru. *Archaeology* 26(4): 289–297.
             New York.
1978   Moche Art of Peru (exhibition catalogue). Museum of Cultural History,
             University of California, Los Angeles.
Doyle, Gerald A.
1960   Metal and Pottery Associations. *Panama Archaeologist* 3(1): 48–51. Canal Zone.
Drucker, Philip
1952   La Venta, Tabasco. *Bureau of American Ethnology Bulletin* 153. Smithsonian
             Institution, Washington.
Duque Gomez, Luis
1964   Exploraciones arqueológicas en San Agustín. *Revista Colombiana de Antropología*
             Sup. 1. Bogotá.
1970   Los Quimbayas. Instituto Colombiano de Antropología, Bogotá.
1979a   El oro en las prácticas religiosas de los Muiscas. *Boletín Museo del Oro* 2
             (mayo-agosto): 1–18. Bogotá.
1979b   La Pieza del Museo. *Boletín Museo del Oro* 2 (mayo-agosto): center fold. Bogotá.
Duque Gomez, Luis, and Julio César Cubillos
1979   Arqueología de San Agustín. *Publicación de la Fundación de Investigaciones*

Arqueológicas Nacionales 4. Bogotá.

Easby, Dudley T., Jr.

1955a   Sahagún y los orfebres precolombinos de México. *Anales del Instituto Nacional de Antropología e Historia* 9: 85–117. Mexico.

1955b   Los vasos retratos de metal del Peru. *Revista del Museo Nacional* 24: 137–153. Lima.

1956   Sahagún Reviviscit in the Gold Collection of the University Museum. *University Museum Bulletin* 20(3): 2–15. University of Pennsylvania, Philadelphia.

1961   Fine Metalwork in Pre-Conquest Mexico. *In* S. K. Lothrop et al., Essays in Pre-columbian Art and Archaeology: 35–42. Harvard University Press, Cambridge.

1969   Aspectos técnicos de la orfebrería de la Tumba 7 de Monte Albán. *In* Memorias del Instituto Nacional de Antropología e Historia 3: 343–394. Mexico.

Elera A., Carlos G.

1984   Características e implicaciones culturales en dos tumbas disturbadas de Huaca La Merced, Complejo Arqueológico de Batán Grande, Lambayeque, Costa Norte del Perú. Unpub. report submitted to the Instituto Nacional de Cultura, Lima.

Emmerich, André

1965   Sweat of the Sun and Tears of the Moon. University of Washington Press, Seattle.

1979   The Jan Mitchell Collection of Pre-Columbian Gold. *Apollo* (August): 94–101. London.

Epstein, Stephen M., and Izumi Shimada

n.d.   Metalurgía de Sicán. *Beitrage zur allgemeinen und vergleichenden Archäologie.* Bonn. In press.

Escalera Ureña, Andres, and María Angeles Barriuso Pérez

1978   Estudio científico de los objectos de metal de Ingapirca (Ecuador). *Revista Española de Antropología Americana* 8: 19–47. Madrid.

Espinosa, Gaspar de

1913a   Relación hecha por Gaspar de Espinosa . . . (1517). *In* J. T. Medina, ed., El Descubrimiento del Océano Pacífico . . . 2: 154–182. Imprenta Universitaria, Santiago de Chile.

1913b   Relación é proceso quel licenciado Gaspar de Espinosa ∴ . . 1519. *In* J. T. Medina, ed., El Descubrimiento del Océano Pacífico . . . 2: 272–317. Imprenta Universitaria, Santiago de Chile.

Evans, Oswald H.

1909–10   A Note on the Gilded Metalwork of Chiriqui, Central America. *Nature* 82: 457. London.

Falchetti [de Sáenz], Ana María

1976   The Goldwork of the Sinú Region, Northern Colombia. Unpub. M. Phil. diss., Institute of Archaeology, University of London.

1978   Pectorales acorazonados. *Boletín Museo del Oro* 1 (mayo-agosto): 28–34. Bogota.

1979   Colgantes 'Darien.' *Boletín Museo del Oro* 2(enero-abril): 1–55. Bogotá.

Fernández, D. León, ed.,

1886   Colección de Documentos para la Historia de Costa Rica 4. Paris.

Fernández Guardia, Ricardo

1968   Reseña Histórica de Talamanca. 2nd ed. Imprenta Nacional, San José.

Fisher, J. R.

1976   Gold in the Search for the Americas. *Gold Bulletin* 9 (2): 58–63. Johannesburg.

Fonseca Zamora, Oscar

1979   Informe de la primera temporada de reexcavación de Guayabo de Turrialba. *Vínculos* 5(1–2): 35–52. San José.

1983   Historia de las excavaciones en la región de Guayabo. *In* Comptes Rendus des Communications du Neuvième Congrès International d'Études des Civilisations Précolombiennes des Petites Antilles: 201–218. Montreal.

Garcilaso de la Vega, El Inca

1966   Royal Commentaries of the Incas. (Ed. by H. V. Livermore). 2 vols. University of Texas Press, Austin.

González, Alberto Rex

1979   Pre-Columbian Metallurgy of Northwest Argentina. *In* E.P. Benson, ed., *Pre-Columbian Metallurgy of South America*: 133–202. Dumbarton Oaks, Washington.

González Guzmán, Raúl

1971   Informe preliminar sobre las investigaciones arqueológicas realizadas en El Cafetal, Distrito de Tonosí, Provincia de los Santos, Panamá. *In* Actas del 2 Simposium Nacional de Antropología, Arqueología y Etnohistoria de Panamá:

143–174. Panama.

Gordon, Robert B., and John W. Rutledge

1984   Bismuth Bronze from Machu Picchu, Peru. *Science* 223: 585–586. Washington.

Groot de Mahecha, Ana María

1980   Buritaca 200. *Boletín Museo del Oro* 3 (mayo-agosto): 21–34. Bogotá.

Grossman, Joel W.

1972   An Ancient Gold Worker's Tool Kit. *Archaeology* 25(4): 270–275. New York.

Haberland, Wolfgang

1973   Stone Sculpture from Southern Central America. *In* The Iconography of Middle American Sculpture: 134–152. The Metropolitan Museum of Art, New York.

Hartman, C. V.

1901   Archaeological Researches in Costa Rica. Royal Ethnological Museum, Stockholm.

Helms, Mary W.

1977   Iguanas and Crocodilians in Tropical American Mythology and Iconography with special reference to Panama. *Journal of Latin American Lore* 3(1): 51–132. Los Angeles.

1979   Ancient Panama. University of Texas Press, Austin.

1981   Cuna Molas and Coclé Art Forms. *Working Papers in the Traditional Arts* 7. Institute for the Study of Human Issues, Philadelphia.

Herrera y Tordesillas, Antonio de

1944–47   Historia General de los Hechos de los Castellanos, en las Islas, y Tierra-Firme de el Mar Occeano. 10 vols. Editorial Guarania, Asuncion.

Holmes, William H.

1888   Ancient Art of the Province of Chiriqui, Colombia. *Sixth Annual Report of the Bureau of American Ethnology*: 3–187. Smithsonian Institution, Washington.

Ichon, Alain

1980   L'Archéologie du Sud de la Péninsule d'Azuero, Panama. *Études Mésoaméricaines, Série 2* (3). Mission Archéologique et Ethnologique Française au Mexique, Mexico.

Jane, Cecil, ed.

1929   Voyages of Columbus. Select Documents . . . 1. (Trans. and ed. by Cecil Jane). The Hakluyt Society, London.

Johnson, Frederick

1948   Caribbean Lowland Tribes: The Talamanca Division. *Bureau of American Ethnology Bulletin* 143(4): 231–252. Smithsonian Institution, Washington.

Jones, Julie

1974   Gold and the New World. *In* El Dorado, the Gold of Ancient Colombia (exhibition catalogue): 11–19. Center for Inter-American Relations and the American Federation of Arts, New York.

1979   Mochica Works of Art in Metal. *In* E. P. Benson, ed., Pre-Columbian Metallurgy of South America: 53–104. Dumbarton Oaks, Washington.

Joralemon, Peter David

1976   The Olmec Dragon, *In* H. B. Nicholson, ed., Origins of Religious Art and Iconography in Preclassic Mesoamerica: 27–71. Los Angeles.

Kauffmann Doig, Federico

1973   Manual de Arqueolgía Peruana. 5th ed. Peisa, Lima.

Knauth, Percy, et al.

1974   The Metalsmiths. Time-Life Books, New York.

Köln, Kunsthaus Math. Lempertz.

1966   Aussereuropäische Kunst (sales catalogue), December 14 and 15. Cologne.

Kosok, Paul

1959   El Valle de Lambayeque. *In* Actas y Trabajos del 2 Congreso Nacional de Historia del Perú 1: 49–67. Lima.

1965   Life, Land and Water in Ancient Peru. Long Island University Press, New York.

Kroeber, Alfred L.

1944   Peruvian Archaeology in 1942. *Viking Fund Publication in Anthropology* 4. New York.

Ladd, John

1964   Archaeological Investigations in the Parita and Santa Maria Zones of Panama. *Bureau of America Ethnology Bulletin* 193. Smithsonian Institution, Washington.

Lange, Frederick W., and Richard M. Accola

1979   Metallurgy in Costa Rica. *Archaeology* 32(5): 26–33. New York.

Lange, Frederick W., and Doris Z. Stone, eds.

1983   The Archaeology of Lower Central America. University of New Mexico Press, Albuquerque.

Lapiner, Alan
1976   Pre-Columbian Art of South America. Harry N. Abrams. New York.
Lathrap, Donald W.
1980   El Ecuador Antiquo, Cultura, Cerámica y Creatividad, 3000–300 AC (exhibition catalogue). Field Museum of Natural History, [Chicago]. Guayaquil.
Lechtman, Heather N.
1973   The Gilding of Metals in Precolumbian Peru. In W. J. Young, ed., Application of Science in Examination of Works of Art: 38–52. Museum of Fine Arts, Boston.
1976   A Metallurgical Site Survey in the Peruvian Andes. Journal of Field Archaeology 3(1): 1–42. Boston.
1977   Style in Technology. In H. Lechtman and R. Merrill, eds., Material Culture: 3–20. West Publishing, St. Paul.
1979   Issues in Andean Metallurgy. In E. P. Benson, ed., Pre-Columbian Metallurgy of South America: 1–40. Dumbarton Oaks, Washington.
1980   The Central Andes. In T. A. Wertime and J. D. Muhly, eds., The Coming of the Age of Iron: 267–334. Yale University Press, New Haven.
1981   Copper-Arsenic Bronzes from the North Coast of Peru. Annals of the New York Academy of Science 376: 77–122. New York.
1984a   Andean Value Systems and the Development of Prehistoric Metallurgy. Technology and Culture 25(1): 1–36. Chicago.
1984b   Pre-Columbian Surface Metallurgy. Scientific American 250(6): 56–63. New York.
Lechtman, Heather, Antonieta Erlij, and Edward J. Barry, Jr.
1982   New Perspectives on Moche Metallurgy. American Antiquity 47(1): 3–30. Washington.
Legast, Anne
1980   La Fauna en la orfebrería Sinú. Publicación de la Fundación de Investigaciones Arqueológicas Nacionales 7. Bogotá.
1982   La fauna mítica Tairona. Boletín Museo del Oro 5 (enero-abril): 1–18. Bogotá.
Leningrad, Hermitage Museum
1976   Zoloto dokolumbovoi Ameriki, katalog vystaki (exhibition catalogue, loan from The Metropolitan Museum of Art to the Ministry of Culture, USSR). Soviet Artist, Moscow.
Lévi-Strauss, Claude
1955   Tristes Tropiques. Librairie Plon, Paris.
Lima, Museum Gold of Peru
1970   Catalogue, Museum Gold of Peru (collection catalogue). Miguel Mujica Gallo Foundation, Lima.
Linares [de Sapir], Olga F.
1976   Animals that were Bad to Eat were Good to Compete With. University of Oregon Anthropological Papers 9: 3–19. Eugene.
1977   Ecology and the Arts in Ancient Panama. Studies in Pre-Columbian Art and Archaeology 17. Dumbarton Oaks, Washington.
Linares [de Sapir], Olga F., and Anthony J. Ranere, eds.
1980   Adaptive Radiations in Prehistoric Panama. Peabody Museum Monographs 5. Harvard University Press, Cambridge.
Linares [de Sapir], Olga F., P. D. Sheets, and E. J. Rosenthal
1975   Prehistoric Agriculture in Tropical Highlands. Science 187: 137–145. Washington.
Linares [de Sapir], Olga F., and Richard White
1980   Terrestrial Fauna from Cerro Brujo (CA-3) in Bocas del Toro and La Pitahaya (IS-3) in Chiriqui. Peabody Museum Monographs 5: 181–193. Harvard University Press, Cambridge.
London, Sotheby & Co.
1966   African, Pre-Columbian, Pacific North-West Coast, Eskimo, Oceanic, and Indian Art (sales catalogue), March 29. London.
Long, Stanley
1964   Cire-perdue Copper Casting in Pre-Columbian Mexico. American Antiquity 30(2): 189–192. Washington.
1967   Hornas de piedra y su uso en la metalúrgica chibcha. Unpub. report. Archivo Museo del Oro, Bogotá.
López de Gómara, Francisco
1964   Cortés, the Life of the Conquerer by his Secretary. (Trans. and ed. by L. B. Simpson). University of California Press, Berkeley & Los Angeles.
Los Angeles, The Los Angeles County Museum

1964   Gold Before Columbus (exhibition catalogue). The Los Angeles County Museum, Los Angeles.
Lothrop, Samuel K.
1937   Coclé, Part 1. Memoirs of the Peabody Museum of Archaeology and Ethnology, Harvard University 7. Cambridge.
1941   Gold Ornaments of Chavin Style from Chongoyape, Peru. American Antiquity 6(3): 250–62. Menasha.
1942   Coclé, Part 2. Memoirs of the Peabody Museum of Archaeology and Ethnology, Harvard University 8. Cambridge.
1950   Archaeology of Southern Veraguas, Panama. Memoirs of the Peabody Museum of Archaeology and Ethnology, Harvard University 9(3). Cambridge.
1951   Gold Artifacts of Chavin Style. American Antiquity 16(3): 226–40. Menasha.
1952   Metals from the Cenote of Sacrifice, Chichen-Itza, Yucatan. Memoirs of the Peabody Museum of Archaeology and Ethnology, Harvard University 10(2). Cambridge.
1956   Jewelry from the Panama Canal Zone. Archaeology 9(1): 34–40. Cincinnati.
1963   Archaeology of the Diquís Delta, Costa Rica. Papers of the Peabody Museum of Archaeology and Ethnology, Harvard University 51. Cambridge.
Lothrop, Samuel K., W. F. Foshag, and Joy Mahler
1957   Pre-Columbian Art, Robert Woods Bliss Collection. Phaidon Press, London.
Lyon, Patricia J.
1966   Innovation through Archaism. Ñawpa Pacha 4: 31–61. Berkeley.
MacCurdy, George G.
1911   A Study of Chiriquian Antiquities. Memoirs of the Connecticut Academy of Arts and Sciences 3. New Haven.
Mason, J. Alden
1942   New Excavations at the Sitio Conté, Coclé, Panama. In Proceedings of the 8th American Scientific Congress 2: 103–107. Washington.
Mathewson, C. H.
1915   A Metallographic Description of Some Ancient Peruvian Bronzes from Machu Picchu. American Journal of Science 11: 525–602. New Haven.
McGimsey, Charles R., III
1968   A Provisional Dichotomization of Regional Styles in Panamanian Goldwork. In Actas y Memorias del 37 Congreso Internacional de Americanistas 4: 45–55. Buenos Aires.
Menzel, Dorothy
1960   Archaism and Revival on the South Coast of Peru. In A. F. C. Wallace, ed., Men and Cultures: 596–600. Philadelphia.
1947   The Archaeology of Ancient Peru and the Work of Max Uhle (exhibition catalogue). R. H. Lowie Museum of Anthropology, University of California, Berkeley.
Mitchell, Russell H., and James F. Heidenreich
1965   New Developments on the Azuero Peninsula, Province of Los Santos, Republic of Panama. Panama Archaeologist 6(1): 13–26. Canal Zone.
Morison, Samuel Eliot
1942   Admiral of the Ocean Sea, A Life of Christopher Columbus. Little, Brown and Company, Boston.
Moseley, Michael E.
1978   Peru's Golden Treasures (exhibition catalogue). Field Museum of Natural History, Chicago.
Moseley, Michael E., and Kent C. Day, eds.
1982   Chan Chan: Andean Desert City. University of New Mexico Press, Albuquerque.
Motolinía, Toribio de
1950   History of the Indians of New Spain. (Trans. and ed. by E. Andros Foster). Cortes Society, Berkeley.
Muller, Priscilla E.
1972   Jewels in Spain, 1500–1800. The Hispanic Society of America, New York.
Müller, Theodor
1972   Das Altärchen der Herzogin Christine von Lothringen in der Schatzkammer der Münchner Residenz under verwandte Kleinkunstwerke. Zeitschrift für bayerische Landesgeschichte 35(1): 69–77. Munich.
New York, The Metropolitan Museum of Art
1970   Before Cortés, Sculpture of Middle America (exhibition catalogue). The Metropolitan Museum of Art, New York.
1972   Gold (exhibition). The Metropolitan Museum of Art, New York.
1972/73 Bulletin (winter). The Metropolitan Museum of Art, New York.

New York, The Museum of Primitive Art
1969   Precolumbian Art in New York (exhibition catalogue). The Museum of Primitive Art, New York.
1974   Rituals of Euphoria (exhibition catalogue). The Museum of Primitive Art, New York.

Nolan, James
1980   Prehispanic Irrigation and Polity in the Lambayeque Sphere, Peru. Unpub. Ph.D. diss., Department of Anthropology, Columbia University, New York.

Nordenskiöld, Erland
1921   The Copper and Bronze Ages of South America. *Comparative Ethnographical Studies* 4. Göteborg.

Northover, J. P.
1983   The Exploration of Long-distance Movement of Bronze in Bronze and Early Iron Age Europe. *Institute of Archaeology Bulletin* 19: 45–72. University of London.

Oman, Charles
1968   The Golden Age of Hispanic Silver, 1400–1665. Victoria and Albert Museum, London.

Otis, F. M.
1859   The New Gold Discoveries on the Isthmus of Panama. *Harper's Weekly*, August 6: 499–500. New York.

Oviedo y Valdés, Gonzalo Fernández de
1944–45   Historia General y Natural de las Indias. 14 vols. Editorial Guanaria, Ascuncion.

Pedersen, Asbjorn
1976   El ajuar funerario de la tumba de la Huaca Menor de Batán Grande (Lambayeque, Perú). *In* Actas del 41 Congreso Internacional de Americanistas 2: 60–73. Mexico.

Perez de Barradas, Jose
1954   Orfebrería Prehispánica de Colombia, Estilo Calima. 2 vols. Banco de la República, [Bogotá]. Madrid.
1958   Orfebrería Prehispánica de Colombia, Estilos Tolima y Muisca. 2 vols. Banco de la República, [Bogotá]. Madrid.
1965–66   Orfebrería Prehispánica de Colombia, Estilos Quimbaya y Otros. 2 vols. Banco de la República, [Bogotá]. Madrid.

Plazas [de Nieto], Clemencia
1975   Nueva Metodología para la Clasificación de Orfebrería Prehispánica. Jorge Plazas Editor, Bogotá.
1977–78   Orfebrería prehispánica del altiplano nariñense, Colombia. *Revista Colombiana de Antropología* 21: 197–244. Bogotá.
1978   'Tesoro de los Quimbayas' y piezas de orfebrería relacionadas. *Boletín Museo del Oro* 1 (mayo-agosto): 21–28. Bogotá.
1983   Gold Objects from Primavera. *Pro-Calima* 3: 40–42. Basel.

Plazas [de Nieto], Clemencia, and Ana María Falchetti [de Sáenz]
1981   Asentamientos prehispánicos en el bajo río San Jorge. *Publicación de la Fundación de Investigaciones Arqueológicas Nacionales* 11. Bogotá.

Plazas [de Nieto], Clemencia, Ana María Falchetti [de Sáenz], and Juanita Sáenz
1979   Investigaciones arqueológicas en el río San Jorge. *Boletín Museo del Oro* 2 (sept-dic): 1–18. Bogotá.

Posnansky, Arthur
1957   Tihuanacu, The Cradle of American Man 3–4. Ministerio de Educación, La Paz.

Pozorski, Sheila
1980   The Moche Pyramids of Peru. *Carnegie Magazine* (November): 23–30. Pittsburgh.

Ralegh, Sir Walter
1848   The Discovery of the Large, Rich, and Beautiful Empire of Guiana. (Ed. by R. H. Schomburgk). The Hakluyt Society, London.

Ravines, Rogger
1980   El gran Chimú y el Chimocápac. *In* R. Ravines, ed., Chanchan: metrópoli Chimú. *Fuentes e Investigaciones para la Historia del Perú* 5: 21–101. Lima.

Records of the Past
1904   Gold Plates and Figures from Costa Rica. *Records of the Past* 3(9): 282–286. Washington.

Reichel-Dolmatoff, Gerardo
1971   Amazonian Cosmos. University of Chicago Press, Chicago.
1975a   Contribuciones al conocimiento de la estratigrafía cerámica de San Agustín, Colombia. Biblioteca del Banco Popular, Bogotá.
1975b   The Shaman and the Jaguar. Temple University Press, Philadelphia.

1981   Things of Beauty Replete with Meaning. *In* Sweat of the Sun, Tears of the Moon (exhibition catalogue): 17–33. Natural History Museum of Los Angeles County, Los Angeles.

Reichel-Dolmatoff, Gerardo, and Alicia Dussán de Reichel
1958   Reconocimiento arqueológico en la hoya del río Sinú. *Revista Colombiana de Antropología* 6: 29–158. Bogotá.

Restrepo Tirado, Ernesto
1929   Ensayo Etnográfico y Arqueológico de la Provincia de los Quimbayas en el Nuevo Reino de Granada. Eulogio de las Heras, Seville.

Rivet, Paul, and H. Arsandaux
1946   La métallurgie en Amérique précolombienne. *Travaux et Mémoires de l'Institut d'Éthnologie* 39. Paris.

Rondón S., Jorge
1965–66   Ferreñafe prehispánico. *Ferruñap* 3(25): 7–15. Chiclayo

Roosevelt, Anna Curtenius
1979   The Goldsmith. *In* A. C. Roosevelt and J. G. E. Smith, eds., The Ancestors (exhibition catalogue): 66–101. Museum of the American Indian, New York.

Rosshandler, Leo
1976   The Meaning of Gold to the Ancient Peruvians. *In* Gold for the Gods (exhibition catalogue): 15–20. Royal Ontario Museum, Toronto.

Rowe, John H.
1967   Form and Meaning in Chavin Art. *In* J. H. Rowe and D. Menzel, eds., Peruvian Archaeology, Selected Readings: 72–103. Palo Alto.

Sahagún, Bernardino de
1959   General History of the Things of New Spain, Book 9. (Trans. and ed. by C. E. Dibble and A. J. O. Anderson.) *Monographs of the School of American Research and the Museum of New Mexico* 14(10). Santa Fe.
1963   General History of the Things of New Spain, Book 11. (Trans. and ed. by C. E. Dibble and A. J. O. Anderson.) *Monographs of the School of American Research and the Museum of New Mexico* 14(12). Santa Fe.

Sander, Dan, R. H. Mitchell, and R. G. Turner
1958   Report on Venado Beach Excavations. *Panama Archaeologist* 1: 26–28. Canal Zone.

Sauer, Carl Ortwin
1966   The Early Spanish Main. University of California Press. Berkeley and Los Angeles.

Saville, Marshall H.
1920   The Goldsmith's Art in Ancient Mexico. *Indian Notes and Monographs* 7. Museum of the American Indian, Heye Foundation, New York.

Scheele, Harry, and Thomas C. Patterson
1966   A Preliminary Seriation of the Chimu Pottery Style. *Ñawpa Pacha* 4: 15–30. Berkeley.

Schuler-Schömig, Immina von
1981   A Grave-lot of the Sonso Period. *Pro Calima* 2: 25–27. Solothurn.

Scott, David A.
1980   The Conservation and Analysis of Some Ancient Copper Alloy Beads from Colombia. *Studies in Conservation* 25: 157–164. London.
1983a   Depletion Gilding and Surface Treatment of Gold Alloys from the Nariño area of ancient Colombia. *Journal of the Historical Metallurgy Society* 17(2): 99–115. London.
1983b   The Deterioration of Gold Alloys and some Aspects of their Conservation. *Studies in Conservation* 28: 194–203. London.

Scott, David A., and Warwick Bray
1980   Ancient Platinum Technology in South America. *Platinum Metals Review* 24(4): 147–157. London.
n.d.   Pre-Hispanic Platinum Alloys. *In* H. Lechtman and A. M. Soldi, eds., Technología en el Mundo Andino 2. Mexico. In press.

Service, Elman R.
1975   Origins of State and Civilization. W. W. Norton and Co., New York.

Sharer, Robert J.
1984   Lower Central America as seen from Mesoamerica. *In* F. W. Lange and D. Z. Stone, eds., The Archaeology of Lower Central America: 65–84. Albuquerque.

Sheets, Payson D.
1984   The Prehistory of El Salvador. *In* F. W. Lange and D. Z. Stone, eds., The Archaeology of Lower Central America: 85–112. Albuquerque.

Shimada, Izumi
1978   Economy of a Prehistoric Urban Context. *American Antiquity* 43(4): 569–592. Washington.
1981   Temples of Time. *Archaeology* 34(5): 37–45. New York.
1982   Horizontal Archipelago and Coast-Highland Interaction in North Peru. *In* L. Millones and H. Tomoeda, eds., El Hombre y su Ambiente en los Andes Centrales. *Senri Ethnological Studies* 10: 137–210. National Museum of Ethnology, Senri, Japan.
1983   The Formation of the Middle Sicán Polity. Paper presented at the 49th Annual Meeting of the Society for American Archaeology, Portland.
n.d.a   The Sicán Culture. *In* La Cultura y Historia de Lambayeque, Perú (tentative title). Editorial Mendoza, Chiclayo/Lima. In press.
n.d.b   Batán Grande and Cosmological Unity in the Andes. *In* R. Matos and S. Turpin, eds., Papers of the International Andean Colloquum. Institute of Archaeology, University of California, Berkeley. In press.
n.d.c   Perception, Procurement and Management of Resources. *In* S. Masuda, I. Shimada and C. Morris, eds., Andean Civilization and Ecology. University of Tokyo Press, Tokyo. In press.
Shimada, Izumi, [et al.]
1981   Batan Grande—La Leche Archaeological Project. *Journal of Field Archaeology* 8(4): 405–556. Boston.
Shimada, Izumi, Carlos G. Elera A., and Melody Shimada
1982   Excavaciones efectuadas en el centro ceremonial de Huaca Lucía–Chólope, del Horizonte Temprano, Batán Grande, costa norte del Perú. *Arqueológicas* 19: 109–210. Lima.
Shimada, Izumi, Stephen Epstein, and Alan K. Craig
1983   The Metallurgical Process in Ancient North Peru. *Archaeology* 36(5): 38–45. New York.
Shimada, Melody, and Izumi Shimada
n.d.   Prehistoric Llama Breeding and Herding on the North Coast of Peru. *American Antiquity*. New York. In press.
Snarskis, Michael J.
1978   The Archaeology of The Central Atlantic Watershed of Costa Rica. Unpub. Ph.D. diss. Department of Anthropology, Columbia University, New York.
1979   Turrialba. *American Antiquity* 44(1): 125–138. Washington.
1981   The Archaeology of Costa Rica. *In* Between Continents/Between Seas: Precolumbian Art of Costa Rica (exhibition catalogue): 15–84. Harry N. Abrams, New York, and The Detroit Institute of Arts.
1983   Casas Prehistóricas en Costa Rica. *In* Comptes Rendus des Communications du Neuvième Congrès International d'Études des Civilizations Précolombiennes des Petites Antilles: 219–238. Montreal.
1984   Central America: The Lower Caribbean. *In* F. Lange and D. Z. Stone, eds., The Archaeology of Lower Central America: 195–232. Albuquerque.
Stone, Doris Z.
1954   Apuntes sobres las esferas grandes de piedra, halladas en el río Diquís o Grande de Térraba, Costa Rica. *Boletín Informativo del Museo Nacional de Costa Rica* 1(6): 6–10. San José.
1963   Cult Traits in Southeastern Costa Rica and their Significance. *American Antiquity* 28(3): 339–359. Salt Lake City.
1977   Pre-Columbian Man in Costa Rica. Peabody Museum Press, Cambridge.
Stone, Doris Z., and Carlos Balser
1965   Incised Slate Disks from the Atlantic Watershed of Costa Rica. *American Antiquity* 30(3): 310–329. Salt Lake City.
1967   Aboriginal Metalwork in Lower Central America. Editorial Lehmann, San José.
Tamalameque
1555   Averiguaciones en Tamalameque sobre los Manyllas que Mando Hazer Juan de Azpeleta a los Yndios de su Encomienda de Anpihuegas. Justicia, Legajo 610–612, folios 2520–25. Archivo General de Indias, Seville.
Tayler, D. B.
1974   The Ika and their Systems of Belief. Unpub. Ph.D. diss. Oxford University.

Tello, Julio C.
1937a   Los trabajos arqueológicos en el departamento de Lambayeque. *El Comercio,* January 29–31. Lima.
1937b   El oro de Batán Grande. *El Comercio,* April 18. Lima.
Thompson, J. Eric S.
1962   A Catalog of Maya Hieroglyphs. University of Oklahoma Press, Norman.
Time Magazine
1962   Costa Rica, Vanishing Treasure. *Time Magazine,* October 12: 22–23. New York.
Topic, John R., Jr.
1982   Lower-Class Social and Economic Organization at Chan Chan. *In* M. E. Moseley and K. C. Day, eds., Chan Chan: Andean Desert City: 145–175. Albuquerque.
Torres de Araúz, Reina
1972a   Algunas consideraciones etnográficas e históricas sobre el vestido cucua. *Patrimonio Histórico* 1(2): 35–47. Panama.
1972b   Natá Prehispánico. Centro de Investigaciones Antropológicas, Universidad de Panamá.
Torres de Araúz, Reina, and Oscar A. Velarde B.
1978   El parque arqueológico de El Caño. *Revista Patrimonio Histórico* 2(1): 201–221. Panama.
Torres de Mendoza, Luis
1869   Información hecha en México sobre averiguar si los indios . . . regalaron al Marqués del Valle joyas y otras alhajas . . . *Colección de documentos inéditos relativos al descubrimiento, conquista, y organización . . . de América y Oceania . . .* 12: 531–540. Madrid.
Tushingham, A. D.
1976   Gold of the Gods (exhibition catalogue). Royal Ontario Museum, Toronto.
Tushingham, A.D., Ursula M. Franklin, and Christopher Toogood
1979   Studies in Ancient Peruvian Metalworking. Royal Ontario Museum, Toronto.
Uribe Alarcón, María Victoria
1977–78   Asentamientos prehispánicos en el altiplano de Ipiales, Colombia. *Revista Colombiana de Antropología* 21: 57–195. Bogotá.
Valcárcel, Luis E.
1937   Un valioso hallazgo arqueológico en el Perú. *Revista del Museo Nacional* 6(1): 164–168. Lima.
1938   El lote de objetos de oro de La Merced, Lambayeque. *El Comercio,* May 14. Lima.
Vázquez, Ricardo
1982   27-HM: Un sitio en Cartago con tumbas de cajón. Unpub. Licenciatura tesis, Universidad de Costa Rica, San José.
n.d.   Excavaciones de muestreo en el Sitio Nacascolo, Bahía Culebra. *Journal of the Steward Anthropological Society.* Urbana. In press.
Von Winning, Hasso
1968   Pre-Columbian Art of Mexico and Central America. Harry N. Abrams, New York.
Waterbolk, H. T., and J. J. Butler
1965   Comments on the Use of Metallurgical Analysis in Prehistoric Studies. *Helinium* 5: 227–251. Wetteren, Belgium.
Willey, Gordon R., and Jeremy A. Sabloff
1974   A History of American Archaeology. Thames and Hudson, London.
Wing, Elizabeth S.
1980   Aquatic Fauna and Reptiles from the Atlantic and Pacific Sites. *Peabody Museum Monographs* 5: 194–215. Harvard University Press, Cambridge.
Young, Philip
1971   Ngawbe: Tradition and Change among the Western Guaymí of Panama. *Illinois Studies in Anthropology* 7. University of Illinois Press, Urbana.
1976   The expression of Harmony and Discord in Guaymí ritual. *In* M. Helms and F. Loveland, eds., Frontier Adaptations in Lower Central America. Institute for the Study of Human Issues, Philadelphia.
Zevallos Q., Jorge
1971   Cerámica de la cultura Lambayeque. Universidad Nacional de Trujillo.